YOUTH MAF
IN BRI

Contemporary ⌐⌐⌐
of austerity

Edited by Shane Blackman and Ruth Rogers

First published in Great Britain in 2017 by

Policy Press
University of Bristol
1-9 Old Park Hill
Bristol
BS2 8BB
UK
t: +44 (0)117 954 5940
pp-info@bristol.ac.uk
www.policypress.co.uk

North America office:
Policy Press
c/o The University of Chicago Press
1427 East 60th Street
Chicago, IL 60637, USA
t: +1 773 702 7700
f: +1 773-702-9756
sales@press.uchicago.edu
www.press.uchicago.edu

© Policy Press 2017

British Library Cataloguing in Publication Data
A catalogue record for this book is available from the British Library

Library of Congress Cataloging-in-Publication Data
A catalog record for this book has been requested

ISBN 978-1-4473-3054-7 paperback
ISBN 978-1-4473-3052-3 hardcover
ISBN 978-1-4473-3055-4 ePub
ISBN 978-1-4473-3056-1 Mobi
ISBN 978-1-4473-3053-0 epdf

The rights of Shane Blackman and Ruth Rogers to be identified as editors of this work has been asserted by them in accordance with the Copyright, Designs and Patents Act 1988.

All rights reserved: no part of this publication may be reproduced, stored in a retrieval system, or transmitted in any form or by any means, electronic, mechanical, photocopying, recording, or otherwise without the prior permission of Policy Press.

The statements and opinions contained within this publication are solely those of the author and not of the University of Bristol or Policy Press. The University of Bristol and Policy Press disclaim responsibility for any injury to persons or property resulting from any material published in this publication.

Policy Press works to counter discrimination on grounds of gender, race, disability, age and sexuality.

Cover design by Andrew Corbett
Front cover image: Jason Dodd
Printed and bound in Great Britain by TJ International, Padstow
Policy Press uses environmentally responsible print partners

To Debbie Cox and Peter Watts

Contents

List of tables and figures

Tables

Figures

Notes on contributors

Patrick Ainley is Professor of Training and Education at the University of Greenwich. He has been a researcher, reader and professor at the University of Greenwich since 1995. His research expertise is in the further education to higher education interface.

Frances Atherton is a Senior Lecturer in the Faculty of Education and Children's Services at the University of Chester. She is involved in ethnographic research with homeless people in Chester and has an interest in qualitative research methodologies and their philosophical foundations.

Susan Batchelor is a Senior Lecturer in Criminology in the School of Social and Political Sciences at the University of Glasgow (based in the Sociology subject area and the Scottish Centre for Crime and Justice Research). Her research is on youth, gender, culture and crime, with a particular focus on young women and violence.

Shane Blackman is Professor of Cultural Studies, Canterbury Christ Church University. He is an editor of the *Journal of Youth Studies* and *YOUNG: Nordic journal of youth research*.

Linda Brooks is a volunteer and Treasurer for the Canvey Island Youth Project, which helps disadvantaged young people aged between 11 and 25 with advice and support on homelessness, benefits, drugs and alcohol. It also helps young people in urgent hardship.

Emma Davidson is a Leverhulme Trust Research Fellow in the School of Social and Political Science at the University of Edinburgh. Her research is concerned with young people's everyday lives, their relationships and social/spatial geographies.

Eldin Fahmy is a Senior Lecturer at the University of Bristol. He has researched and published widely in the areas poverty, social exclusion and citizenship, specifically in relation to youth poverty, social inclusion and participation, and is one of the editors of the *Journal of Poverty and Social Justice*.

Alistair Fraser is a Lecturer in Criminology and Sociology at the University of Glasgow (based in Sociology subject area and the Scottish

Centre for Crime and Justice Research). His research focuses on youth gangs and social change.

Carlie Goldsmith is Director of North RTD (Research Training and Development), a small social research company that specialises in research on crime, criminal justice and inequality. She is also a tutor at the Free University Brighton where she teaches modules on social inequality and criminological theory.

Mary Jane Kehily is Professor of Gender and Education at The Open University, specialising in the field of childhood and youth studies. She is a former editor of *Children and Society* and *Gender in Education*.

Leona Li Ngai Ling is a Senior Research Assistant, Tutor and Honorary Lecturer at the Department of Sociology and Centre for Criminology, University of Hong Kong.

Jane McKay is a Senior Lecturer in Education Studies in the Faculty of Education and Children's Services at the University of Chester. Her research interests are in children's rights, notably in the field of special educational needs and disability, and vulnerable groups.

Robert McPherson is a PhD student at Canterbury Christ Church University. His PhD is an ethnographic study on a city-centre pub, studying young people's alcohol consumption within the Canterbury night-time economy. He teaches sociology, cultural studies and youth studies.

Seán Murphy is a Senior Lecturer in Youth Work at Teesside University. He has developed key specialisms in youth work practice, childhood and youth studies, children's rights, globalisation, youth work history, and contemporary youth policy.

Kim Robinson is a Lecturer in Social Work at Deakin University in Australia. She has worked in a variety of social work settings, including drug and alcohol services, local government, a major public women's hospital, community health and a centre for the care of refugee torture and trauma. In addition she worked at the University of Kent for 10 years prior to returning to Australia.

Ruth Rogers is a Reader in Social Justice and Inclusion at Canterbury Christ Church University. Her research and publications are in the areas of social exclusion, marginalisation and youth transitions, particularly among looked after children.

Anthony Ruddy is an Intelligence Specialist at North Yorkshire County Council and an ESRC Research Fellow at the University of York. His main research interests are centred on youth poverty and youth transitions in the UK, which are the key themes explored in his PhD research in the Social Futures Institute at Teesside University.

Peter Squires is Professor of Criminology and Public Policy at the University of Brighton. He is author of *Rougher Justice: Anti-Social Behaviour and Young People* and the editor of *Asbo Nation: The Criminalisation of Nuisance*.

Claire Tupling is a Lecturer in Postgraduate Studies at the University of Derby. Her research interests include social class inequalities in contemporary education and the history of working-class schooling.

Jenny van Krieken Robson is a Senior Lecturer at the University of East London based in the Cass School of Education and Communities. She has broad experience in working with children and families facing challenges in accessing public services and involving them in service redesign and evaluation.

Lisa Whittaker previously worked as a Research Assistant at the University of Glasgow, and now works as Research Engagement Officer for Tenovus Cancer Care, Cardiff.

Lucy Williams is a Senior Visiting Research Fellow at the University of Kent. She has been involved in community work and research with refugees and asylum seekers since 1998. Her current research, carried out in homeless shelters, detention centres and in 'Section 4' accommodation, focuses on migrants facing forced return to countries of origin.

Acknowledgements

This book largely emerged from a conference hosted by Canterbury Christ Church University in 2014 and new authors who subsequent ly agreed to write chapters for the proposal. The conference 'Where now for social justice? The marginalisation of young people in the UK' included excellent papers from delegates from across the UK, many of whom went on to contribute chapters to this book. Consequently, we would like to express gratitude to Canterbury Christ Church University for supporting the conference, with particular thanks to the Research Centre for Children, Families and Communities, the Faculty of Art and Humanities, the School of Media, Art and Design, the Faculty of Education, and Equality and Diversity.

Finally, we would like to thank each and every one of the young people who gave up their time to participate in the research and share their views. This also includes Sarah Christie for organising the front cover, and Isobel Tudor for agreeing to be the model on the cover. Thanks are due to Debbie Cox, Peter Watts, Andy Furlong, Robert MacDonald, Andy Birtwistle, Peter Mills, the anonymous reviewers of our book proposal, and especially thanks are owed to all at Policy Press for their support.

Foreword

Robert MacDonald

Why do we study youth? One could argue that there is nothing *inherently* interesting about young people. Especially now that so much 'youth cultural' activity has become commodified, commercialised, mainstream and, in fact, consumed by adults, it is difficult to see how young people are *de facto* any more, or less, sociologically fascinating than people older or younger than them.

This might appear to be an odd opening salvo for a new edition about youth in the UK but, just as sociologists question the taken-for-granted assumptions of others, it is fair to do the same reflexively and ask: 'What is Youth Studies for?'

In trying to answer that question (see MacDonald, 2011), I think we need to look beyond the particular characteristics or practices of young people (for example, their youth cultures and identities) to look at **'youth as a life-phase'**. In so doing, we conceive of youth as essentially transitional: a period of movement between the dependence of childhood to the anticipated independence of adulthood. This has become one of the dominant approaches to studying youth in the Global North (Coles, 1995; Furlong, 2017) – and the chapters in this book contain plenty of evidence of the value of this perspective. If new social trends emerge it is feasible that they will be seen here first, or most obviously, among the coming, new generation of young adults: youth as harbingers of the future society. If the economy can no longer provide sufficient standard employment it is likely that young people, as new entrants to the labour market, will be among the first to feel the effects. If house prices outstrip incomes, it will be young adults not yet on the 'housing ladder' who are most likely to be excluded. If 'choice biographies' replace 'normal' ones, if the conventional work ethic dissipates, if family forms become less standard, if radical politics or parties gain force, if patterns of social inequality loosen or take on unfamiliar forms, it is likely that we will see these changes first in the youth phase, as young people make transitions to adult life. This is one very important reason for studying youth: doing so allows us to undertake close-up investigation of wider processes of social change – and social continuity – and, as such, to answer questions of wide relevance for social science (Furlong and Cartmel, 2007). *Youth Marginality in Britain* contains many excellent examples of exactly this sort of detailed, current, empirical, sociological analysis both of forms and spheres of youth experience (eg of the justice and care systems, of training and education, of leisure, of systems for citizenship and asylum, in media representation, on the street) and the situations and lives of groups of young people in transition (eg as young mothers, care leavers, students, apprentices, migrants and asylum seekers, consumers, workers).

A second reason for studying 'youth' is that we can then interrogate the way that powerful social actors create and construct '**youth as a social category**' through discourses that serve ideological purposes and that can work against the real interests of young people. For instance, youth scholars have long documented how the twin discourses of 'youth as trouble / in trouble' have shaped popular, political and academic representations of youth and informed the governance of young people through successive waves of state intervention (Hebdige, 1988; Griffin, 1993). Since the early industrial era, young people have been constructed as a vulnerable group needing of special treatment and care in a hostile world and, simultaneously, as an uncivilised, threatening presence requiring discipline and control (Gillis, 1974; Pearson, 1983). The power of these twin discourses has meant that Youth Studies itself (and perhaps this tendency is represented in the foci of this volume) has often had an unspoken preference for studies of the disadvantaged, the impoverished, the rebellious and deviant, and those at the margins, at the expense of research about the 'better off', the apparently conformist, and the advantaged.

The recent (re-)emergence of a political economy perspective in Youth Studies is to be welcomed exactly because it enables a wider, critical perspective on the material and ideological processes and powerful actors that construct 'youth' in certain ways (and not others) (see Côté, 2014; Sukarieh and Tannock, 2015, 2016; France and Threadgold, 2016). For instance, recent research about 'youth and social exclusion' in the Middle East and North Africa (MENA) countries has drawn heavily on this sort of perspective in showing how autocratic, corrupt states manipulate 'narratives of youth' in order to maintain 'political stability' and power (Calder et al, 2017). Also drawing heavily on Global South research, Sukarieh and Tannock (2016) point out that 'doing' Youth Studies need not be limited to active, direct research – interviews, surveys, ethnography – with young people (albeit that very much of the research of Youth Studies scholars, and the content of the *Journal of Youth Studies*, is exactly that sort of research). Indeed, they argue that Youth Studies has done too little to expose the 'enormous influence' that 'the activities, interests and agendas of elite social actors such as international development agencies, high level policy makers, think tanks and foundations, trade unions and faith groups' have had 'on young people's lives as well as on the significance and nature of youth more generally' (p 1284). In this vein, Côté (2014) has argued that, over several decades, young people *as a whole* have experienced substantial degradation of their material position vis-à-vis other age groups, particularly in respect of income from wages. Partly this has been achieved via policy measures that have enacted ideologically the extension of the (life) phase of youthful dependency. We can see one practical, small example of this in the UK in the way that an individual aged 21 years carries very many adult entitlements in law, such as the right to vote, to join the armed forces, to have sex, to marry, to work, to become an MP, and so on. Yet people of this age are now represented, defined and constructed in welfare policy as 'not fully adult'. Thus, those people aged under 25 years are, from 2017, as part and parcel of the continued retrenchment of welfare spending under austerity, now disallowed from claiming housing benefits – because of an assumed, continuing dependence on parents. Even more glaringly, recent policy makes it legal for employers to pay this group of workers (i.e. young adults) a lower (minimum) wage than is paid to other people (even if they are doing the same work). It is difficult to imagine how such a set of circumstances might be countenanced for any other social group.

The ideological nature of 'youth as a social category' is brought to attention by the array of suffixes that are typically appended to 'youth'. Rarely are these 'positive'. A book of my own, written with Jane Marsh (2005), purposefully added a question mark to the couplet 'Disconnected Youth' so as to interrogate the common assumptions of difference and deficiency that are alleged against young people. As the editors of *Youth Marginality in Britain*, Shane Blackman and Ruth Rogers, make clear in their introduction, a plethora of normative labels are ready to hand and enjoy widespread currency in policy and academic discourse in the UK – and more widely: the dismal 'ds' – the 'disaffected', 'disengaged', 'detached' (and 'disconnected'); the 'hard to reach' continues to be a stubborn lament of welfare practitioners and think tanks, transmogrifying into the 'hard to help'; 'socially excluded youth' stands as a blander, less offensive 'youth underclass'; the 'NEET' acronym was invented to replace 'Status Zero' because it was thought to be less judgemental and has now become a significant UK export, a device to label and sort 'successful' from 'unsuccessful' young people across several different countries. Names matter. Representations of youth are 'overburdened' with unspoken but powerful assumptions (Ball et al, 2000). Labels carry implied explanations, not just descriptions, with those listed here defining young people by something they are not, something that they do not have or, generally, their presumed social and economic distance and dislocation from 'the rest', from 'us'. The editors are to be commended for avoiding this trap of easy, catchy labels by exploring 'youth marginality'; a term and concept that draws attention to the different dimensions and forms of marginality that can face young people and, crucially, to the processes of marginalisation that can be enacted against young people and against youth as a social category. Their approach is one that highlights the meaning of these things to young people,through research with them, and which draws attention to young people's active engagement with and resistance to marginalisation.

A book about youth, marginality and austerity could not be more timely. Young people are facing particularly tough times (Shildrick et al, 2015). Never likely to be as newsworthy as 'child poverty' or 'pensioner poverty', nevertheless it is 'youth poverty' that is worthy of urgent attention, as the chapters here by Fahmy and Ruddy each show. Young adults (18- to 29-year-olds) in the UK are now the socio-demographic group who are most likely to experience material deprivation, with an alarming upward trend since 1999. Across every different measure of poverty, young people are especially disadvantaged compared to other age groups (Fahmy, 2015). The UK government's austerity programme from 2010 onwards heavily forefronted 'welfare reform', and young people have been particularly hard hit by this more punitive regime for the provision of what used to be called 'social security' (Watts, 2014). Not only are they now denied support to which previous generations were entitled (eg student grants, housing benefit) compared with other age groups, they are now more likely to face punitive sanctions (ie denial of benefit payments for infringement of tightened rules and tests) (Watts, 2014; see also Brooks' chapter in this volume). Some already deprived groups of young people, such as homeless young people, face an even greater risk of sanction, often leading to even worse and less secure housing situations, food poverty, anxiety and depression, and disengagement from welfare and employment services (North East Homelessness Think Tank, 2016). This report implies that the latter outcome is an *unintended* consequence of 'welfare reform'; it is, of course, quite plausible that this is an *intended* consequence of these changes. Services for young people have also faced heavy austerity cuts. Between April 2010 and April 2016, £387 million was cut from youth service spending across the UK. This meant that 603 youth centres closed, 3,652 youth work jobs were lost, and 138,898 places for young people in youth projects were cut (Unison, 2016). This has local and personal resonance. In North East England, on Teesside's social housing estates, many of the youth centres, sports clubs and libraries in which Jane Marsh and myself used to meet and interview young people during the 1990s and 2000s for *Disconnected Youth?* (MacDonald and Marsh, 2005) have now been closed because of cuts to local authority spending. Austerity combines with deeper political, social and economic changes to make conditions precarious for youth. Five years on, the author of one of the most authoritative studies of the English riots of 2011 suggested that the underlying conditions that sparked those disorders had become more severe.[1] Of course, there is a generational dimension to some of these issues. A 2014 policy briefing from the European Youth Forum pointed to a wider context of rising rates of youth unemployment, increased levels of poverty and social exclusion and a growing inequality between older and younger generations. Related to this, the UK's decision to leave the EU has been seen as betraying the aspirations of the younger generation (over 70% of whom voted to 'remain'; Cresci, 2016).

Alongside this material attack on the provisions and prospects for young people, youth have been subject to a domineering insistence that somehow their predicament is their responsibility. In Nancy Fraser's terms (2000; see also Mackie, 2017), not only have they suffered social injustice from the politics of distribution (of resources) but also they face injustice in respect of the politics of recognition; that is, their circumstances are misrecognised and presented as a consequence of their own flaws and failings. This can be seen with what is one of the dominant tropes of British politicians, policy makers, think tanks, and welfare practitioners: those who are not successful in their transitions from school to employment are deficient, with the most fashionable 'lack' currently being of aspiration ('grit', 'resilience', 'character', 'social capital', 'skills', 'qualifications' and 'experience' are also regularly cited as the things young people are lacking). Elsewhere I have described this as *voodoo sociology* (MacDonald, 2016): an insistence, against the weight of substantial available evidence, that the problems of youth unemployment can be magically resolved by recanting the mantra of 'raise aspirations'. Some very well-known research and theory from Youth Studies – about the role of 'opportunity structures' – reveals the stupidities here (Roberts, 2009) and, at a basic level, simple labour market statistics can confound this voodoo sociology. For instance, in Middlesbrough, Teesside, in March 2015 there were 3.3 unemployed claimants for every notified vacancy. Experts agree that not all vacancies are 'notified'; there are more jobs on offer than this. Experts also agree, however, that there are more people looking for jobs than are registered to claim unemployment benefits. That in Teesside typically 28 young adults apply for every *single* manufacturing and engineering apprenticeship would seem to confirm this point (TVU, 2014). The same pattern can be seen on a bigger canvas. In the US in 2011, the McDonald's fast food chain held a hiring day. They were looking to recruit 50,000 new staff. They had one million applications (eventually taking on 62,000 new workers[2]). Similarly, 'welfare to work programmes' falter when there are limited numbers of decent jobs to which the unemployed can be moved. For instance, the UK government's flagship 'Work Programme' for the long-term unemployed has a success rate in Teesside of 8% (ie it was able to help fewer than one in ten participants into lasting employment) (*Northern Echo*, 2013). In other words, talk of making people more 'employable' requires us to properly understand that 'employability' is a feature of the demand side as well as the supply side. In the depression of 1930s' Britain, the million 'unemployables' vanished when wartime labour demand deemed them employable.

To conclude, I think a contemporary book about youth marginality and austerity in Britain inevitably raises questions, even if these sometimes remains implicit in the chapters here, about the *provenance*, *extent* and *reach* of marginality, and how best we theorise youth in relation to processes of class reproduction and inequality. There comes a temptation when thinking about 'youth as a social category' to see the *uniformity* and commonality of youth experiences (Woodman and Wyn, 2015). This is particularly the case during historic periods – as now – when there is clearly opportunity to conceive of youth as a group that faces intergenerational inequality (Roberts, 2012). There are pressures that affect *all* young people in Britain as they look towards adulthood under conditions of government-pursued austerity: for example, rising house prices, particularly in relation to incomes; diminishing financial 'pay-offs' from a university degree; high rates of unemployment and underemployment; the spread of precarious employment; worsened retirement pensions; fewer and reduced welfare state entitlements; the loss of opportunities provided by EU membership; and, all in all, a greater risk of downward social mobility. Nevertheless – and of course – not all young people face these conditions from the same starting point. Class inequalities – and those connected to gender, ethnicity, disability, nationality and migration status, sexuality and other well-known forms of domination and inequality – cross-cut with age and generation *just as they always have done* (Hall and Jefferson, 1976). *Patterns* of inequality and *processes* of class reproduction might be less clear or more complex than previously (this reminds us of the privileged position youth researchers possess in relation to these pressing empirical questions), but this does not mean that class inequalities have melted away with the heat of austerity programmes, heightened marginality or obvious intergenerational inequality. At the same time as I was reading about how those already experiencing extreme disadvantage (homeless young people in North East England) faced an increased and unequal risk of welfare benefit sanctions (see earlier), national newspapers carried a story that betrayed the privilege of other young people in the same part of the UK. This story told of how the summer ball of Durham University's student 'Champagne Society' had descended into a 'drunken drug fuelled orgy' (*The Telegraph*, 11 November 2016). Tickets sold at £99 each, revellers received two free bottles of champagne and £45,000 was spent at the bar. These are tough times for young people in Britain – but much less tough for some.

Notes

[1] Tim Newburn, quoted in the *Guardian*, 5 August 2016, https://www.theguardian.com/uk-news/2016/aug/05/conditions-that-caused-english-riots-even-worse-now-says-leading-expert

[2] This acceptance rate of 6.2% meant it was harder to get a job at McDonalds than a place at Yale University, as one commentator noted at the time: http://www.motherjones.com/politics/2011/05/mcdonalds-national-hiring-day

References

Ball, S., Maguire, M. and Macrae, S. (2000) *Choice, Pathways and Transitions Post-16: New Youth, New Economies in the Global City.* London: Routledge/Falmer.

Byrne, D. (1999) *Social Exclusion.* Milton Keynes: Open University Press.

Calder, M., MacDonald, R., Mikhail, D., Murphy, E. and Phoenix, J. (2017) *Marginalization, Young People in the South and East Mediterranean, and Policy: An analysis of young people's experiences of marginalization across six SEM countries, and guidelines for policy-makers.* EU Framework 7 Power2Youth Programme, Brussels.

Coles, B. (1995) *Youth and Social Policy.* London: Routledge.

Côté, J. (2014) 'Towards a new political economy of youth', *Journal of Youth Studies*, 17, 4: 527–43.

Cresci, E. (2016) 'Meet the 75%: the young people who voted to remain in the EU', *Guardian*, 24 June 2016, http://www.theguardian.com/politics/2016/jun/24/meet-the-75-young-people-who-voted-to-remain-in-eu

European Youth Forum (2014) Policy Paper on Youth Employment. http://www.youthforum.org/assets/2014/06/0166-13_PP_Employment_Final1.pdf

Fahmy, E. (2015) 'On the frontline: the growth of youth deprivation in Britain, 1990–2012', *Discover Society*, 20. http://discoversociety.org/2015/05/05/on-the-frontline-the-growth-of-youth-deprivation-in-britain-1990-2012/

France, A., and Threadgold, S. (2016) 'Youth and political economy: towards a Bourdieusian approach, *Journal of Youth Studies*, 19, 5: 612–28.

Fraser, N. (2000) 'Rethinking recognition', *New Left Review*, 3, 107–20.

Furlong, A. (ed) (2017) *The Handbook of Youth and Young Adulthood*. London: Routledge.

Furlong, A. and Cartmel, F. (2007) *Young People and Social Change: New Perspectives*. Milton Keynes: Open University Press.

Gillis, J. (1974) *Youth and History*. New York: Academic Press.

Griffin, C. (1993) *Representations of Youth*. Cambridge: Polity Press.

Hall, S. and Jefferson, T. (1976) *Resistance through Rituals*. London: Hutchinson.

Hebdige, D. (1988) *Hiding in the Light*. London: Comedia/Routledge.

MacDonald, R. (2011) 'Youth, transitions and un(der)employment: plus ça change, plus c'est la même chose?', *Journal of Sociology*, 47: 427–44.

MacDonald, R. (2016) 'Voodoo sociology, unemployment and the low-pay, no-pay cycle', Blog for SARF (Social Action & Research Foundation). http://www.the-sarf.org.uk/voodoo-sociology/

MacDonald, R. and Marsh, J. (2005) *Disconnected Youth? Growing up in Britain's Poor Neighbourhoods*. Basingstoke: Palgrave.

Mackie, A. (2017) 'Life on the see-saw: young people, Nancy Fraser and Social Justice', presentation to Young People's Transitions conference, Edinburgh University, April.

North East Homelessness Think Tank, (2016) *Benefit Sanctions and Homelessness*. http://youthhomelessnortheast.org.uk/wp-content/uploads/NEHTT-final-report-2015.pdf

Northern Echo (2013) 'Results of Government's Work Programme in the North-East "appalling" – Labour', 27 June. http://www.thenorthernecho.co.uk/news/local/teesvalley/middlesbrough/10513443.Results_of_Government_s_Work_Programme_in_the_North_East__appalling____Labour/?action=complain&cid=11750335

Pearson, G. (1983) *Hooligan: A History of Respectable Fears*. London: Macmillan.

Roberts, K. (2009) 'Opportunity structures then and now', *Journal of Education and Work* 22(5): 355–68.

Roberts, K. (2012) 'The end of the long baby-boomer generation', *Journal of Youth Studies*, 15, 4: 479–97.

Sukarieh, M., and Tannock, S. (2015) *Youth Rising? The politics of youth in the global economy*, London: Routledge.

Sukarieh, M., and Tannock, S. (2016) 'On the political economy of youth: a comment', *Journal of Youth Studies*, 19, 9: 1281–9.

Shildrick, T., MacDonald, R., and Antonucci, L. (2015) 'Hard times for youth', *Discover Society*. http://discoversociety.org/2015/05/05/focus-hard-times-for-youth/

TVU (Tees Valley Unlimited) (2014) *Tees Valley Skills Strategy 2014-20*. https://www.teesvalleyunlimited.gov.uk/.../tees_valley_skills_strategy_20..

Unison (2016) *A Future at Risk: Cuts in Youth Services*, London: Unison. https://www.unison.org.uk/content/uploads/2016/08/23996.pdf

Watts, B. (2014) 'Benefits sanctions are adding to bleak prospects for young people', Joseph Rowntree Foundation blog post. https://www.jrf.org.uk/blog/benefits-sanctions-are-adding-bleak-prospects-young-people

Woodman, D. and Wyn, J. (2015) *Youth and Generation*. London: Sage.

Part One:
Youth policy, pariahs and poverty

ONE

Critically theorising young adult marginality: historical and contemporary perspectives

Shane Blackman and Ruth Rogers

Introduction: 'austerity isn't over'

This introductory chapter will contextualise some of the key theoretical developments relating to young people's experiences of social marginalisation in Britain. First, we examine the disparity between populist labels used by government and media to describe young people who experience marginality in the UK. Second, we develop a theory of advanced youth marginality through the work of Loic Wacquant and John Westergaard. Third, we argue that there is a commonality of argument between Thomas Malthus and Charles Murray that defines the young adult poor through the use of biological metaphors such as a 'redundant population'. Finally, we seek to advance the debate into new areas, by considering the political relationship between youth marginality and anomie. We maintain that young adults in Britain are subject to forms of biopolitical control by governmental and media organisations.

Popular images and punitive sanctions: young adults in Britain

The British tabloid media thrives on images of youth misrepresentation, showing marginalised young adults in dangerous spaces living on edge-of-town housing estates, in urban tower blocks or under rural isolation. Youth tend to be visually projected as either hooded and threatening, or wearing skimpy outfits suggesting low sexual morality (Blackman et al, 2015, p52). Young people's social exile is delivered through stereotypical caricatures enhanced by a narcissistic vision of young people addicted to mobile devices. These confining portrayals fail to capture the agency that young people use when they engage in social space, to gather and create bonds, to establish cultural memory and to affirm social relationships. Lisa Mckenzie (2015, p195) identifies that 'stigma and stereotypes' dominate how the young adult poor are represented and also denied self-conscious reflection of their situation. For young people, being in the park or on the street corner is a space of everyday action, where the hub of 'doing nothing' becomes active (Corrigan, 1976).

Across Britain, diverse sources suggest that young people face poverty and lack of opportunity. Watts (2014), writing for the Joseph Rowntree Foundation, states: 'Benefits sanctions are adding to bleak prospects for young people'. Natalie Gil (17 November 2014) in *The Guardian* states: 'Robbed of their futures ... austerity cuts hit young people hardest'. According to poverty.org.uk (2016), 'Young adults are much more likely to live in low-income households than older working-age adults: 31% compared to 19%. This has been the case since at least the mid 1990s.' On 22 February 2015, Daniel Boffey from *The Guardian* reported 'Youth unemployment rate is worst for 20 years, compared with overall figure' (Boffey, 2015). Telfer (2012) assesses the general situation for young people as one where there is high unemployment, 10% of young adults are not in work or full-time education and, furthermore, that 2.1 million young adults aged 16–24 are living in low-income households. David Gordon, reporting on the findings of *Poverty and Social Exclusion in Scotland and the UK*, states:

> Almost 18 million people cannot afford adequate housing conditions; 12 million people are too poor to engage in common social activities; one in three people cannot afford to heat their homes adequately in the winter and four million children and adults aren't properly fed by today's standards. (Gordon, 2014, p2)

Gordon continues, this means that 'around 2.5 million young people live in homes that are damp and around 1.5 million young people live in households that cannot afford to heat their homes'. A key factor in many young people's lives relates to lack of income, variable income and a low income overall, described as in-work poverty. In the 21st century, it is clear that hardship and means testing are two policies that persistently follow young people.

Little has changed in terms of neo-liberal strategies to reduce unemployment. As Tawney (1909, p363) argued at the beginning of the 1900s, people who apply for benefit are defined by the state as 'idle and vicious'. Furthermore, he maintains that the state 'denies point-blank that there is such a thing at all as distress due to economic causes'. Thus, Tawney states that under neo–liberalism, the policy is to make relief 'unattractive', to give only the 'minimum' except to those who are 'absolutely destitute', so as 'to repel all except those on the verge of starvation' (p364).

Today, benefit sanctions according to Crawshaw (2013) and Rogers (2013) have focused on behaviourist approaches and restrictive principles impacting on the poor and on young people, with a focus on punitive policies regulating lifestyles. On Jobseeker's Allowance sanctions, Sanders (2016, p201) notes that young people have to cope with the 'threat of three years without benefits for those who fail to comply with job search requirement three times'. The Office for National Statistics (2014) states: 'There were a total of 5.84 million decisions to apply a Job Seekers Allowance sanction (i.e. an adverse sanction decision) between April 2000 and December 2013, including 1.03 million under the new sanctions regime, introduced in October 2012'. Garthwaite (2016, p9) states: 'The estimated amount of money lost to claimants though Job Seekers Allowance sanctions imposed in 2013/14 was in the region of £328 million, with almost £5 million lost to Employment and Support Allowance claimants who have a sickness or disability'. This evidence reveals that the conditionality of sanctions applied to young people has been effective in denying them access to the benefits they are entitled to. Owen Jones states:

> Benefit fraud – costing an annual £1.2 billion, or 0.7 per cent of social security spending – is treated as a despicable crime, while tax avoidance – with an estimated £25 billion a year – is even facilitated by the state, with accountancy firms that promote such tax avoidance seconded to government to draw up tax laws. (Jones, 2014, pxv)

In *The Guardian* on 13 April 2016, Garside reported that: 'Figures show thousands more government inspectors are employed tackling benefits fraud than dealing with abuse of the tax system'. The article notes that Angus Robertson MP is concerned that a Conservative government is more focused on the 'poorest in society abusing benefits than with the super-rich evading their taxes'. Owen Jones (2014, p193) argues: 'the real scroungers are to be found not at the bottom of society, but at the top'. The austerity measures imposed by governmental and institutional sanctions curtail young people's access to services, increasing their vulnerability and reducing their options. Using C. Wright Mills' (1959) structural argument, it is apparent that young adults on benefits see their 'private troubles' transformed into negative 'public issues'.

In the ethnographic chapters in this book by Brooks (Chapter Four), Kehily (Chapter Six), Davidson and Whittaker (Chapter Twelve), McPherson (Chapter Fifteen) and Ruddy (Chapter Sixteen), we get a personal sense of how negative labels applied at national level are experienced in a personal way, increasing young people's feeling of anomie.

Advanced youth marginality

Under the social and cultural conditions of marginality, young adults are unable to do normal and everyday things, such as having the opportunity to contribute, participate, produce and consume. Being marginal separates young adults from being normal; that is, they are outside the mainstream. Marginality is not defined by unemployment alone; for us, marginality also encompasses low pay, underemployment and the insecurity of precarious employment (Standing, 2012). We identify youth marginality as a multilayered and multidimensional form of social and personal oppression. Marginality operates as a series of structural, cultural and emotional experiences, where social exclusion both preserves and intensifies discrimination, stereotypes and prejudice.

One way in which this is achieved is through language as a discourse of contemporary memory, biography and history. Two theorists, Loic Wacquant and JohnWestergaard, have influenced our approach. From the outset, we define the social exclusion of young adult people as an advanced form of social marginality, as theorised by Wacquant (2008, p25) in terms of the social structuring of poverty based on unemployment, the precarity of jobs, decaying neighbourhoods and heightened stigmatisation. For Wacquant, advanced youth marginality is a curse of dispossession with the removal of 'social dignity' (p30). Under structural processes of social fragmentation and demoralisation, young adults suffer the hardship of media accusations pouring the 'the weight of public scorn' (p29) on them, with the result that 'youths in devastated neighbourhood(s) ... assessed their success and failures almost exclusively in personal terms' (p180).

We take Wacquant's approach to young adult marginality at a structural level and see it as also relevant at the micro-individual level to understanding young people's actions. In the chapters in this book by Brooks (Chapter Four), Kehily (Chapter Six), Batchelor et al (Chapter Seven), Davidson and Whittaker (Chapter Twelve) and Ruddy (Chapter Sixteen), young people speak about their social and personal aspirations at an individual level, demonstrating the ordinariness of their hopes and how their values are common throughout society, but also demonstrating Wacquant's theory that their experience is deemed personal rather than shared.

We apply Westergaard's (1992, p575) idea of the 'fashion in social speculation'. His aim for sociology was to cut through the temporality of fashions in social policy to explore how faddish notions require critical investigation. For MacDonald (1997, p6), negative labels that describe youth marginality are 'an ideological red herring which diverts attention from the real causes of poverty and the real problems faced by the poor'. For example, a range of terms that have been used to describe young people under hardship are: marginal, 'underclass', precariate, yobs, hooligans, disconnected, dispossessed, socially excluded, outcasts, feckless, new rabble, scum, zonards, outsiders, lumpen proletariat, disadvantaged, vulnerable. The proliferation of these labels, according to Wacquant (2008, p245), 'speaks volumes on the state of symbolic derangement afflicting the fringes and fissures of the recomposed social and urban structure'. For Westergaard (1992, p581), these labels are 'powerful myths, which social science then has a responsibility to explode'. However, at the same time, one feature of the UK debate on youth marginality has been the concern to critique or overturn stereotypes that MacDonald et al (2014, p1) argue have been promoted 'by politicians, think tanks and the media'. We maintain that due to the heightened moral and political context of young people's marginality, it has been found that authors who produce studies on poverty and inequality among young adults have to disprove stereotypes or inaccurate information before they can legitimately advance their main findings.

Thus Westergaard's (1992, p581) key strategy is to identify 'ideological fashions', to reveal bias and inaccuracy. To do this, Westergaard elaborates that sociology 'needs its *agents provocateurs* who flaunt new fashions' (p581). For example, Imogen Tyler (2013, p4) applies Julia Kristeva's concept of the abject to critically analyse how government policy and media representation construct and define young people as marginalised through terms including '"chavs", rioters and scroungers'. For Tyler, the lived process of social abjection promotes an ideology of young people who are upheld, according to her, as a series of 'revolting subjects'. For example, the tabloid media often combine stigma with fertility – see the *Mail Online* headlines 'Vile product of Welfare UK' (3 April 2013) and 'Benefit broods' (31 December 2012). The evocative images and moral discourse summoned up by such headlines return the analysis to the notion of a 'redundant population' and Social Darwinism, described by Hansen et al (2014, p76) as 'pathologising poverty', where the biological and the medical are fused to shape cultural and social debates.

Young adults – a 'redundant population': from Malthus to Murray

'Strivers versus shirkers' was the Chancellor George Osborne's clarion call at the 2012 Conservative party conference (Jowit, 2013). For Hughes et al (2014, p3) this was evocative of the 'underclass thesis from the 1980s and the Poor Laws of the 1880s, where people were positioned in the binary of "deserving" and "undeserving" poor'. Contemporary political comment confirms this position, as advanced by Hellen (2014) – 'Rise of the new underclass costs £30bn' – and Wilson's (2014) 'Britain's expanding underclass'.

We argue that the approach developed by Thomas Malthus in *An essay on the principle of population* (1798) and Charles Murray in *'Underclass': A disaster in the making* (1989) examines lower-class young adults through a biological approach. Specifically, there is a commonality between Malthus and Murray, who identify the young adult working class in biological terms as a 'redundant population' without purpose, through the metaphors of fear about 'vice' and 'fertility' and as a projected economic burden and a social threat to society.

Malthus's (pp19, 41, 107) idea of a 'redundant population' suggested that the poor possessed values and morality that were different from the rest of society. For him, the poor are too concerned with natural passion – what he calls 'vices'. Malthus states: 'no check whatever has existed to early marriages, among the lower classes'. He continues: '[the] lower classes of people in Europe may at some future period be much better instructed than they are at present; they may be taught to employ the little spare time they have in many better ways than at the ale-house' (p88). Lydia Morris (1994, p11) identifies coercion as a key explanation within Malthus's work: she argues that for him 'the poor need to be made to recognise and accept responsibility.'

Malthus's essay on population played a significant role in influencing Social Darwinism and the ideas of eugenics, a term coined by Francis Galton (1883). Porter et al (2008, p118) note: 'Galton was directly influenced by and made reference to Malthus in his presidential address before the Division of Demography of the seventh International Congress of Hygiene' (1892). According to Raymond Williams (1980, p92), 'There is a direct link back to Malthus and the thought

8

that the unfit should be prevented from breeding' (see Macnicol, 1989). Welshman (2013, pp76-77) identifies that these ideas resurface periodically, such as the 'cycle of deprivation in the 1970s'.

An example of youth recycled as a social problem can be found in the work of Charles Murray. In *Underclass: The Crisis Deepens*, Murray (1994, p115) talks about *The New Rabble*, who he defines thus:

> Illegitimacy in the lower classes will continue to rise and, inevitably, life in lower class communities will continue to degenerate—more crime, more widespread drug and alcohol addiction, fewer marriages, more dropout from work, more homelessness, more child neglect, fewer young people pulling themselves out of the slums, more young people tumbling in. (Murray, 1994, p115)

Malthus's understanding of the system of relief through the Poor Laws parallels that of Murray's position on benefits and sanctions related to the youth 'underclass'. Murray (1989) states: 'the underclass spawns illegitimate children without a care for tomorrow. Its able-bodied youth see no point in working and feel no compulsion either. They reject society while feeding off it, giving the cycle of deprivation a new spin.' For Murray, the key problem is with high teenage pregnancy and absent young adult fathers (Murray, 2001, p19). Both Malthus and Murray create an image of the lower classes breeding in an uncontrollable manner, as though they were animals that 'run wild' (Murray, 1989, p33).

Murray's ideas have defined the radical right's approach towards young people on benefits. Throughout Murray's major studies – *Losing ground* (1984), *Underclass: A disaster in the making* (1989), *Underclass: The crisis deepens* (1994), *The bell curve* (1996) with Herrnstein, and *In our hands: A plan to replace the welfare state* (2006) – we see the development of a series of ideas. As MacDonald (1997, p11) points out, these seek to blame the poor for their social condition, by arguing that social disadvantage is caused by both 'maternal deprivation' and 'paternal deprivation'. However, in *The bell curve*, Murray rekindles the link between poverty and the discredited eugenic movement, with its focus on discouraging reproduction among the poor: blame is fixed on 'unmarried and unschooled teenagers' (Peretz, 1995, p154). Fraser (1995, p8) states: '*The Bell Curve* builds a brief on behalf of eugenics and the continued rule of the cognitive elite'.

Through *The bell curve* and *In our hands* (2006), Murray has argued for the abolition of the welfare state and its replacement with a single payment of cash of $10,000 to each benefit claimant called the *Plan*. His right-wing policy agenda is particularly harsh on young mothers under 21 and young males who are unemployed. Boyle (2007, p3) states that *In our hands* 'shows his visceral hatred for the two groups'. The populism of Murray's approach bore fruit where the idea of a one-off payment was the defining feature of the Channel Five programme *The Great British Benefits Handout*, where a family is given their £26,000 annual benefits allowance in one lump sum. Although key advisers to the programme included Professor Guy Standing to support the families, the programme features benefits as entertainment, for example when the money is delivered 'gangster style' in a suitcase. Sophie Wilkinson (2016) states: 'you can't help but baulk at the tastelessness of turning this into a reality TV format that plays out more like a win–or–lose game than the social experiment it purports to be'. In 'popular factual entertainment' reality TV, as noted by Skeggs and Wood (2008), there is little control over circumstances for participants, because their lives are already precarious, but through the confessional device of self-narration the audience becomes absorbed, watching vulnerability as unfolding entertainment (Windle, 2010, p260).

Anomie and youth marginality: the state of exception and the return of biology

We identify in the chapters of this book a strong link between young people's experience of poverty, hardship and anomie. Anomie can be defined by a breakdown of norms governing social interactions. For Emile Durkheim, anomie is concerned with the breaking of social bonds in culture and society, first outlined in Durkheim's PhD thesis, *The division of labour in society* in 1893, then applied in *Suicide* in 1897. Durkheim (1893/1933, p5) states: 'It is this anomic state that is the cause, as we shall show, of the incessantly recurrent conflicts, and the multifarious disorders of which the economic world exhibits so sad a spectacle'.

Contemporary neo-liberal economic policies assert the priority of competition over welfare. Both Bauman (2004, p51) and Giroux (2009, p169) argue that the growth of social disadvantage and the emergent *précarité* has reached a position where social exclusion has defined young people as 'waste.' The apparent economic burden of marginal young adults means that they are identified as disposable through current austerity measures, which define welfare as the threat to economic growth itself (Chadderton and Colley, 2012, p329). Park (1928, p893) first introduced the notion of the 'marginal', where it manifested itself in 'moral turmoil' in the mind of the individual as an 'intensified self-consciousness, restlessness, and malaise'. Park sought to capture real lives and real problems with human interest. As Matza (1969, p33) writes, Park 'was immersed in the concrete details of the everyday life of his subjects'. Sociologically thinking, we see the connection between Durkheim's normlessness of anomie and Park's idea of the marginal. For young adults themselves, marginality is shaped through their inability to participate as a result of discrimination or social exclusion. This is felt at a personal level, where marginality is in essence the fate of 'being ignored', 'left out' or 'not cared for'. Chadderton and Colley (2012, p34) argue that: 'marginalised young people are displaced at best into various waiting room strategies of government (such as Connexions and various training or pre-vocational preparation schemes) and at worst the dangerous spaces of those who have no hope'. Without social and cultural integration, young marginal adults feel their 'everyday life' is of less value. They are being pushed to the sidelines, where they experience anomie (see Chapter Two and Chapter Three).

We see Giorgio Agamben's (2005) theory of the 'state of exception' as a useful explanation in relation to young marginal adults trapped in a zone of anomie by the state and the media. We interpret advanced social marginalisation through two of Agamben's ideas: first, through the language of war, violence and conflict; and second, through biopolitical control. Agamben argues that the state of exception describes the form of governance or rule today whereby, under a state of emergency, government uses a vocabulary of war to justify punitive powers. We argue that the use of language as a destructive form of emotion creates an unpredictable alliance, between tabloid media messages of stigma and government accusations of the burden of youth, and creates emptiness for young adults without feelings. Here anomie describes the breakdown in cultural norms experienced most acutely by young adults, who feel blamed or accused through negative labels.

This leads us to believe that young adults who are labelled in negative terms are subject to a loss of identity within the wider community, creating feelings within young people of personal and social disintegration – an anomic state. Populist terms, including 'waifs', 'strays' or 'scum', follow an undifferentiated, demonising pattern or a collective target with an accusatory tone. Bourdieu et al (1999) argue that young adults are faced with the 'weight of the world of social suffering' through being defined publicly as 'feral' or 'lazy'. The power behind emotive language cuts young people off, or makes them feel isolated or overburdened, as Turner and Stets (2005, p265) state: 'emotions can make individuals strike out, tear down, or detach themselves from social structures'. The great fear of social exclusion for young people, according to Julkunen (2009, p163), is that they experience 'the process of becoming detached from the moral order or from the prevailing norms in society'.

Alongside the executive power of government, the media promotes a fictitious threat or narrative of fear against young adults, who are repetitively defined as 'scroungers' on benefits (Gordon, 2014). In *Homo Sacer*, Agamben (1998, p103) uses the notion of an 'accursed' or stigmatised person, as someone who is 'excluded' from the 'community and from all political life', where their 'existence is reduced to a bare life stripped of every right'. Under governmental and institutional power, *Homo Sacer* 'is in a continuous relationship with the power that banished him precisely insofar as he is at every instant exposed to an unconditioned threat'. This corresponds to the media image of young people in social exile on edge-of-town housing estates or in urban tower blocks: at the margins of society. Meek (2016, p17) argues that Agamben's 'critical conception of the media can be related to his argument that the modern state has reduced the individual to a condition of bare life or biological existence'. Giroux (2009, p169) argues that, for Agamben, biopolitics is the 'founding moment of politics' and also the current historical moment; that exhibits force and danger. Here we note Humphreys' (2006, p687) argument that the technologies of biopolitical control are a means whereby young adult marginality is affirmed through biological and cultural categories that define the state of exception as the creation of a zone of anomie. Thus, Agamben (2005, p59) suggests that state power 'seeks to annex anomie through the state of exception', that is to say a paradigm of governance based around a fiction of violence. Or, as the tabloid media assert, it is a 'War on scroungers' (*Daily Express*, 28 August 2011).

The structure of this book

This book is divided into three parts:

- **Part One** is on youth policy, pariahs and poverty. It explores the tensions of change and continuity at the level of critical theory, policy analysis, media representation and the subjective experience of marginality.
- **Part Two** covers intersections of youth marginality: class, gender, ethnicity and education. It examines the diversity of intersections

relating to youth marginality across social class, gender and racial boundaries.

• **Part Three** focuses on resistance and ethnography. It highlights the importance of young people's personal, familial and collective experiences of poverty and austerity and the strategies of resistance or risk, while they are also experiencing disconnection and discrimination.

A key aim is to challenge the dominant notions of youth marginalisation and the representation of youth as 'trouble', through critical analysis and participatory research methods to project young people's 'real' experience and voice. Some chapters highlight degrees of resistance, where the struggle to survive in the face of stigma can generate counter-practices or refusal. Within the struggle of poverty and insecurity, the cultures of survival observed were found to be both fragile and contradictory.

In **Chapter Two**, Squires and Goldsmith focus on the social exclusion of youth and the conservative ideology of the 'broken society'. They address young people's marginality through a critical analysis of political ideology to argue that the wellbeing of young adults has diminished as a result of 'tough justice'. They question the neo-liberal approach to young adults with its focus on risk and compliance measures, where punitive innovations encourage a rolling back of youth social policy, while at the same time young people receive sanctions, disciplines and punishments.

In **Chapter Three**, Fahmy draws on data from the *2012 UK Poverty and Social Exclusion Survey* (2012 PSE-UK), to examine the nature, extent and social distribution of youth deprivation and social exclusion among 16–29 year olds living in Britain.. He uses household income data with direct observations to examine young people's living standards and exclusion from customary norms. This offers insight into the social profile of vulnerability among young people, which extends beyond relative low-income measures. Also, by comparing data for the PSE from 1990, 1999 and 2012, Fahmy explores the changing profile of vulnerability to youth disadvantage and how this can be seen as a reflection of wider changes in the context of youth transitions.

In **Chapter Four**, Brooks chronicles the impact of the Conservative government's austerity measures experienced at a local charity in Essex. Linda is a volunteer and treasurer at the charity and draws from first-hand experience of working with young adults to provide insights into the impact of austerity measures. Here, youth marginality is investigated through real-life examples, to show how the government austerity measures increase social disadvantage for young people in the local community.

In **Chapter Five**, Blackman and Rogers present a textual analysis of newspaper headlines and reality TV programmes that exploit forms of popular culture, such as successful television series, to convey a political and moral message that reinforces the marginality of young adults in society. They argue that selective visual imagery and a constructed language of fear shape the intersection of government policy and media coverage on young people (Ilan, 2015). They identify two types of media representations: first, through the image of the 'scrounger'; and second, through the image of 'mockery', whereby young adults are projected as scroungers and marginalised thorough mockery, which combine to show young people as a burden, rather than as an asset, for society.

In **Chapter Six**, Kehily considers the phenomenon of young motherhood in the UK and the ways in which it may be viewed in policy and popular discourse. Based on a five-year, ESRC-funded study of how women make the transition to motherhood in new times, she argues that early motherhood occupies a distinctive place within the context of late modern social change, marked in this case by changing gender relations and women's increased participation in the workforce. The chapter explores how social differences between women may be played out in the cultural sphere of representations and practices of consumption. She argues that the stigmatised figure of early motherhood, configured colloquially as the marginal 'pramface girl', can be understood within the context of the local – community, family, biography and intergenerational perspectives.

In **Chapter Seven**, Batchelor, Whittaker, Fraser and Ling look at leisure among marginalised youth in the East End of Glasgow. The qualitative data focus on the relative immobility of young people's leisure lives, which are primarily located in and around the family home. Marginalised youth have increasingly few free public spaces available to them, resulting in an apparent upsurge in free time spent in private space indoors and online. They identify declining participation in street-based leisure as a result of increased surveillance and social control, by parents and police, and wider neo-liberal processes of market-led regeneration and the commercialisation of urban amenities. The young people experience a retreat into private and domestic spaces in an effort to survive, and adopt creative ways to engage in commercialised leisure, albeit in marginal ways.

In **Chapter Eight**, Robinson and Williams focus on young Afghan men's asylum claims in terms of their family background, citizenship and immigration status within the care system under vulnerability. All of the research participants have had their asylum claims considered 'unfounded', are classified as Appeals Rights Exhausted, and face return to Afghanistan. Their narratives speak of a dangerous place, where they have no links or connections, yet their description of the UK is often negative and they are critical of the support they have received here (Tyler, 2013). The findings illustrate how immigration policies affect the daily lives of these young people, who are caught between two unpalatable futures – one back in Afghanistan and one living in destitution and illegality in the UK.

In **Chapter Nine**, Robson discusses recent research conducted with a team of teachers and family workers supporting Roma young people who arrived in the United Kingdom as European Union migrants. Using participants' voices reveals a prevailing negative discourse on Roma. Robson reflects on the way in which frequent media representations of English Gypsies as the 'other' are experienced as racism, and are also circulated through social media. She argues that dominant discourses in education settings constrain responses to injustice.

In **Chapter Ten**, Ainley argues that raising school education to 18 has served to divide young people into two official categories: 'students' or 'apprentices'. The concern is that this division will ultimately result in a 'vocational' curriculum in schools from aged 14+ that, despite claiming 'parity of esteem', will result in the marginalisation of young people who fail to embark on an academic route. His critical and political analysis argues that the new vocational route will create a permanently marginalised minority, a reconstituted reserve army of labour, ratcheted up to include large numbers of employed people in permanently insecure, often part-time, unskilled and low-paid jobs. He concludes this is not a 'youth problem' that young people have to overcome by acquiring 'skills': it is an economic problem, for which education can no longer be substituted as a solution.

In **Chapter Eleven**, Tupling critically examines the case study of one free school to challenge whether free schools are really designed to be responsive to the needs of local communities. She addresses whether free schools fail to reflect the diversity of local communities, or fail to offer increased educational opportunities for the most disadvantaged pupils, despite the requirement that their admission criteria are fair and transparent. Drawing on Anderson's (2006) concept of 'imagined communities', she demonstrates how the term 'community' is employed in local political and popular discourses to identify, and to secure a school for, the ideal pupil.

In **Chapter Twelve**, Davidson and Whittaker see young people as becoming the 'new poor', as they struggle to cope with increasingly precarious transitions into in(ter)dependent living. Care leavers across the UK continue to experience marginalisation and have poorer outcomes than their peers across a number of domains, from educational performance and employment through to health and housing. They focus on marginality within a specific group of young people who, as care leavers, are vulnerable to service cuts associated with austerity in the UK. They focus on young adults, giving prominence to their voices and experiences and the importance of long-term, personal relationships while in care.

In **Chapter Thirteen**, Murphy examines the contemporary issues surrounding the policing of disadvantaged communities, to develop an understanding of how rights become qualified or suspended during encounters with the police. His approach considers the status of marginalised young people within Wacquant's (2014) theory of 'advanced marginality', and conceptualises [b]othered youth within a wider framework of the *institutional mistrust of youth*. He explores the controversies surrounding the (mis)use of stop and search powers, and how such discretionary powers can reproduce inequalities, injustice and resentment. He assesses the impact of [b]othering, resistance and marginalisation on the lives of disadvantaged youth and their community through examining the loss of legitimacy and the tensions emerging from over-policing and under-protection of young people and communities.

In **Chapter Fourteen**, McKay and Atherton examine young people's social play in terms of how space is negotiated with the police. They consider the important role of resistance at places of intersection, where the desire to define a new liberty or a free space can involve opposition, resistance and transgression. Places for expression are either provided or sought out by young people, but subject to adult interruption, where young people are framed by wider social and political contexts that set the boundaries, rules and possibilities for their lives. They demonstrate how marginalisation occurs in the micro-interactions of the mundane, and how it is overlooked by protagonists. They relate their findings to the wider competing discourses of risk and marginality.

In **Chapter Fifteen**, McPherson presents ethnographic examples taken from a study focused on young people in the Canterbury night-time economy. He examines the media framing of the contemporary alcohol consumption practice known as 'binge' drinking, and how negative media representations of young people and this practice has produced what he describes as a 'moral marginality' in the UK. He uses data to argue that young people intentionally manage their levels of desired and actual intoxication that also incorporates aspects of perceived risk and possible resistance.

In **Chapter Sixteen**, Ruddy focuses on the experiences of young people growing up in contexts of multiple deprivation in a small, deindustrialised town in North East England. Through the use of the subjective narratives of young people, he interrogates the interplay between youth poverty and material inequality, youth cultural resistance and the day-to-day lives of young people from marginalised communities. Significant hardship and deep poverty intersect with structural economic and social degeneration, and as a result discrimination and individual victimisation run through the respondents' biographies. He offers an insight into the lives of young adults, who experience different forms of marginalisation as part of their struggle of transition to adulthood.

In **Chapter Seventeen**, Rogers and Blackman consider the contemporary issues affecting young adults in the UK as a result of economic insecurity following the Brexit vote. They address the three sections of the book relating to advanced marginality. First, they assess the austerity measures and sanctions applied to young people, resulting in increased social disadvantages. Second, they explore the critical intersections of social class, gender and ethnic identities within educational, political, cultural and popular discourses as they impinge upon the question of young people and social marginalisation. Finally, they examine the degrees of resistance and autonomy among young people, whereby agency appears vulnerable and young people struggle to maintain an independent voice.

References

Agamben, G. (1998) *Homo Sacer: Sovereign power and bare life*. Stanford, CA: Stanford University Press.

Agamben, G. (2005) *State of exception*. Chicago: University of Chicago Press.

Anderson, B. (2006) *Imagined communities: Reflections on the origin and spread of nationalism*. London: Verso.

Barron, L. (2013) 'The sound of street corner society: UK grime music as ethnography', *European Journal of Cultural Studies*, 16, 5: 531-47.

Bauman, Z. (2004) *Wasted lives: Modernity and its outcasts*. Oxford: Polity.

Blackman, S., Doherty, L. and McPherson, R. (2015) 'Normalisation of hedonism? Challenging convergence culture through ethnographic studies of alcohol consumption on young adults – a feminist exploration', in P. Staddon (ed) *Women and alcohol: Social perspectives.* Bristol: Policy Press: 45-64.

Boffey, D. (2015) 'Youth unemployment rate is worst for 20 years, compared with overall figure', https://www.theguardian.com/society/2015/feb/22/youth-unemployment-jobless-figure

Bourdieu, P. et al (1999) *The weight of the world: Social suffering in contemporary society.* Translated by P.P. Ferguson. Palo Alto, CA: Stanford University Press.

Boyle, C. (2007) *In our hands: A plan to replace the welfare state.* Washington, DC: The American Enterprise Institute. http://www.conallboyle.com/BasicIncomeNewEcon/MurrayReview.pdf

Chadderton, C. and Colley, H. (2012) 'School-to-work transition services: Marginalising 'disposable' youth in a state of exception?', *Discourse: Studies in the cultural politics of education*, 33, 3: 329-43.

Corrigan, P. (1976) *Schooling the Smash Street kids.* London: Macmillan.

Crawshaw, P. (2013) 'Public health policy and the behavioural turn: The case of social marketing', *Critical Social Policy*, 33, 4: 616-37.

Daily Express (28 August 2011) 'War on scroungers', www.express.co.uk/news/uk/267673/War-on-scroungers

Durkheim, E. (1893/1986) *The division of labour in society.* London: Sage.

Durkheim, E. (1897/1951) *Suicide.* New York: The Free Press.

Fraser, S. (1995) (ed.) *The bell curve wars: Race, intelligence, and the future of America.* New York, NY: Basic Books.

Galton, F. (1883/1907) *Inquiries into human faculty and its development.* London: J.M. Dent & Sons.

Garside, J. (13 April 2016) 'Benefit fraud or tax evasion: Row over the Tories' targets', https://www.theguardian.com/uk-news/2016/apr/13/benefit-or-tax-evasion-row-over-the-tories-targets

Garthwaite, K. (2016) *Hunger pains: Life inside foodbank Britain.* Bristol: Policy Press.

Gil, N. (17 November 2014) 'Robbed of their futures: How austerity cuts hit young people hardest', *The Guardian.* https://www.theguardian.com/education/2014/nov/17/robbed-of-their-futures-how-austerity-cuts-hit-young-people-hardest

Giroux, H. (2009) *Youth in a suspect society: Democracy or disposability?* New York: Palgrave Macmillan.

Gordon, D. (2014) 'The impoverishment of the UK', www.poverty.ac.uk/sites/default/files/attachments/The_Impoverishment_of_the_UK_PSE_UK_first_results_summary_report_March_28.pdf

Greenwood, W. (1933) *Love on the dole*. London: Cape.

Hancock, L. and Mooney, G. (2013) '"Welfare Ghettos" and the "Broken Society": Territorial stigmatization in the contemporary UK. Housing', *Theory and Society*, 30, 1, 46-64.

Hancox, D. (18 February 2016) 'Party politics: Why grime defines the sound of protest in 2016', *The Guardian*. www.theguardian.com/music/2016/feb/18/party-politics-why-grime-defines-the-sound-of-protest-in-2016

Hansen, H., Bourgois, P. and Drucker, E. (2014) 'Pathologizing poverty: New forms of diagnosis, disability, and structural stigma under welfare reform', *Social Science & Medicine*, 103, 1: 76-83.

Hellen, N. (17 August 2014) 'Rise of the new underclass costs £30bn', *The Sunday Times*. http://www.thesundaytimes.co.uk/sto/news/uk_news/Society/article1447828.ece

Hughes, G., Cooper, C., Gormally, S. and Rippingale, J. (2014) 'The state of youth work in austerity England – reclaiming the ability to "care"', *Youth and Policy*, 113: 1-14.

Humphreys, S. (2006) 'Legalizing lawlessness: on Giorgio Agamben's state of exception', *European Journal of International Law*, 17, 3: 677-87.

Ilan, J. (2015) *Understanding street culture: Poverty, crime, youth and cool*. Basingstoke: Palgrave.

Jones, O. (2014) *The establishment*. London: Penguin.

Jowit, J. (8 January 2013) 'Strivers v shirkers: The language of the welfare debate', *The Guardian*. www.theguardian.com/politics/2013/jan/08/strivers-shirkers-language-welfare

Julkunen, I. (2009) 'Youth, unemployment and marginalisation', in A. Furlong (ed) *International Handbook of Youth and Young Adults*. London: Routledge: 157-66.

MacDonald, R. (ed) (1997) *Youth, the 'underclass' and social exclusion*. London: Routledge.

MacDonald, R., Shildrick, T. and Furlong, A. (2014) '"Benefits Street" and the myth of workless communities', *Sociological Research Online*, 19: 3, www.socresonline.org.uk/19/3/1.html

Macnicol, J. (1989) 'Eugenics and the Campaign for Voluntary Sterilization in Britain between the Wars', *The Society for the Social History of Medicine*, 2, 2: 147-69.

Mail Online (3 April 2013) 'Vile product of Welfare UK', www.dailymail.co.uk/news/article-2303120/Mick-Philpott-vile-product-Welfare-UK-Derby-man-bred-17-babies-milk-benefits-GUILTY-killing-six.html

Mail Online (31 December 2012) 'Benefit broods', www.dailymail.
co.uk/news/article-2255203/200-families-claiming-housing-
benefit-10-children-taxpayers-face-150million-benefit-broods.html

Malthus, T. (1798) *An essay on the principle of population*. London: J.
Johnson.

Matza, D. (1969) *Becoming deviant*. Englewood Cliffs, NJ: Prentice-Hall.

McKenzie, L. (2015) *Getting by: Estates, class and culture in Austerity
Britain*. Bristol: Policy Press.

Meek, A. (2016) *Biopolitical media*. London: Routledge.

Mills, C. Wright (1956) *The power elite*. New York: Oxford University
Press.

Mills, C. Wright (1959) *The sociological imagination*. New York: Oxford
University Press.

Morris, L. (1994) *Dangerous class*. London: Routledge.

Murray, C. (1984) *Losing ground*. New York: Basic Books.

Murray, C. (1989) 'Underclass': A disaster in the making', *The Sunday
Times Magazine*, 27 November: 26-45.

Murray, C. (1994) *Underclass: The crisis deepens*. London: Institute of
Economic Affairs.

Murray, C. (2006) *In our hands: A plan to replace the welfare state*.
Cambridge: AEI Press.

Murray, C. with Herrnstein, R. J. (1994) *The bell curve*. New York:
Free Press.

Office for National Statistic (2014) First Release. https://www.gov.uk/
government/uploads/system/uploads/attachment_data/file/382255/
stats_summary_may14_final_v1.pdf

Park, R. (1928) 'Human migration and the marginal man', *American
Journal of Sociology*, 33, 6: 881-93.

Peretz, M. (1995) 'Equality: An endangered faith', in S. Fraser (ed.)
The Bell Curve Wars: race, intelligence, and the future of America. New
York, NY: Basic Books: 148-55.

Porter, N., Bothne, N. and Jason, L. (2008) *Interconnectedness and the
Individual: New research*. New York: Nova Science Publishers Inc.

Poverty.org (2016) 'Young adults in low-income households', http://
www.poverty.org.uk/34/index.shtml

Rodger, J. (2013) 'Regulating the poor: Observations on the structural
coupling of welfare, criminal justice and the voluntary sector in a big
society', in H. Kemshall (ed) *Crime and social policy*. Oxford: Wiley-
Blackwell: 59-76.

Sanders, T. (2016) 'Concluding thoughts: the consequence of a "not-so-big society"', in M. Harrison and T. Sanders (eds) *Social policies and social control: New perspectives on the 'not-so-big' society*. Bristol: Policy Press.

Shildrick, T., Macdonald, R., Webster, C. and Garthwaite, K. (2012) *Poverty and insecurity: Life in low-pay, no-pay Britain*. Bristol: Policy Press.

Skeggs, B. and Wood, H. (2008) *Reality television and class*. London: Palgrave.

Standing, G. (2012) *The precariat: The new dangerous class*. London: Bloomsbury.

Steinbeck, J. (1939) *The grapes of wrath*. New York: The Viking Press.

Tawney, R. H. (1909) 'The theory of pauperism', *The Sociological Review*, October: 361-74.

Telfer, S. (2012) 'Austerity in the UK – Spotlight on young people', Joseph Rowntree Foundation. https://www.jrf.org.uk/austerity-uk-spotlight-young-people

Thomson, R. and Kehily, M.J. (2011) 'Figuring families: generation, situation and narrative in contemporary mothering', *Sociological Research Online*. www.socresonline.org.uk/16/4/16.html

Turner, J. and Stets, J. (2005) *The sociology of emotions*. Cambridge: Cambridge University Press.

Tyler, I. (2013) *Revolting subjects: Social abjection and resistance in neoliberal Britain*. London: Zed Books Ltd.

Wacquant, L. (2008) *Urban outcasts: A comparative sociology of advanced marginality*. Cambridge: Polity.

Watts, B. (2014) 'Benefits sanctions are adding to bleak prospects for young people', https://www.jrf.org.uk/blog/benefits-sanctions-are-adding-bleak-prospects-young-people

Westergaard, J. (1992) 'About and beyond the underclass: Some notes on influences of social climate on British Society', *Sociology*, 26: 575-87.

Welshman, J. (2006/2013) *Underclass: A history of the excluded 1880–2000*. London: Bloomsbury.

Wilkinson, S. (2016) 'As a social experiment, 'The Great British Benefits Handout' fails from the beginning', VICE, 10 February. www.vice.com/en_uk/read/channel-5-great-british-benefits-handout-social-experiment-342

Williams, R. (1980) *Problems in materialism and culture*. London: Verso.

Wilson, S. (2014) *Britain's expanding underclass*, 25 Augus, http://moneyweek.com/britains-expanding-underclass/

Windle, J. (2010) '"Anyone can make it, but there can only be one winner": modelling neoliberal learning and work on reality television', *Critical Studies in Education*, 51, 3: 251–63.

TWO

Broken society, anti-social contracts, failing state? Rethinking youth marginality

Peter Squires and Carlie Goldsmith

Introduction

Central to our analysis is a critical reinterpretation of the pervasive conservative 'common sense' regarding inequality and the social exclusion of substantial sections of contemporary working-class youth, and concerning crime and disorder. We begin by engaging with three core components structuring and sustaining this social exclusion of youth: the ideology of the 'broken society'; the variety of anti-social 'contracts' and compliance processes to which many marginalised young people have become subject; and the failing state with which they frequently have to deal. We question each of these components of neo-liberal political ideology and the way in which they combine to blame the victims of failing neo-liberal governance for a wide range of social problems, utilising their ascribed culpability to justify tougher compliance measures, sanctions, disciplines and punishments. In contrast, we argue that it has been the pursuit of neo-liberal free market policies that has exacerbated contemporary inequalities, while fostering a powerful ideology of individualism that has generated the precarious situation of marginalised youth as collateral harm.

Our argument presents the claim that, as neo-liberalism fails youth, so too it fails as governance. Yet states do not fail, overnight, or even all at once; a failing state can still be strong and dangerous. But the more that states fail to achieve certain minima of human rights and social provisions, and the more they slip down the 'quality of life' league tables, then the less they reflect a collective public interest, the less legitimacy they possess and the more broken the social and cultural contract upon which they depend.

The broken society?

The 'broken society' discourse played a key role in the re-working of Conservative Party strategies for welfare reform, family policy, youth 'disaffection' and crime control (Cameron, 2008a; Driver, 2009). According to Mooney (2009), the notion of a 'broken society' – echoing the moralistic tone of the 'broken windows' analysis on crime and community decline (Wilson and Kelling, 1982) that came to dominate crime prevention thinking in the final decades of the 20th century – appeared to suggest a different way of understanding social problems in contemporary Britain. However, as Mooney concluded, this view was 'largely underpinned by an individualistic and moralistic view of poor people as a distinctive group apart from "mainstream" society ... and a thinly disguised culture of poverty argument that people experiencing poverty are lacking in the capacity to escape poverty, gripped by fatalism and apathy' (Mooney, 2009, p447). In turn, such attitudes were said to fuel crime, anti-social behaviour and youthful violence and disorder.

Characteristic of neo-liberal politics, the emerging 'broken society' commentary blamed individuals for social problems (Finlayson, 2010) and was implicit in much of the output of Iain Duncan Smith's Centre for Social Justice policy think tank. The Centre's influential report *Dying to belong* (Centre for Social Justice, 2009), which underpinned several strands of Cameron Conservative public policy – on gangs and youth violence, on families and social responsibility – famously inverted the widely accepted relationship between cause and consequence, when it described a youthful generation being lost 'as they plunged *through* violence and criminality *to* hopelessness and despair' (Centre for Social Justice, 2009, p9). Britain's gang culture was said to be the product of such environments, often to be found in the country's deprived and marginalised communities. Just as the causes are laid at the feet of feckless or irresponsible individuals, so, according to Bauman (2008), neo-liberal politics encourages individuals to find their own 'individual solutions to socially generated problems, and to do it individually, using their own skills and individually possessed assets'.

If individuals have to solve their own problems by hard work and a strong dose of social responsibility, it is then but a short step to the idea that 'dysfunctional' or broken families might be 'turned around' by appropriate intervention (Kirby, 2009). This is precisely the aim of the Troubled Families programme (Bond-Taylor, 2014), a punitive form of social welfare (Phoenix, 2009) closely aligned with crime and disorder management, which, as Hancock and Mooney have argued, performs the routine but 'increasingly pervasive' surveillance and intervention 'to regulate and control working class lives and communities' (Hancock and Mooney, 2013). Accordingly, under the Conservative-led Coalition government of 2010–15, welfare reform became increasingly characterised by conditionality and benefit sanctions, measures which eventually meshed with the Troubled Families programme and a corresponding array of anti-social behaviour measures, thereby establishing a wide-ranging regime of compliance management interventions.

Welfare, conditionality and sanctions

When, in *Punishing the poor* (2009), Loic Wacquant described similar regime changes, from 'welfare' to 'workfare', in the US, he outlined a process whereby the benevolent 'left hand' of the state withdrew, and the more punitive 'right hand' extended, replacing social supports with social controls. In the UK, by contrast, perhaps especially in England and Wales, it is difficult to describe so abrupt a transformation, notwithstanding the austerity-driven expenditure cuts underpinning the 'welfare reform' agenda. Although significant aspects of the welfare reform programme appear primarily intended to demonstrate a lowering of the cost of the benefit system to the notional 'tax-payer', it remains the case that substantial sums are still being invested in social support, although the purpose of this support is no longer to meet 'liveability' needs, but rather to incentivise, cajole and coerce people into employment. Universal Credit, Iain Duncan Smith's comprehensive new welfare support system and the Work Programme, which replaced the former Jobseeker's Allowance, became compulsory for all unemployed benefit claimants over 25 who had been out of work for a year (nine months for those aged 18–24). Claimants are referred to government-selected service providers, the majority being private companies, tasked with helping the unemployed back into work. Formal agreements or 'claimant commitments' are drawn up, outlining the support and services offered to the unemployed, and the obligations of claimants are spelled out. The service providers, like the agencies involved in the Troubled Families programme, are paid according to the results they achieve – sustained job placements. Evaluation of the programme by the National Audit Office (NAO) in 2014 revealed that over 2 million claimants were expected to have been referred to the programme by March 2016, at a cost of £2.8 billion (NAO, 2014). Roughly one in four of those referred were finding employment (although only 11% of those deemed 'harder to help'), but the target threshold implied only moving 'into employment lasting six months or longer' (NAO, 2014, p4). Six months hardly constitutes secure and stable employment, especially for the lower-skilled sectors in which a majority of placements were being achieved. Savings of £41 million were reported by the NAO compared with 'similar levels of performance on previous welfare-to-work programmes', but a loss of £11 million was reported (anticipated to rise to £25 million) relating to payments made to contractors for non-validated employment placements (that is, payments for employment placements not achieved). The NAO concluded overall that 'the Work Programme has ... struggled to improve outcomes for harder-to-help groups ... and there are signs that some people receive very little support' (NAO (Summary), 2014, p8).

Tellingly, the reference to the outcomes for 'harder-to-help' groups is complemented by a discussion of the 'parking' of these 'difficult' groups – effectively, the warehousing of the unemployable. Similar issues have been identified in earlier 'welfare-to-work' programmes, and in other reports on the Work Programme (House of Commons Work and Pensions Select Committee, 2013). Alongside the programme's lack of effective support for needy people and perverse incentives for contractors to claim payments for services not delivered, the evidence clearly suggests a policy intended to discipline and disentitle those excluded from the labour market, rather than meet their needs.

Similar issues arise in respect of the 'benefit sanction' processes, the complementary compliance control systems intended to 'responsibilise' claimants and reduce the length of time that people spend in receipt of welfare benefits. Beatty et al (2015) reviewed the toughened regime of benefit sanctions installed after 2012 by the Welfare Reform Act of that year. They note that not only were the length and severity of benefit sanctions increased, but there has also been a significant step change in the frequency with which they are applied – for example, the number of Jobseeker's Allowance (JSA) sanctions applied almost tripled from a rate of 2.5 per 100 claims to 7.1 per 100 in 2014. The monthly average number of JSA sanctions rose from 35,500 a month prior to October 2012 to a monthly average of 84,800 after this date. Likewise, there was a threefold increase in Employment and Support Allowance (ESA) sanctions from 1,400 per month in March 2013 to 5,400 in March 2014.

While the key rationale for the sanction system concerned the need to change claimant behaviour in order to reduce unemployment, Beatty et al suggested that there is 'no robust evidence to support this claim' (Beatty et al, 2015), leading to questions being asked regarding both the fairness and effectiveness of the benefit sanctions. Overall, Beatty et al concluded that rather than benefit sanctions fostering a culture change among claimant groups, they in fact often have counterproductive effects, piling additional hardships upon the already most vulnerable, further excluding those facing the greatest barriers to mainstream employment opportunities.

During the first few months of 2015, Frances Ryan produced a series of compelling reports in *The Guardian* newspaper, detailing 60 suicides under investigation by the Department for Work and Pensions, where it was thought that a benefit sanction decision had been the immediate trigger to the claimant killing himself or herself (Ryan, 2015a). Following an inquest suicide verdict on another claimant, a Jobcentre adviser described the 'constant and aggressive' pressure she was placed under by management to meet performance targets 'almost by persecuting people' (Ryan, 2015b; O'Hara, 2015). Later in 2015, the aggressive culture of benefit conditionality and sanctioning was exposed by a battery of Freedom of Information requests, revealing that over 80 people a month were dying after being declared 'fit for work'. In total, 2,380 people died between December 2011 and February 2014, shortly after being declared fit for work and rejected for sickness and disability benefits or ESA. A further 7,200 claimants died after being awarded ESA and having been placed in the work-related activity category in order to be prepared for a return to work (Ryan, 2015c).

Such evidence of the pressure placed on claimants reflects the broad conclusions reached by Griggs and Evans, who acknowledged that there was a substantial 'gulf between the rhetoric and the evidence for the effects of sanctions in welfare reform. The gulf is not just on evidence, but also in different approaches to preventing poverty and promoting opportunity' (Griggs and Evans, 2010). UK governments have committed themselves both to evidence-based policy making and eliminating child poverty by supporting 'hard-working families' (although often invoking the unfortunate language of 'strivers and skivers' when doing so). Yet, as Griggs and Evans conclude, there is still rather limited evaluation of the real consequences of benefit sanctions in practice, and 'policy-makers continue to justify extending sanction-backed conditionality on moral grounds while taking an ambivalent attitude to the evidence' (Griggs and Evans, 2010, p7). The available qualitative evidence tends to suggest that, while sanctions might induce labour market compliance, they have relatively little effect on underlying motivations to work and anyway are typically only evaluated in the short term. They fail to take account of a range of social factors, such as the institutionalisation and recycling of poorer quality employment opportunities (unstable jobs and lower pay), the reproduction of long-term family poverty, poorer outcomes for children, poorer health and damaging consequences for especially disadvantaged groups. Few studies go on to explore the wider criminogenic consequences of benefit sanctions (Griggs and Evans, 2010, p7).

Arriving at such troubling conclusions about the Work Programme, about welfare conditionality and benefit sanctions, about the 'soft controls' and about compliance measures of austerity, returns us to the core paradox of 'broken society' 'common-sense'. The central concerns of the 'broken society' argument, first articulated in the original Centre for Social Justice *Breakdown Britain* report of 2006, included family breakdown, educational failure, worklessness and economic dependence, addictions and indebtedness (CSJ, 2006). The institutionalisation of long-term social disadvantage and poorer outcomes for children are a direct consequence of welfare conditionality and benefit sanctions. Such measures deepen and extend family poverty. It becomes difficult to avoid the conclusion that the government's tough measures reproduce the very 'broken society' of fragmenting relationships, fractured communities, social exclusions and, especially, marginalised youth that they claim to address.

The related case of indebtedness, a parallel world of compliance, individualisation and responsibilisation, is also instructive. For aside from the social and opportunity costs associated with the Conservative-led Coalition's high-profile decision to increase student loans and to abolish the Education Maintenance Allowance, the longer-term picture reveals 'a steady and problematic increase in personal debt in the UK' over the last two decades (Ben-Galim and Lanning, 2010). Almost two thirds of people on annual incomes below £10,000 exhibit 'problematic levels of indebtedness' (Walker et al, 2015). Debt is especially problematic for families in relative poverty. Research for Citizens Advice has shown that debt clients were typically poor, 'with a high proportion of people in receipt of means tested benefits' (Edwards, 2003). Walker has noted that 'for a growing number of people, personal debt supplements their existence in a relatively low wage and insecure employment landscape' (Walker, 2011, p526). Despite this, the largely unregulated pay-day loan and 'personal debt industry' exercises its own disciplinary compliance, confirming, often physically reinforcing, a sense of individual responsibility for poverty and perceived financial mismanagement. Just as the compliance processes within systems of benefit sanctioning serve mainly to institutionalise inequality and social exclusion so, likewise, it is hardly in the interests of the debt industry either to abolish debt or to allow debtors to escape (Walker et al, 2015).

This is certainly not the first time that problems of poverty, inequality and disadvantage have been refracted through the moralising language of just deserts, culpability and irresponsible lifestyle choices; on the contrary, there is a long history of this stretching back into the early 19th century and beyond. As Golding and Middleton astutely noted, over thirty years ago, the British have long exemplified a difficulty in distinguishing poverty from crime (Golding and Middleton, 1982). This criminalised conception of the disadvantaged – especially poor families and their marginalised young people – is the necessary precursor to the new systems of (anti-social) contractual governance embodied in our contemporary measures for 'troubled families' interventions, youth employment and training, and the youth justice and anti-social behaviour management practices to which we now turn.

Anti-social contracts?

We propose to discuss the various areas of policy mentioned above within a single frame, that of anti-social contracts. In the first place, each of the four policy areas – troubled families policy, youth employment and training, youth justice policy and ASB management policy – impinges directly or indirectly upon the problematic question of marginalised youth.

As Guy Standing has noted, 'youth make up the core of the precariat' (Standing, 2011, p66). Standing describes three such 'precarity traps', although he rather overlooks a fourth:

- The first precarity trap relates to disadvantaged, broken and dysfunctional family backgrounds.
- The second involves the loss of positive masculine role models, including ambition, access to networks or what used to be called the 'work ethic'.
- The third, partly a consequence of the second, concerns the drift into peripheral, non-economic (or illegitimate economic) roles, including addiction, apathy and gangs, where alternative kinds of role model might be found. Standing describes gang membership, disaffection and petty criminality as 'part of the wider precarity trap for young men' (Standing, 2011).

Hallsworth and Lea have referred to this as a kind of 'self-warehousing' (2011, p22), the internalisation of a sense of failure and responsibility, the most abject forms of which are reflected in the escalating suicide and parasuicide[1] rates among young, economically marginal, males (Fenton, 2016). The final precarity trap overlooked by Standing concerns criminalisation itself and the impact of criminal convictions and periods of imprisonment on subsequent career opportunities and future employability.

This infamous NEET (Not in Education, Employment or Training) generation, caught in a fractured transition between family dependence and full labour market involvement and economic independence, is increasingly confronted by attitudinal, behavioural and, especially, criminal justice policies preoccupied by risks, riots and radicalisation. Increasingly, surveillance and control, and governance through crime and disorder management, are presented as logical and rational responses to the problems of marginalised youth. In each of the areas addressed, the governance of youth goes beyond the compliance management described already and instead takes on a profoundly anti-social and frequently counterproductive contractual form, where behaviour is closely regulated, responsibility is fixed in a rigid one-dimensional fashion and significant consequences follow breaches of the contract.

Contractual principles run throughout the Troubled Families and anti-social behaviour interventions, most conspicuously so in the varieties of Acceptable Behaviour Contract designed to nip in the bud 'offensive and disorderly' behaviour of younger children, but which do so by potentially jeopardising the social housing tenancies of the families involved (Stephen and Squires, 2004). Similarly, contractual aspects form part of the system of police 'final warnings', in that young people have to agree the offence of which they are accused and also consent to undertake such activities as form part of the final warning programme. Essentially, similar arrangements underpin the referral order (RO), first introduced in 2002, and available to youth courts in the case of offenders aged 10–17 who are in court charged with an offence for the first time. As the Ministry of Justice *Referral order guidance* stipulates, the young offender must *admit* the offence with which they are charged and then 'under the order the young offender agrees a contract with the [referral] panel which can include reparation or restitution to their victim, for example, repairing any damage caused or making financial recompense, as well as undertaking a programme of interventions and activities to address their offending behaviour' (Ministry of Justice, 2015).

As noted earlier (Squires and Stephen, 2005, pp100-2), the contractual elements of these orders, forms part of a wider strategy of 'responsibilisation governance', derived from a conception of the contractual balance between rights and duties, which is frequently invoked in contemporary public policy, especially crime and disorder management. Some commentators have criticised ROs for the way in which they attempt to graft an artificial notion of restorative justice onto what is actually an enforcement process (Haines, 2000). Our main concern about this order has concerned the doubtful kind of contract on which it is based. In our own research, despite receiving assurances about how 'contracts' and agreements were very carefully compiled in full discussion with young people themselves, we continued to find examples of young people who either could not remember the compliance requirements of their own contracts, or did not actually understand what they meant (Squires and Stephen, 2005). There might also be something ethically doubtful about requiring a young person aged 10–12 to commit to such a contract.

The new public space protection order (PSPO) extends a 'conditional control'[2] principle even wider, and can impose behavioural conditions on anyone using the designated area. No prior convictions are required and the behaviour which is regulated comprises that which is 'unreasonable' rather than illegal, although 'likely to have, a detrimental effect on the quality of life of others in the locality' (Home Office, 2014). This suggests that the PSPO falls squarely into the sphere of 'pre-criminal regulation', reiterating the sense of 'institutional mistrust' experienced by marginalised young men over recent years (Brown, 1998; Kelly, 2003). Breach of a PSPO is a criminal offence, which can be punishable by a £100 fixed penalty notice or a fine. Among a number of critics, Liberty has argued that the PSPO is too vaguely drawn and open-ended, while the grounds for appeal are especially narrow (Liberty, 2015). There seems every indication that the 'usual suspects', especially marginalised young men, will continue to be at the focus of the new legislation, just as they were in respect of preceding anti-social behaviour powers (Bottoms, 2006; Bannister and Kearns, 2012).

In sum, a pervasive sense of distrust, sustained in part by decivilising and criminalising discourses of youth (France, 2007), have perpetuated a sense that youth itself – or at least that visible, urban segment of it – is somehow deemed 'anti-social' by its very nature. Extraordinary measures are considered necessary. Ferguson (drawing upon Habermas) refers to these measures as 'juridification processes' – 'when actions or behaviours become subjects of statute law as part of a wider trend towards extending the reach of the law into the domains of the lifeworld' (Ferguson, 2016, p195). These extraordinary measures, which become even more markedly unjust and anti-social when the young people in question are deemed to be members of a gang – for which some of the most oppressive police powers and punitive forms of racist surveillance and 'dragnet justice' are reserved (Bridges, 2013; Williams and Clarke, 2016) – are themselves often divisive, unfair and profoundly anti-social. Squires originally introduced the concept of 'anti-social policy' in 1990. Referring to this 'anti-social' quality, it involved 'policies which have widened inequalities and exacerbated social tensions, restricted rights to welfare, increased the numbers suffering poverty or homelessness, or undermined the aspirations of many while leading even more people to suspect that their overall quality of life is declining or increasingly "precarious"' (Squires, 1990, p2).

For many young people, the essential contract relationship at the heart of social citizenship, that of belonging, has been shattered. This suggests a *broken contract* rather than a 'broken society'.[3] Young people are variously described as 'disaffected', 'disconnected', 'excluded', 'non-participating' or 'marginalised', although the language is ambiguous or simply wrong. Sometimes it is a question of what young people are *connected to*, rather than simple 'disconnection'. In place of the wider social contract, expressed in an idea of citizenship, young people, as we have seen, are increasingly confronted by a formidable array of disciplinary contracts relating to behaviour, compliance and performance. Some are specifically tailored to the needs of individuals, others are more generic in nature or designed for designated groups, but all deploy sanctions, penalties and exclusions as a consequence of breach or non-performance. Of all the anti-social and quasi-contracts gaining comment and attention in recent years, few have attracted more attention than *zero-hours* contracts.

It is important to acknowledge that zero-hours contracts are not confined exclusively to young people, but young people certainly feature among the most insecure, temporary and poorly paid sections of the labour market.[4] A survey commissioned by the trade union Unite suggested that, across the UK, 5.5 million people were subject to zero-hours contracts, most of them young people. Of those on the contracts, 36% said they were not entitled to holiday pay and over three quarters received no sick pay (Butler, 2013). Supporters emphasise the flexibility that such contracts offer to employers with fluctuating work patterns (such as seasonal work) and even facilitate choices for some employees about when and how much to work. The benefits of labour market flexibility, traded off against job security and workforce sustainability, makes a certain kind of narrow, econometric, business sense. However, facilitating the effective management of risk, reducing the costs of recruitment and training, and even, for some less scrupulous employers, as a means of avoiding particular employment obligations, the day-to-day operation of zero-hours contracts tells a different story. This involves a picture of employees living permanently as if 'on-call', reluctant to turn down work for fear that it may not be offered again (being 'zeroed down'), while attempting to juggle the flexible incomes from flexible working with the largely *inflexible* demands of housing costs, running a home, caring for children and synchronising access to tax credits and other income benefits (Pennycook et al, 2013; Adams and Deakin, 2014).

There appears to be relatively little empirical sociological research into the anti-social and exclusionary consequences of shifting employees onto zero-hours contracts. Notwithstanding this, employment commentators have drawn attention to the break, signified by zero-hours contracts, with an inclusive Keynesian social contract which, as Levitas has argued, understood social inclusion as a form of social citizenship, an aspect of labour market participation (Levitas, 1996). By contrast, according to Elliott (2013), zero-hours contracts re-establish a precarious 'reserve army' of low-waged, low-skilled and low-opportunity, temporary labour. As Elliott notes, these are precisely the kinds of conditions that the union movement as a whole sought to overcome.

In place of an idea of working associated with respect and aspiration (Sennett, 2004), a standard of living and the dignity of labour – notions barely grasped by contemporary management discourses on the 'work–life balance' – zero-hours contracts establish anti-social, coercive and exploitative performance and compliance systems. These detract from a sense of belonging, reinforce social divisions and exclusions, and resemble, in all relevant respects, the wider regime of anti-social contracts impinging upon the lives of the youngest and poorest. This is especially the case with evidence emerging that jobcentre staff – in an effort to put further pressure on jobseekers and to fill notified vacancies – were able to 'sanction' benefit claimants under the new universal credit system, if they did not apply for, and show willingness to accept, certain zero-hours jobs (Mason, 2014). This was despite concerns that such work could disrupt training and apprenticeship opportunities, tying young workers into permanent insecure and low-paid employment.

As we have indicated, it is not so much 'society' that is broken, but rather the relationship between sections of the population and the state. At this point, we turn to the final aspect of our argument.

Conclusion: the failing state?

Any discussion of 'state failure' will inevitably beg important questions, rooted in political theory and philosophy, about: the various roles and purposes of states; what they seek to achieve; and the discourses of rights and wellbeing with which they surround themselves. One approach might be to draw on some of the state's own language – the rhetorics of 'inclusion', society, rights and responsibilities, social justice and opportunity – deployed by politicians and purporting to represent contemporary values and realities. Prime Minister David Cameron, for instance, frequently referred to the values of 'One Nation'. Earlier he had championed the cause of 'the Big Society', each concept articulating a loosely framed veneer of values that stressed 'belonging' or inclusion.

Such values can represent a framework of ideas from which to draw conclusions about the effectiveness of states and policy systems in living up to their stated ideals. There are still many difficulties here, not least the fact that states tend to write their own stories. Governance also applies to the capacity to maintain accurate records of key areas of policy performance. Yet one of the signs that a state may be disengaging from an area of policy and practice may well be the fact that reliable records are no longer kept. Failing to clearly define or to count the number of families living in poverty might be a sign that tackling family poverty has ceased to be a policy priority (Pantazis et al, 2006). Likewise, endless changes in the methods for calculating the unemployment total (and the figure for those genuinely seeking work) suggests that the welfare and needs of the unemployed themselves are no longer paramount (Gregg, 1994). Tolerating wide margins of error in the police recording of crime and artificial limits on the reporting of violence in the Crime Survey for England and Wales (Walby et al, 2016) might also imply that the state is rather happier with the comforting myths of falling crime.

Another means by which to assess state performance might be to draw on a more comparative approach, judging the performance of states against a group of similar nations, 'European partners', OECD nations, or similar. Of course, in the wake of Brexit, it may well be said that Britain has declared itself rather less interested in such comparisons. Even so, the exceptional work of Wilkinson and Pickett in *The spirit level* (2010) provides a compelling portrait of the relations between inequality and a range of social problems (including mental disorders, crimes, infant mortality rates and poor health), but it is the comparative regime analysis developed by Pantazis and Pemberton (2009) that gives us a direct purchase on the question of state performance.

Pantazis and Pemberton's work feeds directly into the discussion of anti-social policies and failing states, for their concern is with differing kinds of state and policy regime and the production of social harms. Like Wacquant (2009), they recognise that socioeconomic outcomes such as mass incarceration, widening patterns of inequality and the increasingly marginal status of many young, working-class men, is not an inevitable outcome of inexorable social and economic forces, but the result of clear *political* decisions. Their article then proceeds to itemise the greater or lesser harms associated with social democratic, corporatist and neo-liberal state regimes. They then match these regime types to a range of policy outcomes data,[5] relating to a series of social, material and psychological needs such as: basic physical health, infant and neo-natal mortality, life expectancy, education and literacy, economic activity, 'personal autonomy', housing, material and environmental deprivation, social and political participation, as well as security, 'autonomy' and 'recognition' (Pantazis and Pemberton, 2009). The conclusions they draw from this international survey centre on the consistently poor performance of the neo-liberal regime type, which, they say, appears to assume that 'the benefits accrued through economic growth outweigh the inequalities that are inherent in this form of [state] organisation' (Pantazis and Pemberton, 2009, p231). They note that while some 'may benefit from the freeing of the market, a series of collateral harms result which far outweigh those occurring in other regimes'. The UK, they note, is also 'marked by high levels of economic insecurity, reflected in the persistence and extent of relative poverty and inequality' (Pantazis and Pemberton, 2009, p232).

In a similar vein, the Unicef child welfare 'Score sheet' for 2013 (Unicef, 2013) placed the UK 16th (out of 29) 'affluent countries', but significantly below virtually all other Western European societies, on a series of five measures of wellbeing (material wellbeing, health and safety, education, behaviours and risk, and housing and environment). The UK ranked especially lowly on educational opportunity, behaviours and risks, and health and safety.

Translating these figures into the specific example of violence victimisation, Danny Dorling, supported by Bellis et al's (2011) research on accident and emergency hospital admissions, has made a strong empirical case that inequality and deprivation are powerful drivers of violent victimisation (Dorling, 2005). Marginalised young men living in 'deprived areas' are over three times more likely to access A&E services following a violent assault.[6] Drilling even further into these disproportionate violence figures, Office for National Statistics data for the period 2011–13 show that, even as *overall* homicide rates have fallen, young black men are four and a half times more likely to be victims of homicide than young whites (ONS, 2014). As Dorling has concluded, murder rates are increasingly concentrated in the poorest areas. Murder (and interpersonal violence) has become significantly concentrated in the poorest and most deprived parts of Britain (Shaw et al, 2005). As Dorling concludes, 'murders are at the tip of the pyramid of social harm and their changing numbers and distributions provide one of the key clues as to where harm is most and least distributed' (Dorling, 2005, p40).

In effect, even this least 'ideological' and most 'intimately' individual of crimes can be seen to reveal the profound influence of social forces and political choices. In turn, these choices are shaped by priorities, reflecting contrasting political ideologies, which have allowed the growth of inequality and tolerated the existence of poverty, while driving the social exclusion and disentitlement to which the marginalised young and the least qualified have been subject.

At the same time, as Dorling has noted, there appears to be something in the British outlook that accepts as natural the pattern of social inequalities and the harmful injuries of class associated with it. Even as the rift between the richest and the poorest began to stretch still wider following the political changes of the 1980s, overhauling the principles of collectivism and universalism that had sustained key features of what was once the 'welfare state', so an even more virulent and vituperative series of attitudes towards the poor and marginal took hold, deriding the poor for their 'failure' and condemning the young as violent, 'chavs' and 'scum' (Hayward and Yar, 2006; Tyler, 2008, 2013; Pickard, 2014). The irony that the principal victims of the 'broken society' are blamed for its condition represents just one further aspect of this British paradox.

The 'broken society' analysis with which we began this discussion is not just a question that concerns the simple distribution of harms and victimisation, but it has also concerned the organisation of a power to stigmatise, criminalise, ostracise and punish. This is the power to *produce* a criminality against which society's moral and juridical forces might be deployed, to demonstrate once and for all the feckless and irresponsible condition of the poor and their need for discipline, supported by compliance processes, sanctions and punishment.

To take our commentary full circle, we conclude by referring briefly to the excellent Institute for Public Policy Research study *Make me a criminal* (Margo and Stevens, 2008). Drawing on cross-European evidence of diminished social provisions and falling quality of life indicators for young people, the authors demonstrate conclusively the precarious and overwhelmingly criminogenic contexts in which marginalised young people in the UK are forced to live. Taken together, the withdrawal of social supports, the rates of educational exclusion and underachievement, the disrupted family backgrounds and the collapse of the youth and young adult labour markets have disrupted and disaffected more than one generation. The injustices they face, including short-term, transitional and low-paid training opportunities, offer rather little consolation for the hostile ideological climate facing many young working-class people. In turn, the strategies they adopt, such as street socialisation, nuisance behaviours, substance misuse, peer group activities and gang formation – 'delinquent solutions' all over again (Downes, 1966) – are further demonised, regulated and criminalised. In sum, the anti-social governance of contemporary marginalised youth invariably produces and reproduces the problems it bemoans. This is not a broken society, more a failure of government.

Notes

[1] Parasuicides are suicide attempts or acts of intentional self-harm where there is no result in death. They are non-fatal acts in which a person deliberately causes injury to him or herself. Of course, some parasuicide attempts can result in death where the person miscalculates the seriousness of an act of self-harm or where medical help is not available. Such incidents then become suicides.

[2] Section 59 of the Anti-social Behaviour, Crime and Policing Act 2014.

[3] This may not be the only broken 'contract' discussed in similar terms, for, following evidence of the numbers of former military personnel, either in prison, suffering PTSD or related psychological conditions, or homeless, a number of commentators have voiced concerns about the 'Armed Forces Covenant' (Gillan and Norton-Taylor, 2007). The Ministry of Defence reissued the covenant in 2011.

[4] An early legal discussion of zero-hours contracts, from 2002, concluded: 'there is no doubt that the casual/zero hours worker personifies precarious work and that many such workers are among the worst treated in the labour market' (Leighton, 2002: 77). It adding: 'such one-sided working relationships

are unusual in other EU states ... there is often some incredulity on the part of lawyers ... that such a working relationship can be legally valid' (Leighton, 2002: 72).

[5] From the World Health Organization, Unicef, the International Labour Organization and the Organisation for Economic Co-operation and Development.

[6] Furthermore, following the introduction of A&E police reporting protocols involving gang-related and weapon violence, there are strong grounds for thinking that gang-involved young people are especially reluctant to visit A&E, when the injuries they have sustained are not thought to be serious or life-threatening (see Squires, 2011).

References

Adams, Z. and Deakin, S. (2014) *Re-regulating zero hours contracts*. London: Institute of Employment Rights.

Bannister J. and Kearns, A. (2012) 'Overcoming intolerance to young people's conduct', *Criminology and Criminal Justice*, 13, 4: 380-97.

Beatty, C., Foden, M., McCarthy, L. and Reeve, K. (2015) *Benefit Sanctions and Homelessness: A Scoping Report*. Sheffield Hallam: Centre for Regional Economic and Social Research.

Bauman, Z. (2008) *The absence of society*, www.jrf.org.uk/publications/absence-society.

Bellis, M. A., Hughes, K., Wood, S., Wyke, S. and Perkins, C. (2011) 'National five-year examination of inequalities and trends in emergency hospital admission for violence across England', *Injury Prevention*, 17: 319-25.

Ben-Galim, D. and Lanning, T. (2010) *Strength against the shocks. Low income families and debt*. London: Institute for Public Policy Research.

Bond-Taylor, S. (2014) 'The politics of ASB within the "Troubled Families" Programme', in S. Pickard (ed) *Anti-Social Behaviour in Britain: Victorian and Contemporary Perspectives*. Palgrave Macmillan.

Bottoms, A. E. (2006) 'Incivilities, offence and social order in residential communities', in A. von Hirsch and A.P. Simester (eds) *Incivilities: Regulating Offensive Behaviour*. Oxford: Hart Publishing.

Bridges, L. (2013) 'Thecase against joint enterprise', *Race and Class*, 54, 4: 33-42.

Brown, S. (1998) *Understanding youth and crime: Listening to youth?*, Buckingham: Open University Press.

Butler, S. (2013) 'Zero-hours contracts: 5.5m Britons "are on deals offering little guaranteed work"', *The Observer*, 8 September.

Cameron, D. (2008a) 'Fixing our broken society', The Conservative Party. http://conservativehome.blogs.com/torydiary/files/fixing_our_broken_society.pdf

Cameron, D. (2008b) 'There are Five Million People in Britain on Benefits: How do we stop them turning into Karen Matthews', *Daily Mail*, 8 December.

Centre for Social Justice (CSJ) (2006) *Breakdown Britain: Interim Report on the State of the Nation.* London, CSJ Policy Group. http://www.centreforsocialjustice.org.uk/library/breakdown-britain-executive-summary

CSJ (2009) *Dying to Belong: An In-Depth Review of Street Gangs in Britain.* London: Centre for Social Justice.

Dorling, D. (2005) 'Prime suspect: Murder in Britain' in Hillyard, P., Pantazis, C., Tombs, S., Gordon, D. and Dorling, D. (eds) (2005) *Criminal Obsessions: why harm matters more than crime.* London: Pluto Press.

Downes, D. (1966) *The delinquent solution: A study in subcultural theory.* Routledge.

Driver, S. (2009) '"Fixing our broken society": David Cameron's post-Thatcherite social policy', in S. Lee and M. Beech (eds), *The Conservatives under David Cameron: Built to last?*, Basingstoke: Palgrave.

Edwards, S. (2003) *In too deep: CAB clients' experience of debt.* Citizens Advice. https://www.citizensadvice.org.uk/in-too-deep.pdf

Elliott, L. (2013) 'Zero-hours contract workers – the new reserve army of labour?', *The Guardian*, 4 August.

Fenton, S. (2016) 'Self-harm biggest cause of death for young people in the UK, study finds', *The Independent*, 10 May.

Ferguson, R. (2016) *Young people, welfare and crime: Governing non-participation.* Bristol: Policy Press.

Finlayson, A. (2010) 'The broken society versus the social recession', *Soundings*, 44, 1, 22-34.

France, A. (2007) *Understanding youth in late modernity*, Buckingham: Open University Press.

Gillan, A. and Norton-Taylor, R. (2007) 'Care of soldiers compromised by failing Army pact', *The Guardian*, 15 August.

Golding, P. and Middleton, S. (1982) *Images of welfare: Press and public attitudes to welfare.* Oxford: Martin Robertson.

Gregg, P. (1994) 'Out for the count: a social scientist's analysis of unemployment statistics in the UK', *Journal of the Royal Statistical Society. Series A (Statistics in Society)*, 157, 2: 253-70.

Griggs, J. and Evans, M. (2010) *Sanctions within conditional benefit systems: A review of evidence.* Joseph Rowntree Foundation.

Haines, K. (2000) 'Referral Orders and Youth Offender Panels', in B. Goldson (ed) *The New Youth Justice*. Lyme Regis: Russell House Publishing.

Hallsworth, S. and Lea, J. (2011) 'Reconstructing Leviathan: emerging contours of the security state', *Theoretical Criminology*, 15, 2: 141-57.

Hancock, L. and Mooney, G. (2013) '"Welfare ghettos" and the "broken society": Territorial stigmatization in the contemporary UK', *Housing, Theory and Society*, 30, 1, 46-64.

Hayward, K. and Yar, M. (2006) 'The 'chav' phenomenon: Consumption, media and the construction of a new underclass', *Crime, Media, Culture*, 2, 1, 9-28.

Home Office (2014) *Anti-social Behaviour, Crime and Policing Act 2014: Reform of anti-social behaviour powers. Statutory guidance for frontline professionals*. London, Home Office.

House of Commons Work and Pensions Select Committee (2013) *Can the Work Programme Work for all User Groups? First Report of Session 2013–14*. HC 162. London: The Stationery Office.

Kelly, P. (2003) 'Growing up as risky business? Risks, surveillance and the institutionalized mistrust of youth', *Journal of Youth Studies*, 6, 2: 165-80.

Kirby, J. (2009) 'From broken families to the broken society', *The Political Quarterly*, 80, 2: 243-47.

Leighton, P. (2002) 'Problems continue for zero hours workers', *Industrial Law Journal*, 31, 1, 71-8.

Levitas, R. (1996) 'The concept of social exclusion and the new Durkheimian hegemony', *Critical Social Policy*, 16, 46: 5-20.

Liberty (2015) *Campaigning against: Public Space Protection Orders,* www.liberty-human-rights.org.uk/campaigning/public-space-protection-orders-0

Margo, J. and Stevens, A. (2008) *Make me a criminal: Preventing youth crime*. London: Institute for Public Policy Research.

Mason, R. (2014) 'Jobseekers being forced into zero-hours roles', *The Guardian*, 5 May.

Ministry of Justice (2015) *Referral order guidance*. London: Ministry of Justice.

Mooney, G. (2009) 'The "broken society" election: class hatred and the politics of poverty and place in Glasgow East', *Social Policy and Society*, 8, 4: 437-50.

NAO (National Audit Office) (2014) The Work Programme: Department for Work and Pensions: Report by the Comptroller and Auditor General. HC 266, Session 2014-15.

O'Hara, M. (2015) 'As a Jobcentre advisor I got "brownie points" for cruelty', *The Guardian*, 4 February.

ONS (Office for National Statistics) (2014) *Homicide Statistics*. London: The Stationery Office.

Pantazis, C. and Pemberton, S. (2009) 'Nation states and the production of social harm: resisting the hegemony of "TINA"', in R. Coleman and D. Whyte (eds), *State power crime*. Sage, 214-33.

Pantazis, C., Gordon, D. and Levitas, R. (2006) *Poverty and social exclusion in Britain*. Bristol: Policy Press.

Pennycook, M., Cory, G. and Alakeson, V. (2013) *A matter of time: The rise of zero-hours contracts,* The Resolution Foundation.

Phoenix, J. (2009) 'Beyond risk assessment: the return of repressive welfarism,' in McNeil, R. and Barry, M. (eds) *Youth offending and youth justice: Research highlights in social work*. London: Jessica Kingsley.

Pickard, S. (2014) 'The trouble with young people these days: "deviant" youth, the popular press and politics in contemporary Britain. Labelling the deviant: othering and exclusion in Britain from past to present', *French Journal of British Studies*, 19, 1: 91-121.

Ryan, F. (2015a) 'Suicides hi-light the grim toll of benefit sanctions in austerity Britain', *The Guardian*, 3 January.

Ryan, F. (2015b) 'How many benefits claimants have to kill themselves before something is done?', *The Guardian*, 10 February.

Ryan, F. (2015c) 'Death has become part of Britain's benefit system', *The Guardian*, 27 August.

Sennett, R. (2004) *Respect: The formation of character in an age of inequality*. London: Penguin Books.

Shaw, M., Tunstall, H. and Dorling, D. (2005) 'Increasing inequalities in risk of murder in Britain: trends in the demographic and spatial distribution of murder, 1981–2000', *Health & Place*, 11, 1: 45-54.

Squires, P. (1990) *Anti-social policy: Welfare, ideology and the disciplinary state*. Hemel Hempstead: Harvester/Wheatsheaf Books.

Squires, P. (2011) 'Young people and weaponisation', in B. Goldson (ed) *Youth in crisis: 'Gangs', territoriality and violence*. Routledge.

Squires, P. and Stephen, D. E. (2005) *Rougher justice: Anti-social behaviour and young people*. Willan Publishing.

Standing, G. (2011) *The Precariat: The new dangerous class*. London: Bloomsbury Academic.

Stephen, D. E. and Squires, P. (2004) *Community safety, enforcement and acceptable behaviour contracts: An evaluation of the work of the Community Safety Team in the East Brighton 'New Deal for Communities' Area*. University of Brighton, Health and Social Policy Research Centre Report.

Tyler, I. (2008) "'Chav mum chav scum": Class disgust in contemporary Britain', *Feminist Media Studies*, 8, 1: 17-34.

Tyler, I. (2013) *Revolting subjects: Social abjection and resistance in neo-liberal Britain*, London, Zed Books.

Unicef (2013) *The well-being of children: How does the UK score?*, Unicef Score sheet 11: https://353ld710iigr2n4po7k4kgvv-wpengine.netdna-ssl.com/wpcontent/uploads/2013/04/ReportCard11_CYP.pdf

Wacquant, L. (2009) *Punishing the poor: The neo-liberal government of social insecurity*. Duke University Press.

Walby, S., Towers, J. and Francis, B. (2016) 'Is violence increasing or decreasing?: A new methodology to measure repeat attacks making visible the significance of gender and domestic relations', *British Journal of Criminology*, 56, 4.

Walker, C. (2011) "'Responsibilizing" a healthy Britain: personal debt, employment, and welfare', *International Journal of Health Services*, 41, 3: 525-38.

Walker, C., Hanna, P., Cunningham, L. and Ambrose, P. (2015) 'Parasitic encounters in debt: The UK mainstream credit industry', *Theory & Psychology*, 25, 2: 239-56.

Wilkinson, R. and Pickett, K. (2010) *The spirit level; Why Equality is better for everyone*. London: Penguin Books.

Williams, P. and Clarke, B. (2016) *Dangerous associations: Joint enterprise, gangs and racism*. London: Centre for Crime and Justice Studies.

Wilson, J.Q. and Kelling, G.L. (1982) 'Broken windows', *Atlantic Monthly*, 249, 3: 29-38.

Work and Pensions Select Committee (2013) *Can the Work Programme work for all user groups?*, First Report of Session 2013–14 House of Commons, HC 162.

THREE

Youth poverty and social exclusion in the UK

Eldin Fahmy

Introduction

Drawing on analysis of the *2012 UK Poverty and Social Exclusion Survey* (2012 PSE-UK; Gordon, 2016),[1] this chapter examines the nature, extent and distribution of vulnerability to poverty and social exclusion among young adults (18–29-year-olds) living in private households in the UK. The 2012 PSE-UK study is the largest and most comprehensive survey on poverty ever conducted in the UK and updates earlier comparable survey work conducted in 1999. These data can therefore advance our understanding of youth marginality in important ways.

First, it is now well established that household income provides only a partial picture of people's actual command over resources and is wholly uninformative about their actual living conditions and living standards. This emphasises the need to supplement income data with direct observation of living standards in order to examine the relationship between income and deprivation. This is especially important for young adults, given the assumptions typically made in poverty research about the equitable sharing of incomes within households. As we shall see, these assumptions are rather questionable for young adults, given the substantial variation in vulnerability to deprivation within households that this study reveals.

Second, the PSE methodology facilitates meaningful comparisons over time and specifically with the 1999 PSE study. By comparing data for 1999 and 2012, this chapter therefore also examines how the nature, extent and distribution of youth poverty have changed over this period. In doing so, this chapter seeks to examine how the profile of vulnerability to youth disadvantage changes over time and the extent to which variations may be explained by wider changes in the context of youth transitions – most notably as a result of the 2008 economic crisis and subsequent austerity policies that have been pursued in the UK and elsewhere. This chapter reveals the growth in social and material deprivation among UK youth over this period, and should be a stimulus to more concerted policy action to tackle youth poverty and exclusion.

Recession, austerity and the situation of young adults

For the most part, youth interventions have focused on tackling social exclusion rather than poverty, and on promoting a model of inclusion through paid work and associated activation approaches. For New Labour, youth interventions in this area focused primarily on labour market activation, increased welfare conditionality, and targeted casework interventions with 'excluded' youth (Colley and Hodkinson, 2001; France, 2008; Fahmy, 2008). Underpinning this agenda has been a responsibilisation of young people and their families, which obscures a wider withdrawal of the state from its responsibilities for youth social welfare. Subsequent Coalition and Conservative government policies have continued to be premised upon individualised, deficit-based explanations of youth disadvantage, and have considerably reinforced a tendency to neglect the structural causes of disadvantage associated, for example, with poor work, limited opportunities and inadequate incomes (Melrose, 2012). Strategies for addressing youth disadvantage therefore continue to reflect faith in supply-side, labour-market activation programmes and a belief that income and wealth redistribution are inappropriate responses to poverty, especially in relation to the situation of youth.

The revival of cultural and individualist assumptions about the nature and causes of poverty has long since had especial resonance for young people. Characterisations of youth disadvantage as an essentially voluntary condition reflecting poor background and upbringing, and anti–social attitudes and behaviours associated with an apparent 'underclass' has been a persistent theme in public commentary which identified youth as part of the 'undeserving' poor (Macdonald, 1997). Nevertheless, while these deficit models have been keen to identify apparent behavioural drivers of disadvantage, much less attention has been focused on young people's actual living standards and living conditions, or on young people's wider inclusion and wellbeing in these debates.

The extent of youth poverty and unemployment feature prominently in the *EU Youth Strategy, 2010-18* (European Commission, 2012), and young Europeans have suffered disproportionately as a result of rising unemployment, job insecurity and in–work poverty following the post-

2008 economic downturn, especially in southern Europe. Although UK youth unemployment rates have fallen quite quickly since their peak in late 2011, they remain much higher than for older adults. Even during the early/mid-2000s following a period of sustained economic growth, youth unemployment rates remained three times higher than those for older adults (MacInnes et al, 2014). While the UK economy created 1 million jobs in the 2012–14 period, just 40,000 of these went to the under 25s (Gregg et al, 2014). Almost 1.5 million young adults were not in education, employment or training in 2012, with around 250,000 young people being unemployed for over a year. Aside from the obvious human costs (including the scarring effects of youth unemployment), ACEVO (2012) estimated the current costs of youth unemployment at 2012 levels in direct costs and lost factory output to be over £15 billion, with the long-term costs over a 10-year period exceeding £28 billion.

In Britain, young people are increasingly vulnerable to low pay. The proportion of workers aged 16–30 who are low paid has risen steadily since the late 1970s, doubling between 1977 and 2013 (Corlett and Whittaker, 2014). Analysis suggests that the fall in real wages for workers aged 18–25 since 2008 has been so extreme that in real terms, wages are back to levels not seen since the late 1980s (Gregg et al, 2014).

Given these trends in youth unemployment and low pay, it is unsurprising that young adults in the UK are increasingly vulnerable to income poverty. Between 2007 and 2013, average household incomes fell for all working-age adults – but by nearly twice the rate for 22–30 year olds compared with workers aged 31–59 (Bellfield et al, 2014). Comparing the 2000–03 and 2010–13 periods, the proportion of people living in low-income households has increased most for young adults and has fallen most for pensioners, and longer-term changes in intergenerational vulnerability to low income have been even more stark (MacInnes et al, 2014). As a result, by 2012/13 nearly one third (29%) of 19–25 year olds were income poor in the UK (New Policy Institute, 2015). Padley and Hirsch (2014, p22) show that over the 2008–12 period, vulnerability to low income 'is greater and growing most quickly for younger households', and the proportion of younger households with an income insufficient to meet their minimum needs rose by seven percentage points (from 29% to 36%).

In 1999, while young adults in Britain were around 50% more likely than adults aged 30+ to be PSE Poor (i.e. experiencing both low income and low living standards), and were also somewhat more likely to report incomes insufficient to avoid poverty, no significant differences in overall deprivation were evident (Fahmy, 2006). Recent evidence suggests significant improvement in UK youth's evaluation of their financial circumstances (Office for National Statistics (ONS), 2016). However, we might expect that the impact of a substantial, sustained reduction in youth wages and incomes post-2008 will result in significantly greater vulnerability to deprivation for UK youth in future, not least as a result of the withdrawal and/or erosion of services and entitlements for youth associated with the post-2008 austerity agenda.

Despite the vital role that youth services and professional youth work can play in mitigating these impacts of recession – and in supporting successful transitions to adulthood for vulnerable youth – public spending in this area amounted to just £350 million in 2012 in England, or £77 per young person aged 13–19 (House of Commons, 2014, p32). Spending settlements for local authorities have resulted in cuts to youth services, including the complete withdrawal of provision in some areas (Children and Young People Now, 2011), leading Davies (2013) to refer to the funding of youth work as 'radically reshaped and, at worst, wholly erased'. The House of Commons Education Committee similarly emphasises the 'grossly disproportionate' impact of public spending cuts for local youth work and youth services, which throw into stark relief the 'Government's lack of urgency in articulating a youth policy or strategic vision' (House of Commons, 2012, p3).

The wider effects of welfare reform have also weighed on the shoulders of young adults in the UK. Melrose (2012, p1) refers to the disciplinary effects of increased welfare conditionality and sanctioning in driving young people 'to accept low-paid, insecure work and unemployment and thereby entrench their poverty and disadvantage'. The disproportionate impacts of sanctions on vulnerable groups have increasingly been recognised (for example, Oakley, 2014), and young people under 25 have been among those hardest hit by benefit sanctions, prompting speculation that this may be 'a prelude to the gradual removal from the benefit system of all but the most obviously vulnerable young people (such as care leavers)' (Watts et al, 2014).

In the UK, as elsewhere in Europe, recession and austerity policies have undermined young people's economic security and social wellbeing, and compromised routes to independence. These risks are not equally borne, and youth poverty vulnerability continues to reflect enduring social inequalities of class, ethnicity and gender, and life course factors associated with home leaving and childbirth decisions (for example, Vogel, 2002; Aassve et al, 2006; Iacovou and Aassve, 2007; Buchmann and Kriesi, 2011). This chapter addresses this question, using different measures of poverty contained in the PSE-UK studies in 2012 and 1999. The chapter seeks to engage with some critical questions in understanding the contemporary picture of youth poverty vulnerability, including:

- What are minimally acceptable living standards for youth in the UK today, and how many young people experience deprivation according to these standards?
- How does the situation compare with that of older working-age adults, and how have rates of youth poverty changed over time?
- How does youth poverty vulnerability vary using different measures, and for different population subgroups?

The chapter concludes by considering the implications of these findings for policies to tackle youth disadvantage in the UK and internationally.

Introducing the 2012 PSE-UK survey

The 2012 PSE-UK study is the latest in a long line of random sample household surveys, which use consensual methods in order to implement a relative deprivation approach to poverty measurement. In response to widely held concerns about the validity of 'expert' judgements in determining minimally adequate living standards (Piachaud, 1981; Mack and Lansley, 1985), consensual approaches measure deprivation on the basis of public views on the items and activities that all people need to have or do to avoid poverty in the UK today.

This approach builds on Townsend's (1979, 1987) relative deprivation theory in which poverty is understood as an inability to participate in customary or widely approved lifestyles and activities as a result of insufficient resources, principally income. The consensual methodology was pioneered in the 1983 *Poor Britain* survey (Mack and Lansley, 1985) and subsequently refined in the *Breadline Britain* surveys in 1990 (Gordon and Pantazis, 1997) and 1999 (Pantazis et al, 2006a). The consensual approach to poverty measurement is now widely adopted in international survey research practice, including in informing the measurement of material deprivation across EU member states (Guio et al, 2016).

The most recent operationalisation of this two-stage survey design is the *2012 UK Poverty and Social Exclusion Survey* (2012 PSE-UK). First, informed by qualitative development work, a module on public perceptions of necessities was included in the the Office for National Statistics *Opinion Survey* (Britain), and the Northern Ireland Statistics and Research Agency *Omnibus Survey*. Representative samples of the UK public were asked to determine the items and activities that 'all adults should be able to afford and which they should not have to do without'. A second, larger PSE-UK main stage survey was then conducted in summer 2012, in order to estimate how many people and households in fact lack these items because they cannot afford them, and how this relates to household incomes, and wider societal participation, wellbeing and quality of life.

The main stage survey results reported here are based on productive interviews with 8,494 adults aged 18 and over, living in private households, including 986 young adults aged 18–29. As such, the 2012 PSE-UK study is the largest bespoke survey on poverty and social exclusion ever conducted in the UK. It offers an unprecedented contemporary insight into poverty in the UK, by investigating household incomes, people's actual living standards, living conditions and lifestyles. In comparison with the much smaller 1999 PSE-GB study, this means that more detailed subgroup analysis is feasible for young adults, which can provide a more nuanced and precise picture of poverty vulnerability, including the intra-household dynamics of poverty. In order to facilitate meaningful comparisons over time, the same overall measurement approach and survey design and implementation are used in the 1999 and 2012 studies. This means that, notwithstanding the limitations of the 1999 PSE-GB data set, some important longitudinal comparisons of the prevalence of poverty can be made – at least for youth in Britain.

Based on analysis of the PSE-UK Omnibus Surveys for GB and Northern Ireland, this chapter begins by investigating the extent of consensus between young and old on the 'necessities of life' that all people need to have in order to avoid poverty in the UK today. Based on analysis of the PSE-UK main stage survey, it then goes on to investigate how many young people lack these items in the UK today, how this compares with the situation for older working adults, and (for GB respondents) how the extent of deprivation compares with the picture in 1999.

As Bradshaw and Finch (2003) effectively argue, there is no single, universally agreed 'best' measure of poverty, and comparing results derived using a range of different measurement approaches is therefore important. The analysis examines the relationship between youth deprivation, and wider indicators of youth disadvantage, including low income, subjective poverty and social exclusion. One reason for doing so is the widely cited mismatch between monetary and non-monetary poverty estimates (for example, Perry, 2002; Whelan et al, 2004). Based on descriptive analysis of the intra-household distribution of deprivation in 2012, this chapter argues that this may be especially important in understanding the circumstances of young adult marginality.

Youth poverty, deprivation and social exclusion in 2012

This section begins by examining perceptions of necessities, and the extent of deprivation of these items in the UK today. It then considers how youth poverty today compares with the situation in 1999 and how it compares with rates for older working-age adults in the UK today.

What are minimally acceptable living standards for youth in the UK today?

Since its first application in the 1983 *Poor Britain* study (Mack and Lansley, 1985), surveys on public perceptions of the 'necessities of life' in the UK have consistently recorded widespread agreement across social groups (for example by gender, age, occupation, income level and geography) (Pantazis et al, 2006b). Table 3.1 shows older and younger respondents' evaluations of necessities items included in the *2012 ONS Lifestyles and Opinions Survey Necessities* module (undertaken as part of the PSE-UK study). The last column of Table 3.1 displays the relative risk ratios associated with these items – that is, the probability of one group classifying an item as a necessity compared with the other group (for example, in this case comparing young adults aged 16–24 with older adults aged 65+).

In most cases, few significant differences are evident between younger and older people on the items and activities that *all* people need to avoid poverty in the UK today. Nevertheless, some differences remain. While mindful of the risk that ad hoc explanations may reinforce popular stereotypes, it is perhaps unsurprising that younger respondents appear to value appropriate clothes for job interviews, participating in sport and exercise, and celebrating special occasions more highly than older respondents – and that household facilities and items (phone, TV, decent decoration, all-weather shoes, insurance) appear to be more highly valued by older respondents. Moreover, while we might reasonably infer that a broad consensus exists on the 'core' necessities of life in the UK today, age-appropriate measures of youth disadvantage may nonetheless provide a truer (that is, more valid) picture of young adults' experience of poverty and deprivation – though at the cost of undermining strict comparability of measures.

Table 3.1: Perceptions of the necessities of life in 2012: comparing young and old (%)

	All	16-24	65+	RR
Appropriate clothes to wear for job interviews	69	81	52	1.6*
Taking part in sport/exercise activities or classes	56	60	45	1.3*
Celebrations on special occasions such as Christmas	80	91	77	1.2*
Two meals a day	91	96	90	1.1
Visiting friends or family in hospital or other institutions	90	93	86	1.1
All recommended dental work/treatment	82	85	79	1.1
Attending weddings, funerals and other such occasions	79	85	76	1.1
Regular savings (of at least £20 a month) for rainy days	52	57	54	1.1
Regular payments into an occupational or private pension	51	56	51	1.1
Heating to keep home adequately warm	96	94	97	1.0
Replace or repair broken electrical goods	86	85	85	1.0
Washing machine	82	80	81	1.0
Meat, fish or vegetarian equivalent every other day	76	72	75	1.0
Curtains or window blinds	71	75	76	1.0
Damp-free home	94	92	97	0.9
A hobby or leisure activity	70	71	76	0.9
Fresh fruit and vegetables every day	83	69	83	0.8
A warm waterproof coat	79	69	89	0.8*
Telephone at home (landline or mobile)	77	75	89	0.8*
Money to keep your home in a decent state of decoration	69	61	79	0.8*
To be able to pay an unexpected expense of £500	55	52	68	0.8*
A table, with chairs, at which all the family can eat	64	56	77	0.7*
Two pairs of all-weather shoes	54	47	71	0.7*
Household contents insurance	70	51	86	0.6*
Television	51	33	70	0.5*

Note: [] = p>.01 (Pearson Chi Sq., 2 tail)

How many young adults are poor according to contemporary standards, and how does this compare with older working age adults?

Informed by results from the *2012 ONS Necessities* module (and equivalent data in Northern Ireland), the PSE-UK main stage survey then estimated the extent of deprivation of necessities, and the relationship between deprivation and command of resources (income) in private households. Table 3.2 shows the prevalence of overall deprivation of social and material necessities for working–age adults under 30 and aged 30-plus in 2012. On the whole, these data suggest that young adults are more likely to experience deprivation of socially perceived necessities than older working-age people (indicated by mostly positive and significant Relative Risk ratios in Table 3.2).

However, since individual respondents may plausibly lack items because they do not want them, rather than as a result of constrained resources, the PSE also establishes whether respondents lack items because they cannot afford them or by choice. Although questions of affordability also raise concerns about adaptive preferences in shaping 'choices' (Hallerod, 2006), the overall profile of response in Table 3.2 is in any case consistent with overall deprivation. Young adults are consistently more likely to report lacking socially perceived

Table 3.2: Deprivation of social and material necessities in the UK amongst working-age adults by age group, 2012

	% Lacks			% Cannot afford		
	18-29	30-64	RRisk	18-29	30-64	RRisk
Curtains or window blinds	3	2	1.6	2	1	2.2
A table and chairs at all the family can eat	14	11	1.3	8	4	1.7
Household contents insurance	33	19	1.8	20	12	1.7
Damp-free home	28	19	1.5	20	12	1.6
Money to replace/repair broken electrical goods	57	32	1.8	43	27	1.6
Attending weddings, funerals, etc.	17	10	1.6	4	3	1.6
Appropriate clothes for job interviews	16	18	[0.9]	12	8	1.5
Sport/exercise activities or classes	45	55	0.8	16	11	1.4
Two pairs of all-weather shoes	19	11	1.7	12	8	1.4
All recommended dental work/treatment	35	25	1.4	25	18	1.4
Regular occupational or private pension payments	79	55	1.4	38	29	1.3
Fresh fruit and vegetables every day	18	12	1.5	9	7	[1.3]
A warm, waterproof coat	12	7	1.8	6	4	[1.2]
Money to keep home in decent decoration	38	25	1.5	26	22	1.2
Regular savings (£20 a month) for rainy days	46	40	1.1	38	33	1.1
A hobby or leisure activity	26	29	0.9	10	9	[1.1]
Two meals a day	3	5	0.7	2	2	[1.0]
Meat, fish or veggie equivalent every other day	8	8	[1.1]	4	5	[0.9]
Heating to keep home adequately warm	12	9	1.3	7	8	[0.9]
Visiting friends or family in hospital, etc.	34	37	[0.9]	3	3	[0.9]
Celebrations on special occasions (e.g. Xmas)	7	7	[0.9]	3	4	[0.7]

Note: [] = p>.01 (Pearson Chi Sq., 2 tail)

necessities because they cannot afford them than the older working-age population.

How have rates of youth poverty changed over time?

While young adults in the UK in 2017 were generally more vulnerable to deprivation than older working adults, what is most striking is the growth in youth deprivation since the 1999 PSE-GB survey. The 1999 PSE-GB study adopts an identical approach to the operational measurement of consensual poverty as the 2012 PSE-UK survey, including sharing many of the same indicators of deprivation. It is possible to compare the prevalence of deprivation among young adults on a consistent basis (at least for the GB sample), as shown in Table 3.3. For all 16 indicators for which comparable data are available, the prevalence of deprivation of socially perceived necessities has either remained constant or increased (sometimes substantially) over the 1999–2012 period. Despite the limitations of the 1999 PSE-GB sample, most of these changes are significant at the .01 confidence level, indicating that we can be confident that these estimates reflect wider trends in the GB youth population over this period. The growth in financial vulnerability is striking, with a substantial increase in the proportion of young adults reporting being unable to afford home contents insurance (up 10 percentage points), to replace/repair broken electrical goods (up 26 percentage points), to maintain the home in decent decoration (up 11 percentage points), and to make regular savings (up 12 percentage points).

How does youth poverty vulnerability vary using different measures?

It is now generally accepted that the empirical overlaps between indirect, income-based measures and other operational measures are not substantial (for example, Hagenaars and de Vos, 1988; Whelan et al, 2001; Bradshaw and Finch, 2003). Advancing poverty analysis therefore involves better understanding the relationship between social and material deprivation and command over resources.

Indirect, income-based poverty estimates on their own provide an especially unreliable estimate of young adults' command over resources and need to be supplemented with direct measures of social and material deprivation and subjective data (felt needs) on perceptions of economic strain, as well as by triangulating findings with other established measurement approaches and policy-relevant indicators. Using the PSE methodology, Table 3.4 first compares the extent of

Table 3.3: Deprivation of socially perceived necessities amongst young adults aged 18-29 in Britain, 1999 and 2012

	% cannot afford		
	1999	2012	Diff (b-a)
Enough money to replace or repair broken electrical goods	16.9	43.1	26.2
Damp-free home	7.4	20.0	12.6
Regular savings (of at least £20 a month) for rainy days*	25.8	37.7	11.9
Enough money to keep home in decent state of decoration	15.1	26.3	11.2
Household contents insurance*	9.9	19.8	9.9
Appropriate clothes to wear for job interviews	5.3	11.8	6.5
Heating to keep home adequately warm*	3.1	7.5	4.4
Two pairs of all-weather shoes	7.7	11.6	3.8
Meat, fish or vegetarian equivalent every other day	1.1	4.4	[3.4]
Fresh fruit and vegetables every day	5.9	8.6	2.6
A hobby or leisure activity	7.7	10.1	2.4
Two meals a day	0.1	2.4	[2.3]
A warm, waterproof coat	4.7	5.6	[0.9]
Visiting friends or family in hospital or other institutions	2.2	2.9	0.8
Celebrations on special occasions such as Christmas	1.9	2.6	[0.8]
Attending weddings, funerals and other such occasions	4.3	4.3	[0.0]
PSE Deprivation (lacks 3+ socially perceived necessities)	26.7	50.7	1.9
PSE Poor (low income *and* lacks 3+ SPN items)	32.7	30.2	[0.9]
PSE Subjective Poverty	18.2	28.6	1.6

Note: [] = p>.01 (Pearson Chi Sq., 2 tail). * = minor differences in question wording in 1999 and 2012

overall PSE Poverty for young adults and for older working-age adults. Individuals are classified as 'PSE Poor' if, as a result of insufficient resources (low PSE-equivalised household income), they are unable to achieve minimally acceptable living standards (lack 3+ socially perceived necessities). Nearly one third (30%) of young adults in the UK are PSE Poor (that is, both income and deprivation poor), compared with 22% of older working-age adults. Based on this optimal deprivation threshold (3+ items), more than half (51%) of young adults in the UK were unable to achieve minimally adequate living standards in 2012, compared with a little over one third (36%) of older working-age adults (though, importantly, were not all living in income-poor households).

Determining the income required to meet consensually defined minimum needs using budget standards methods is an alternative and highly regarded approach to operationalising a relative deprivation approach to poverty. Based on Minimum Income Standards for 2012

(Davis et al, 2012), Table 3.4 compares the proportion of young and older working age–adults classified as MIS Poor, showing that a substantial majority (57%) of young adults were MIS poor in 2012 (compared with 47% of older working-age adults). In summary (and as indicated by the relative risk ratios in Table 3.4), whether we focus on deprivation, minimum income, combined measures or respondents' own subjective evaluations, young adults are approximately 20–40% more likely to experience poverty in the PSE-UK study and these differences are likely to be generalisable to the UK household population.

For the UK as a result of Brexit there is uncertainty in relation to the EU 2020 strategy (European Commission, 2010), which commits EU member states to achieving progress in reducing monetary poverty and (severe) material deprivation. While these indicators imply different thresholds and/or indicators to the PSE measurement approach, they provide a useful, policy-relevant comparison. For the most part, initiatives to combat poverty and social exclusion in the UK and Europe have been informed by income-based estimates which, as Table 3.4 shows, provide an especially misleading picture of young adults' actual living standards (as well as young adults' own perceptions of economic strain). While young adults are at slightly greater risk of living in low-income households, this effect is not significant at the .01 level. Thus, young adults are more likely than older working-age adults to experience every indicator of poverty reported in Table 3.4 with the exception of low household income. These data suggest that an exclusive focus on income measures at the expense of direct

Table 3.4: Comparing income, deprivation and subjective measures of poverty in the UK by age group, 2012 (%)

	18-29	30-64	RR	Diff (a-b)
PSE Poverty (low income *and* lacks 3+ SPN items)	30.2	22.0	1.4	8.2
PSE Deprivation (lacks 3+ SPN items)	50.7	35.8	1.4	14.9
PSE Subjective Poverty	28.6	23.5	1.2	5.1
UK Minimum Income Standard Poverty	57.1	47.2	1.2	9.9
EU2020 targets:				
Poverty	31.9	24.5	1.3	7.4
Severe Material Deprivation (4+ items)	9.6	5.9	1.6	3.7
Material Deprivation (3+ items)	26.2	17.1	1.5	9.1
At-Risk-Of-Poverty (lt 60% median hh income)	19.5	17.0	[1.1]	[2.5]

Note: [] = p>.01 (Pearson Chi Sq., 2 tail)

observation of young adults' living standards and conditions is likely to seriously underestimate the real extent of youth disadvantage.

How many young people are experiencing wider forms of social exclusion?

Youth social exclusion has received considerable policy attention in recent years, most notably within the work of New Labour's Social Exclusion Unit. Although an explicit focus on social exclusion has been less visible in subsequent policy development since 2010, a wider concern with related concepts such as quality of life, wellbeing, and life satisfaction continue to inform UK research, analysis and policy development. The PSE-UK study adopts the Bristol Social Exclusion Matrix (BSEM) (Levitas et al, 2007) as an operational framework based on an understanding of social exclusion as describing both a lack of access to economic resources and entitlements, and an inability to participate in social relationships and activities, resulting in diminished wellbeing. The BSEM comprises three key themes (resources, participation, wellbeing) and 10 domains of exclusion. Table 3.5 presents estimates of the prevalence of multidimensional disadvantage for a selection of indicators across the BSEM domains separately for young adults and for older working-age adults.

   With regard to participation in society, and in line with earlier findings, while young adults typically report more extensive friendship and familial contact, they do not necessarily benefit from stronger social support, and are around 30% more likely to report dissatisfaction with personal relationships in comparison with older working-age adults. Young adults are also significantly more vulnerable than older working-age adults to employment exclusion (including unemployment, living in workless households, and reporting job dissatisfaction) and are less likely to engage in political action on local and national issues. Diminished wellbeing and quality of life is one inevitable consequence of exclusion from resources and wellbeing, and these data suggest that young adults in the UK are substantially more vulnerable to harassment and discrimination, and poor housing conditions and neighbourhood dissatisfaction. Overall, young adults are certainly at heightened risk of multidimensional exclusion across the range of BSEM indicators reviewed here. Indeed, with the exception of social contact there are *no* indicators where young adults are at significantly lower risk than older working-age adults.

Table 3.5: Multidimensional exclusion in the UK by age group, 2012, selected indicators (%)

	18-29	30-64		
	Col%	Col%	Diff.	RR
Resources				
In arrears on any bills in last year	36	21	15	1.7
Had to borrow money from friends, family or other source	41	23	18	1.8
Cannot afford unanticipated, necessary expense of £500	48	34	14	1.4
Not a home owner	48	30	17	1.6
Has (well) below average living standards	13	15	[–2]	[0.9]
Lacks adequate access to 3+ local services	21	21	[0]	[1.0]
Participation				
Speaks to less than 3 relatives monthly	19	26	–8	0.7
Speaks to less than 3 friends monthly	25	32	–7	0.8
Not satisfied with personal relationships	23	18	5	1.3
Low social support (scores lt. 15)	16	16	[–1]	[1.0]
No working age adults in hhld. in paid work	21	18	3	1.2
Unemployed more than 12 months in last 5 years	14	8	6	1.7
Not satisfied with current job (in employment only)	17	14	3	1.2
Does not participate in 9+ common social activities	47	57	[–10]	[0.8]
Not member of any listed organisations	46	43	[3]	[1.1]
Took no action about local or national issue (inc voting)	49	29	19	1.7
Well-being				
Poor mental health (GHQ gt 24)	46	41	6	1.1
Low life satisfaction (ONS lt 6)	21	21	[1]	[1.0]
Multiple problems with accommodation	29	20	9	1.5
Dissatisfied with accommodation	17	9	8	1.9
Neighbourhood dissatisfaction	19	13	6	1.4
Experiencing 3+ neighbourhood problems	27	24	3	1.1
Experienced harassment or discrimination for any reason	28	15	13	1.8

Note: [] = p>.01 (Pearson Chi Sq., 2 tail)

Which groups of young adults are most at risk of poverty?

Table 3.6 summarises how the profile of vulnerability to poverty for young adults living in the UK in 2012 varies in relation to a selection of social and demographic characteristics including employment status, ethnicity, occupational class, settlement type, housing tenure, sex and family type. While the extent and social distribution of youth poverty is partly dependent on our preferred measure of disadvantage, overall these data confirm the findings of existing studies describing the socioeconomic and demographic determinants of youth vulnerability (for example, Iacovou and Berthoud, 2001; Iacovou and Aassve, 2007; Mendola et al, 2008; Fahmy, 2006, 2014).

Overall, vulnerability to youth poverty is strongly predicted by low socioeconomic status in relation to economic activity, occupational class and housing tenure. Poverty is concentrated among unemployed and economically inactive youth, manual workers, and private and social housing tenants. However, lifecourse and demographic factors are also important, with urban youth, black youth, young women and young adults living in households with children all at greater risk of poverty. In addition to the well-established social and demographic predictors of poverty vulnerability, young people's vulnerability to

Table 3.6: PSE poverty, deprivation and low income amongst UK young adults in 2012, selected characteristics (Row %)

		PSE Poor	Deprivation	Low income
Employment status	Working	21	41	17
	Unemployed	59	66	59
	Not econ active	55	64	41
Ethnicity	White	29	50	27
	Asian	29	45	41
	Black	56	86	49
	Other	30	49	23
Occupational class	Professional/managerial	7	28	8
	Intermediate	24	37	18
	Manual	29	57	24
Settlement type	Urban areas	33	55	31
	Rural/sparsely populated	19	35	19
Housing tenure	Owner occupier	9	31	14
	LA/HA renter	59	74	50
	private renter	50	66	39
Co-resident with parents	No parents in HH	43	59	32
	1 parent in HH	24	51	31
	2 parents in HH	10	31	22
Lives with own children	None	19	41	22
	One	55	65	46
	Two or more	63	80	47
Sex	Male	26	44	29
	Female	34	57	29
Family type	Couple with children	48	68	40
	Couple without children	11	25	9
	Lone parent	59	79	53
	Single without children	23	49	23
All		30	51	21

poverty is also strongly associated with the timing of domestic and housing transitions (for example, leaving the parental home, having children). Young adults living independently of their parents, and young adults with their own children (biological or adoptive) are at significantly greater risk of poverty than other young people.

As Table 3.6 indicates, the profile of youth marginality suggests that young adults are more vulnerable to deprivation of social and material necessities than they are to living in households with low incomes. While around one in five (21%) young adults in the UK lived in income-poor households in 2012, over half (51%) were PSE deprived (that is, were unable to afford three or more items considered necessities of life by the UK public). The disparity between monetary (income) and non-monetary (deprivation) poverty measures is therefore especially stark when considering the situation of youth. Since income refers here to total household income (adjusted for differences in household composition and size), it is plausible that this disparity between monetary and non-monetary measures may reflect inequalities in the distribution of resources *within* households.

Since the 2012 PSE-UK collects information on deprivation of necessities for all adults within households (and not just for the household respondent), it is possible to begin to investigate this issue by comparing the extent of young respondents' deprivation with the overall circumstances of the households in which they live. While these data do not provide direct evidence on the distribution of resources within households, they do give us an insight into the effects of an inequitable intra-household distribution of resources on the assumption that an equitable distribution of resources should result in equal exposure to social and material deprivation within households (that is, equal deprivation scores). Table 3.7 therefore compares the level of respondent deprivation for young adults aged 18–29 with mean deprivation scores for the households in which they live for selected characteristics relevant to understanding the intra-household distribution of poverty.

Overall, 45% of young adults share the same level of deprivation as the average for their household (that is, they are neither better nor worse off than their household as a whole). More young adults are worse off in these terms (30%) than are better off (25%), relative to the average scores of the households within which they live. However, when we disaggregate these data by gender and living arrangements, a clearer pattern begins to emerge. Young women are much more likely than young men to report higher levels of deprivation than the mean average for the households in which they live. In other words, young

Table 3.7: Intra-household distribution of deprivation for UK young adults, selected demographic characteristics (Row %)

		Resp. less deprived than HH mean	Same as HH mean	Resp. more deprived than HH mean
Sex	Male	33	46	21
	Female	19	44	37
Co-residence with parents	Lives with two parents	30	40	30
	Lives with single parent	39	45	16
	Lives independently	20	47	33
Has own children	Has no children	30	49	21
	Has 1 child	13	42	45
	Has 2+ children	22	28	50
ALL		25	45	30

women tend on average to be 'worse off' in terms of their actual living standards than other members of their household. Similarly, a smaller proportion of young adults living independently of their parents report being better off than their household as a whole, compared with young adults living with both parents (perhaps reflecting the extent to which parents are able to insulate their children from the full effects of constrained resources). Finally, young parents are substantially more likely to report being 'worse off' in these terms relative to the situation of their households compared with young adults without children.

Conclusion: tackling youth marginality and disadvantage – directions for policy

These findings add to the growing body of evidence documenting the contemporary challenges facing young adults in the UK in making successful transitions to economic independence. First, these results shed further light on non-monetary indicators of youth disadvantage, including socially perceived necessities, economic strain and social exclusion. In comparison with widely quoted, semi-official, low-income estimates, young adults are substantially more likely to experience deprivation of necessities, economic strain (including subjective poverty), and wider exclusion from economic resources, norms of participation, and living conditions.

Second, by adopting a methodologically consistent approach to poverty measurement, which reflects public perceptions of minimally adequate living standards, the chapter documents an alarming growth in youth deprivation of necessities over the 1999–2012 period. In comparison with the 1999 PSE-GB study, the 2012 PSE-UK survey reveals that the proportion of young adults in the UK experiencing unacceptable hardship in living standards (3+ deprivations) has virtually doubled over this period, almost certainly as a result of the precipitous decline in median wages and incomes for young adults in the UK post-2008 (for example, MacInnes et al, 2014; Bellfield et al, 2014; Padley and Hirsch, 2014).

These findings therefore reflect the impacts of the 2008 economic crisis and the effects of subsequent austerity policies for young adults' access to economic and social citizenship rights, including in relation to jobs, decent pay and housing, and income protection. Government action in this area fails to focus on economic inequalities and the structural roots of youth disadvantage and focuses in preference on individualised explanations and solutions (Colley and Hodkinson, 2001; Fahmy, 2008; France, 2008; Melrose, 2012). While sustained economic growth in the pre-2008 period may have disguised deeper changes in social vulnerability to poverty, the demonstrable growth in youth deprivation over the 1999–2012 period means that sustained policy action to tackle the structural roots of youth disadvantage is urgent.

In the UK context, the policy response since 2010 has been to accelerate cuts to youth services, together with widespread use of conditionality, sanctioning and private sector contracting as part of a (re)emerging regime of 'disciplinary welfare' for young adults. This means that persistent and entrenched youth marginality is likely to remain unaddressed. While the UK continues to lack a comprehensive and coherent youth strategy addressing problems of poverty and social exclusion (or indeed *any* wider prioritisation of youth issues), the need to develop new, more effective responses to the problem of youth disadvantage is also a pressing global challenge.

Growing income and wealth inequalities in the UK and internationally also have important implications for the distribution of assets, opportunities and risk across the lifecourse, which are likely to exert a long-term downward pressure on young adults' living standards in addition to any scarring effects of the 2008 recession and subsequent austerity policies. As part of the Europe 2020 agenda, the EU is committed to achieving a 25% reduction in the share of the EU population at risk of poverty and social exclusion by 2020. On the basis of the evidence reviewed here and the Brexit result, young adults in the UK are likely to miss out on this commitment.

Note

[1] The *2012 UK Poverty and Social Exclusion Survey* is funded by the UK Economic and Social Research Council (Ref: RES-060-25-0052). The research team acknowledge the financial support of the ESRC

References

Aassve, A., Iacovou, M., Mencarini, L. (2006) 'Youth poverty and transition to adulthood in Europe', *Demographic Research*, 15: 21-50.

ACEVO (2012) *Youth unemployment: The crisis we cannot afford*. London: ACEVO Commission on Youth Unemployment.

Bellfield, J., Cribb, C., Hood, A. and Joyce, R. (2014) *Living standards, poverty and inequality in the UK: 2014*. London: IFS.

Bradshaw, J. and Finch, N. (2003) 'Overlaps in dimensions of poverty', *Journal of Social Policy*, 32, 4: 513-25.

Buchmann, M. and Kriesi, I. (2011) 'Transition to adulthood in Europe', *Annual Review of Sociology*, 37: 481-503.

Children and Young People Now (2011) 'True scale of council youth service cuts revealed', *Children and Young People Now*, 8 February.

Colley, K. and Hodkinson, P. (2001) 'Problems with bridging the gap: the reversal of structure and agency in addressing social exclusion', *Critical Social Policy*, 21, 3: 335-59.

Corlett, A. and Whittaker, M. (2014) *Low pay Britain*. London: Resolution Foundation.

Davies, B. (2013) 'Youth work in a changing policy landscape', *Youth and Policy*, 110: 6-32.

Davis, A., Hirsch, D., Smith, N., Beckhelling, J. and Padley, M. (2012) *A Minimum Income Standard for the UK in 2012: Keeping up in hard times*. York: Joseph Rowntree Foundation.

European Commission (2010) *Europe 2020: A European strategy for smart, sustainable and inclusive growth*. Brussels: EC.

European Commission (2012) *EU Youth Strategy, 2010–18: Implementation of the renewed framework for European cooperation in the youth field*. Brussels: EC.

Fahmy, E. (2006) 'Youth, poverty and social exclusion', in C. Pantazis, D. Gordon and R. Levitas (eds) *Poverty and Social Exclusion in Britain: The millennium survey*. Bristol: Policy Press.

Fahmy, E. (2008) 'Tackling youth exclusion in the UK: challenges for current policy and practice', *Social Work and Society*, 6, 2: 280-7.

Fahmy, E. (2014) 'The complex nature of youth poverty and deprivation in Europe', in L. Antonucci, M. Hamilton and S. Roberts (eds) *Young people and social policy in Europe*. London: Palgrave Macmillan.

France, A. (2008) 'From being to becoming: the importance of tackling youth poverty in transitions to adulthood', *Social Policy and Society*, 7, 4: 495-505.

Gordon, D. (2016) *Poverty and Social Exclusion Survey, 2012* [data collection]. UK Data Service. SN: 7879, http://doi.org/10.5255/UKDA-SN-7879-1.

Gordon, D. and Pantazis, C. (1997) *Breadline Britain in the 1990s.* Aldershot: Ashgate.

Gregg, P., Machin, S. and Fernández-Salgado, M. (2014) 'The squeeze on real wages – and what it might take to end it', *National Institute Economic Review*, 228, 1: R3-16.

Guio, A.-C., Marlier, E., Gordon, D., Fahmy, E., Nandy, S. and Pomati, M. (2016) 'Improving the measurement of material deprivation at the European Union level', *Journal of European Social Policy*, 26, 3: 219-33.

Hagenaars, A. and de Vos, K. (1988) 'The definition and measurement of poverty', *Journal of Human Resources*, 23, 2: 211-21.

Hallerod, B. (2006) 'Sour grapes: relative deprivation, adaptive preferences and the measurement of poverty', *Journal of Social Policy*, 35, 3: 371-90.

House of Commons (2012) *Education Select Committee Report: Services for young people.* HC 744-I, London: The Stationery Office

Iacovou, M. and Aassve, A. (2007) *Youth poverty in Europe.* York: JRF.

Iacovou, M. and Berthoud, R. (2001) *Young people's lives: A map of Europe.* Colchester: ISER, University of Essex.

Levitas, R., Pantazis, C., Fahmy, E., Gordon, D., Lloyd, E. and Patsios, D. (2007) *The multi-dimensional analysis of social exclusion.* Bristol: University of Bristol.

Macdonald, R. (ed.) (1997) *Youth, the 'underclass' and social exclusion.* Bristol: Policy Press.

MacInnes, T., Aldridge, H., Bushe, S., Tinson, A. and Born, T. (2014) *Monitoring poverty and social exclusion, 2014.* York: JRF.

Mack, J. and Lansley, S. (1985) *Poor Britain.* London: George Allen & Unwin

Matsumoto, M., Hengge, M. and Islam, I. (2012) *Tackling the youth employment crisis: A macroeconomic perspective.* Employment Working Paper 124. Geneva: International Labour Organization.

Melrose, M. (2012) 'Young people, welfare reform and social insecurity', *Youth and Policy*, 108: 1-19.

Mendola, D., Busetta, A. and Aassve, A. (2008) *Poverty permanence among European youth. ISER Working paper 2008-04.* Colchester: ISER.

New Policy Institute (2015) *Why has poverty risen so much for young adults?*, http://npi.org.uk/publications/children-and-young-adults/why-has-poverty-risen-so-much-young-adults/

Oakley, M. (2014) *Independent review of the operation of Jobseeker's Allowance sanctions validated by the Jobseekers Act 2013*. London: DWP.

Office for National Statistics (ONS) (2016) *Young people's well-being and personal finance: UK, 2013 to 2014*. Statistical Bulletin, 11 May.

Padley, M. and Hirsch, D. (2014) *Households below a minimum income standard: 2008/9 to 2011/12*. York: Joseph Rowntree Foundation.

Pantazis, C., Gordon, D. and Levitas, R. (eds) (2006a) *Poverty and social exclusion in Britain: The Millennium Survey*. Bristol: Policy Press.

Pantazis, C., Gordon, D. and Townsend, P. (2006b) 'The necessities of life', in C. Pantazis, D. Gordon and R. Levitas (eds) *Poverty and social exclusion in Britain: The Millennium Survey*. Bristol: Policy Press.

Perry, B. (2002) 'The mismatch between income measures and direct outcome measures of poverty', *Social Policy Journal of New Zealand*, 19: 101-27.

Piachaud, D. (1981) 'Peter Townsend and the Holy Grail', *New Statesman*, 10 September.

Townsend, P. (1979) *Poverty in the United Kingdom*. London: Allen Lane & Penguin Books.

Townsend, P. (1987) 'Deprivation', *Journal of Social Policy*, 16, 2: 125-46.

Vogel, J. (2002) 'European welfare regimes and the transition to adulthood: A comparative and longitudinal perspective', *Social Indicators Research*, 59, 3: 275-99.

Watts, B., Fitzpatrick, S., Bramley, G. and Watkins, D. (2014) *Welfare sanctions and conditionality in the UK*. York: JRF.

Whelan, C., Layte, R. and Maître, B. (2004) 'Understanding the mismatch between income poverty and deprivation', *European Sociological Review*, 20, 4: 287-302.

Whelan, C., Layte, R., Maître, B. and Nolan, B. (2001) 'Income, deprivation and economic strain: An analysis of the European Community Household Panel', *European Sociological Review*, 17, 4: 357-72.

FOUR

Routine sanctions, humiliation and human struggle: qualitative biographies of young people's experience of live marginality

Linda Brooks

Introduction

This chapter outlines the impact of government austerity measures in the context of a registered charity in Essex. Since 2012, the author has been a volunteer and treasurer at the charity. The charity provides a number of different services for young people, aged 11 to 25, including a drop-in centre. The drop-in centre is the main part of the charity's service and it offers a safe, confidential place for young people to talk about a range of issues. Between April 2014 and April 2015, some 433 contacts were recorded, where young people used the drop-in centre for help and support. The highest recorded concerns included welfare benefits, emotional support, food parcels and housing. The most dramatic change in the help provided by the charity has been an increase in practical support; most notably, there was during 2014/15 a 300% increase in requests for food parcels, together with support to look for work or benefits online.

Methods

The research conducted for this chapter is based on observation field notes and informal interviews with young people who use the charity. As part of the research ethics, the manager and the management committee were consulted about the research and they offered their support. All of the young people interviewed in the research gave their consent to take part, and their names have all been changed to ensure confidentiality. The core principal of the charity is confidentiality, and the young people who use the charity are fully aware of this.

Therefore, as the author is a volunteer at the charity, the young people were at ease discussing their experiences with her. She also endeavoured to remain emotionally detached as the experiences were described. However, it should be noted that there may be an issue with power relations, and that some young people may have felt pressurised to speak to the author (Weber, 1968). In addition, the author may not have achieved an unbiased sample, as the most vocal young people may have participated.

The qualitative approach was based on Clifford Geertz's (1973, p18) value of producing grounded descriptions, motivated by empathy with the young people, on the basis that they would be willing to share their thoughts, feelings and experiences in informal interviews as conversation. There were 12 participants: six female and six male, the youngest aged 17 and the eldest aged 27. The length of interview ranged from 20 minutes to 2 hours. The young people were given the opportunity to read transcripts and to correct or withdraw from the research at any time (Fraser, 2004). Additional information was gathered from a small number of employees of the charity.

Background and context

In 2010, a Coalition government was formed in the United Kingdom between the Conservative Party led by David Cameron and the Liberal Democrat Party led by Nick Clegg. The government set out its political position to reduce the record debts in the HM Treasury Spending Review (Treasury, 2010). One of the key areas that the Coalition and subsequent Conservative government focused on was implementing austerity measures to administer change to welfare on the basis that this would provide net savings of £11 billion a year by 2014/15.

The Conservative government continued to implement austerity measures, which included significant cuts to social security (Oxfam, 2013). In Northern Ireland, the Welfare Reform Bill 2012 states that 'a tighter sanctions regime will also provide a greater incentive to comply with the job seeking requirements', suggesting that claimants need to have incentives to find employment (Department for Social Development, 2012), suggesting that claimants need to have incentives to find employment.

David Cameron, the then Conservative Prime Minister, commented in 2014: 'I want us to end the idea that aged 18 you can leave school, go and leave home, claim unemployment benefit and claim Housing Benefit. We shouldn't be offering that choice to young people' (*Andrew*

Marr Show, 2014). This chapter takes issue with these claims. Instead, this research found that the experiences of the young people using the charity illustrated their struggles to achieve the basic needs of shelter and food.

Information and costs on homelessness

The interviews conducted during this research focused on issues related to housing and homelessness. Nine of those interviewed were aged 17 to 23 years old, and were not able to live in the family home. There is evidence that homelessness is increasing, and 52% of individuals needing help with this are aged under 25. Despite this, from April 2017, young people aged 18 to 21 will not be able to apply for Housing Benefit. In 2015 the Chancellor, George Osborne claimed that removing this entitlement would: 'ensure young people in the benefits system face the same choices as young people who work and who may not be able to afford to leave home' (Gentlemen, 2015).

Criticisms of this move have been strong. The youth homelessness charity Centrepoint estimated that 'as many as 80,000 young people (age 18–25) experience homelessness in the UK' (Crisis, 2012). Research conducted by Homeless Link, the umbrella body for homelessness charities, also stated that the number of people sleeping rough in the South East of England has increased by 14% from 2013 to 2014 (Homeless Link, 2014). In addition, research by the charity Crisis indicated that approximately '62% of single homeless people are hidden and may not show up in official figures' (Hurcombe, 2015). Jacqui McCluskey, Director of Policy and Communications for Homeless Link, said:

> 'with rising youth unemployment, a changing welfare system and many families struggling to get by, youth homelessness is likely to get worse. We can't prevent the recession but we can limit the impact it is having on the next generation. The longer someone doesn't have a home, the more likely they are to develop complex problems and become trapped into a cycle of homelessness. If we don't provide access to the right advice, help and support for young people now, we are potentially looking at a much bigger, and more expensive, problem in the future' (Acred, 2014).

Affordable housing in the location where the research was conducted is a problem for young people. To contextualise this, the calculation for Housing Benefit for the young people interviewed is based on the average cost of housing in the adjacent borough of Southend-on-Sea (approximately £66.78 per week). However, in the borough where the charity is based, there are no rooms available in that price range; instead, the room costs are significantly higher. In Canvey Island, the average price of renting a room in a shared property is as much as £108.25 a week. Because of this, staff at the charity spend a great deal of time trying to find accommodation for young people using a range of different methods, for example the local council, newspapers, letting agents and by monitoring shop window adverts. The cheapest room available for rent in the area is approximately £100 per week. Table 4.1 illustrates the living costs for a person on Jobseeker's Allowance (JSA) living in Castle Point, Canvey Island.

In comparison, the minimum amount that the government has stated that a pensioner should have to live on is £151.20 per week. In addition, pensioners claiming Pension Credit can be exempt from paying council tax. This illustrates a significant difference between the weekly incomes between young and older people. It could be argued that this difference of income between the ages is evidence that the government expects young people under the age of 24 to be living at home with a supportive family (Benefits, 2015a).

Table 4.1: Living expenses on Jobseeker's Allowance

	Age 18 to 24	Age 25 or over
JSA weekly amount received	£57.90	£73.10
Room rent (minimum)	£100.00	£100.00
Housing benefit	£66.78	£66.78
Top up paid by claimant (from JSA)	£33.22	£33.22
Balance remaining for council tax, food, clothes, travel	£24.68	£39.88

The following biographical case studies have been grouped into three themes: homelessness; young people's experiences of unemployment; and benefit sanctions. They are designed to highlight the experiences and voices of the participants (Merrill and West, 2009).

Experiences of homelessness

Castle Point has the lowest proportion of housing association stock in Essex (Essex Insight, 2014). One of the young people who came to the charity was 22-year-old Julie, who had two children aged 4 and 5 years. Julie had experienced the impact of low housing association stock, even though she had young children and was a priority case. Julie said she had been burgled in her private rented accommodation and 'no longer felt safe there and did not want to stay in her house'. Julie informed the council of the burglary with her crime number and was advised that she would be put on the waiting list. Julie stayed with a friend, informed the council of her temporary accommodation and the council agreed to this. While Julie was staying with her friend, Julie's landlord for the private rented accommodation gave her notice to leave, as he wanted to refurbish the house, making Julie and her children homeless. During interview, Julie explained: 'I thought I could sort this out myself and went to live with a friend'. However, within a few weeks the friend's Housing Benefit was stopped, because Julie and her children were living there, so Julie and her children were asked to leave. When Julie arrived at the charity, she was advised to contact the council, as she had young children and would be a priority. The council told Julie to contact all her friends and family to find accommodation. She stated, 'I felt awkward and like scum having to ask friends and family'. Eventually, Julie and her children moved in with her elderly grandfather as a temporary measure.

Another user of the charity was 19-year-old David, who had been asked to leave the parental home and was currently homeless. The nearest homeless centre was based 15 miles away and prioritises young people wanting accommodation in the area they had previously lived in. As such, young people from outside the borough are not eligible for emergency accommodation.

Jacob was an 18 year old who had been street homeless for a few weeks, after his parents told him to leave. He was referred to the charity by the homeless centre mentioned previously. Jacob walked over 10 miles from the homeless centre to the charity. The charity telephoned the local council, who did not consider him a priority as he was 18 years old. Jacob was not in receipt of any benefits, as he was waiting for his application to be processed. Jacob had applied to the National Association for the Care and Resettlement of Offenders (Nacro) without success, as there was a long waiting list. The staff at the charity offered Jacob food, which he refused. He appeared despondent, saying 'I know you can't help me', and he left the charity before any further support could be provided. As he left, he said: 'I don't know where I am gonna be, I will keep moving all night'. The field diary at the charity states: 'We have not seen Jacob again, here professional response and personal emotional feeling become difficult to separate, but such experiences are part of working at the charity, and sometimes we do not know if our young people are ok and have found accommodation and support'.

Another young person who had problems with homelessness was 27-year-old Mark. Mark had had a disruptive home life, living with his mother until the age of 14 when he first became homeless, after he said he was 'thrown out because of arguing and fighting with my step-dad'. Mark was still estranged from his mother and had only met his biological father twice. When Mark was homeless, he slept rough, as he said he 'didn't want to go into care or be fostered, I worked wherever I could just to get by and feed myself'. After living rough, Mark became ill and was hospitalised. When he was discharged, 'another step-dad took him in for about 6 months, but the step-dad's wife didn't like me she still don't and I got kicked out again'. Mark said he had 'drifted since then, worked at window cleaning and gardening and rented a room, and settled down a bit'. Mark then managed to rent a flat, but was evicted after an incident with a neighbour. Mark then lived in a tent for 18 months, as he was not considered to be a vulnerable adult and therefore was ineligible for help as a homeless person. Also, Mark would not be included in the local authority's P1E Statutory Government Return for homelessness (Castle Point Borough Council, 2015). During this period of homelessness, Mark was assigned a community psychiatric nurse (CPN), as he had a criminal record and had reoffended. He said: 'I had asked for help finding somewhere to live, but the CPN said the same as me, but they got results, I had asked 7 times no result. They got me in a hostel, then I got a flat. The CPN finished with me then.' The author asked Mark what could have helped him and he replied:

> 'they should re-evaluate who they can help, I think they should help me get settled now. I got a flat and all it had was an oven and a hob, no bed I had to buy one for £20. I am giving out CVs to get a job. I don't want to be living off benefits, I want to show my family who didn't want me that I can do it.'

Jessica was 17 years old and was also homeless and estranged from her family. Her parents were separated. She had previously lived with her mother, but she had then been 'kicked out'. Jessica's father was an alcoholic, who lived in one rented room. Although Jessica stayed with her father at some stage, this was an unsatisfactory arrangement and she said her father could 'not afford to have me at home if I was not contributing to the rent and council tax'. She said: 'My dad threw me out because I could never pay my way'. Jessica did receive benefits and had been sanctioned at least three times: 'my benefits were always on and off'. She continued: 'I was sanctioned because I was living in different places, sofa surfing and never had the right paperwork for the job centre'. Jessica did not know that she would be sanctioned and she said she felt: 'Angry! I arrived at an appointment, but because I did not have all my paperwork I returned later with it but was told I had "missed" the appointment.' Jessica said she felt 'humiliated at having to borrow and angry because it damaged the relationship with my dad', while being sanctioned. Jessica felt her priority while living in such difficult circumstances had been to find safe places to sleep for the night, rather than focusing her attention on ensuring that she had completed the correct forms and followed the official procedures of the benefits agency.

Paul was 24 years old and had been homeless many times. He had previously been involved with taking and dealing drugs, but at the time of the interview said he was not involved with drugs and was not claiming any benefits. Instead, Paul was working full time and said he felt 'settled'. The first time he became homeless was at the age of 18, after being 'kicked out' of his mum's. He said: 'Me and mum don't have a good relationship. She beat me up from the age of 10 and will still do it now.' The first time Paul was homeless, he went into supported housing, but: 'because I abused the system I got kicked out of there too'. After this:

> 'I slept on the street and I did get a tent. To support myself, I was selling drugs as I didn't have any other option. I was using drugs too. Being homeless and not signing on it was easier to sell more bags of drugs. I lived like this for 9 and a half months. I then went to Open Road for drugs counselling but I kept dealing to support myself. This is when I realised I had a severe mental health problem, I just flipped out at anyone.'

At this point in his life, Paul was diagnosed with psychosis, depression and anxiety, and he was prescribed medication. He then received Housing Benefit and moved into private rented housing. The charity helped Paul with his deposit. However, the private rented accommodation was not in the same area but a few miles away, and Paul kept returning to sell drugs. Paul said:

> 'I didn't get along with the landlord, I had a fight with him then left, homeless again. I then slept in my mum's front garden for a year. It was freezing in the winter. I then got caught with drugs and fined but I didn't pay the fine so went to prison for a month. When I come out I got sent to a hostel for ex-offenders for 2 and a half weeks. This was not helpful and horrible people who didn't care or want to help. I was then homeless again, and had a fight in my mum's front garden and she let me back in. I am still living there now 18 months later.'

Asked if he had a CPN, Paul said, 'yes, but they aren't helpful and don't do long term support'. Asked what would have helped him to not have such a disruptive life, Paul replied: 'I think rehab would have helped when I was 17 or 18 years old. Then I was doing cannabis and cocaine.'

Although the decisions and choices made by some of the young people in these small case studies had contributed to their living arrangements, none of the young people interviewed had chosen to leave home and claim unemployment and Housing Benefit, as has been previously suggested by David Cameron (*Andrew Marr Show*, 2014). Instead, every young person had emerged from a disrupted family background, with little opportunity to return home.

Experiences of youth unemployment

This chapter argues that young people have been affected by the 'recession, and by structural changes in the UK economy over several decades' (Simmons et al, 2014). Moreover, the young people at the charity frequently commented that it feels like a 'catch 22' situation – they cannot find work because they do not have the experience, and without work they cannot gain experience.

The negative effects of young unemployment have been researched by Bell and Blanchflower (2010), who argued that 'spells of unemployment while young create permanent scars' and that these continue to 'have harmful impacts on a number of outcomes – happiness, job satisfaction, wages and health – many years later' (Bell and Blanchflower, 2010). Gregg and Wadsworth (2010) also argue that long-term unemployment 'scars' young people and that this will 'feed into the next generation' (Gregg and Wadsworth, 2010).

Two case studies focusing specifically on youth employment are those of Peter and Patsy. Peter (aged 22) and Patsy (aged 19) were a couple and were both long-term unemployed. Peter said he 'got some work for 24 hours per week', but because of this, his partner was not entitled to any benefits. He said: 'We were worse off but were told if I didn't take the job we would be sanctioned'. Peter took the job and this only lasted for two weeks, before he was 'told to go'. This was not the first time this had happened. Peter returned to the charity and asked for counselling. He said, 'I felt depressed, suicidal and felt just like giving up'. Peter continued: 'I felt like it was never going to get better'. Patsy said, 'I didn't know what to do and how to help, I tried to get a job but couldn't get one. I am still trying.'

Since then, Peter has had counselling and mentoring, has started medication and has applied for Employment and Support Allowance (ESA), which took over two weeks to be changed from JSA. Peter has also attended several training programmes and he explained that he was beginning to feel a little more optimistic about finding work and more hopeful that 'survival was possible'. While being penalised and sanctioned had increased his anxiety, he felt that the support he had received had led to him being able to develop a more positive outlook for the future.

Experiences of benefit sanctions

In 2012, the government implemented a new sanctions regime for JSA. The new sanctions regime has specific targets and the maximum number of weeks has been significantly increased – from 26 weeks to 156 weeks (about three years). The new sanctions regime being developed by government provides advisers at jobcentres with 'the flexibility to target stronger conditionality on some jobseekers where they think this is necessary to help move them into work' (Department for Work and Pensions, 2012). The Department for Work and Pensions states that: 'each sanction is considered on a case by case basis and claimants are given five working days to provide their reasons for failing to participate or engage with conditionality requirements' (Department for Work and Pensions, 2013).

However, this chapter argues that the young people at the charity have not been considered on a case-by-case basis. Instead, the young people interviewed had not been informed of the sanction. In addition, in a number of other cases, young people had been sanctioned because they had been at a job interview on the date they were scheduled to sign on, despite informing the jobcentre of the clash in advance. In the charity's records of young people, there has also been a significant increase in the number of sanctions and these have been for a minimum of two weeks or longer.

Similarly, Citizens Advice has data to show that there was an increase in advice queries about JSA sanctions from June 2013, with year-on-year increases of 45%, 40% and 30% per quarter respectively from October 2012 to June 2013. An overall increase of 64% from 2013 to 2014 was attributed to the change in JSA sanctions rules introduced in October 2012 (National Association of Citizens Advice Bureaux, 2014). Furthermore, research conducted by Homeless Link found that young people claiming JSA are the most likely group to be sanctioned (Homeless Link, 2014).

This chapter argues that the implementation of sanctions has had a negative impact on young people's motivation to find employment and on their mental health. Doris (22 years old) said she had been sanctioned because:

> 'I was just a few minutes late for my appointment. I got sanctioned for two weeks. I didn't know I had been sanctioned until my benefit didn't go in the bank. I called the social and they told me I had been sanctioned. I felt really down as I had a row with my partner a few weeks earlier and he had kicked me out, I was sleeping on a friend's sofa and didn't know what to do. It has taken me a long time to sort myself out and it's been hard.'

Leah was a 20-year-old female living in Canvey Island. Leah had missed five or six appointments in 2014 and was told that she may be sanctioned if she did not attend appointments. Because she had been unemployed over a year, she had to travel to Seetec[1] in Southend to attend appointments and to sign on. She had lent a friend some of her benefits and the friend did not pay the money back in time for Leah to travel to Southend, so she missed another appointment. Leah was then sanctioned for three months. When she was told that she would be sanctioned, Leah said: 'Don't sanction me as I can't live, what am I going to do?' She said, 'I didn't know what to do, I felt really angry and wanted to do myself in'. Leah visited the charity for food and said, 'I would not have survived without the charity, I felt so depressed and low'. She continued: 'The first week I just lived off rice and beans, and the thought of doing that for 3 months was terrible ... It is really difficult to get a job and look for work if you don't have any money and feel down ... I didn't have any money to travel to interviews'. Leah had been on training courses and had had two jobs, but just for a few days each. She was currently unemployed.

Beth was 17 years old and pregnant. She lived with her mother, who was on a low income. Her mother's income paid the bills and Beth's 'benefits were used to pay for shopping so we struggled'. Beth said her experience of receiving benefits was: 'difficult because I didn't have a bank account and benefits have to be paid directly into a bank account, we had to use my mum's post office account ... I have been sanctioned twice and I did not know that I was going to be sanctioned.' Beth said she 'felt angry and worried' and 'gutted and very, very angry'.

Richard was a 21 year old, who had been in a care home and had moved into shared accommodation. Richard lived in shared accommodation for eight months and said he did not know that he had to apply for Housing Benefit. He then received a bill for eight months' rent and he did not know what to do, as he believed his rent was being paid. Richard had applied for JSA and was receiving this, but has been sanctioned three or four times because he could not attend the work programme. He applied for a hardship loan, which took two weeks to come through. During this time, he relied on food banks and help from family. Richard said he 'felt down all the time, and embarrassed to keep asking for help'. Richard also felt he didn't understand the system and the importance of attending interviews and the work programme. Richard said he 'felt desperate and always in trouble with debts'.

Robert was a 23-year-old male living in Canvey Island. Robert had been in foster care due to a violent mother. He applied to the council for accommodation when he was 21. He said he wanted to do his own thing, 'not have dinner at 5pm or be in by 10pm'. His experience of the benefits system is good overall, with bad patches. Robert has been sanctioned 10 times and he did think he would be sanctioned, as 'you are sanctioned for anything'. He felt 'low, depressed, worried' when he had been sanctioned. He said he was 'anxious about paying his bills, you don't get any help they just say go to a charity'. He only has the charity for support, as he has no family that will help. He said: 'if you get any hardship money this will only pay for gas and electric, you just can't afford food ... When you are sanctioned your housing benefit stops and you worry that you will be homeless. You have to contact the council and tell them you have been sanctioned then reclaim again ... The first time this happened I didn't know I had to do this'.

Interviews with these young people suggested that there were often problems with them not fully understanding the consequences and expectations of the benefits agency procedures. These particular young people had limited personal resources to help them negotiate the processes of the benefits system. They would struggle with completing paperwork, organising transport and seeking help, before reaching crisis point. The young people would be confused and genuinely surprised when they were sanctioned, and would frequently say: 'I don't know what I have done wrong'.

Towards a culture of survival

The young people at the charity have a wide range of issues to manage, including not only homelessness, but also additional challenges brought about by the limited available and affordable housing, the absence of accommodation for homeless young people within the borough, and difficulties in finding money for deposits and rent in advance. In addition, there are also significant problems with regard to unemployment, including difficulties in applying for benefits, continuation of benefits when changing from JSA to ESA, and sanctions. Some of the young people at the charity experience unemployment and homelessness at the same time. This is a difficult situation to rectify at any age, and it is especially poignant to see a young person trying to cope in this situation.

The stories offered by the young people of their experience affirm Blackman's (1997, p115) narratives of a culture of survival, which 'allow a view into a personal and subjective world where opportunity has been stripped bare'. The sanctions have had a negative impact on the health of young people in this study, who report feeling depressed and not having any money to buy essentials, such as food or travelling expenses to attend interviews. Furthermore, the young people who come to the charity often have low self-esteem and little knowledge of the criteria for receiving benefits. In the author's experience, young people who had been sanctioned and who understood the system would make sure they attended every meeting, training programme and signing on date, because of the fear of losing benefits, as opposed to being motivated and enthusiastic about gaining employment.

Conclusions

Through the voices and experiences of the young people interviewed, this chapter suggests that benefit sanctions are often implemented far too quickly and routinely and lack consideration of challenging individual circumstances. For example, for young people who are homeless – or those who have personality disorders, mental health problems or learning difficulties – these rapid changes are particularly difficult to cope with. The author has seen numerous young people who, as a result of difficult individual circumstances, have fallen through the social safety nets of education, the NHS and social services.

The sanctions system works on the principle that these young people have high levels of resilience, emotional intelligence and alternative resources to fall back on. The manager at the charity commented: 'I think government may know these young people don't have this resilience, as there is support i.e. job advisors, SEETEC but these systems don't work for our young people's complex needs'. The young people need intense work and understanding and may return to the charity on a number of occasions with the same problem of unemployment, homelessness or benefit sanctions.

The young people in the case studies have not made a lifestyle choice to be homeless, unemployed and on benefits; they are caught in a culture of survival, sometimes with hope and at other times with little hope (Blackman, 1997; Shildrick et al, 2012). Throughout the study, the participants' culture of survival was hanging by a thread. The biographical approach enabled subjective experience to emerge as participants felt humiliated, angry and depressed. The lasting finding from the drop-in centre was that young adults require emotional and financial support, and if this is not possible through their family, then other systems need be in place to ensure that help is available. The goal of the charity was to provide a free service to marginalised young people to help provide basic needs – shelter, food and work, and someone who cares. The problem for the young people – and for the charity – was that we became a last resort, not a first resort.

Note

[1] Seetec is a welfare to work company, whereby claimants of social security benefits are placed by Seetec with companies and required to work unpaid or lose their benefit entitlement. Seetec is located in Southend and Leah had to travel over 10 miles to attend appointments and to sign on.

Bibliography

Acred, C. (2014) *Homelessness in the UK*. 2nd edn. Cambridge: Independence Educational Publishers.

Andrew Marr Show (2014) [TV programme] BBC One. 11 May 2014.

Bell, D. and Blanchflower, D. (2010) *Youth Unemployment: Déjà vu?*. Bonn: University of Stirling and IZA.

Blackman, S. (1997) 'Destructing a Giro': A critical and ethnographic study of the youth "underclass"', in R. MacDonald (ed.) *Youth, the 'Underclass' and Social Exclusion*. London: Routledge, 113–29.

Castle Point Borough Council 2015) *P1E Statutory Government Returns,*www.castlepoint.gov.uk

Crisis (2012) *Crisis Research Briefing: Young, hidden and homeless*. London: Crisis.

Department for Social Development (2012) *Welfare Reform Bill 2012: Regulatory Impact Assessment*. London: Crown Copyright.

Department for Work and Pensions (DWP) (2012) *The Jobseeker's Allowance (Sanctions) (Amendment) Regulations 2012, SI No. 2568*. London: Crown Copyright.

DWP (2013) *Freedom of information request 2011/2013*. London: Crown Copyright.

DWP Benefits (2015a) *Jobseeker's Allowance (JSA)*. London: Crown Copyright.

DWP Benefits (2015b) *Pension Credit*. London: Crown Copyright.

Essex Insight (2014) *Essex Local Authority Portraits*. Essex Insight.

Fraser, S. (2004) *Doing research with children and young people*. London: Sage Publications.

Geertz, C. (1973) *The Interpretation of cultures*. New York: Basic Books.

Gentlemen, A. (2015) 'Austerity cuts will bite even harder in 2015 – another 12bn will go'. *The Guardian*. 1 January 2015. https://www.theguardian.com/society/2015/jan/01/austerity-cuts-2015-12-billion-britain-protest

Gregg, P. and Wadsworth, J. (2010) 'Unemployment and inactivity in the 2008–2009 recession', *Economic and Labour Market Review*, 4, 8: 44–50.

Homeless Link (2014) *Young and homeless*, www.homeless.org.uk

Hurcombe, R. (2015) *Hidden homelessness*. Homeless Link. www.homeless.org.uk

Merrill, B. and West, L. (2009) *Using Biographical methods in social research*. London: Sage.

National Association of Citizens Advice Bureaux (2014) *Evidence. Response to the call for information for the Independent Review of Jobseeker's Allowance Sanctions*. London: Citizens Advice Organisation.

Oxfam (2013) *Oxfam case study: The true cost of austerity and inequality.* Oxford: Oxfam GB.

Shildrick, T., MacDonald, R., Webster C. and Garthwaite, K. (2102) *Poverty and insecurity: Life in low-pay, no-pay Britain.* Bristol: Policy Press.

Simmons, R., Thompson, R. and Russell, L. (2014) *Education, work and social change.* Basingstoke: Palgrave Macmillan.

Treasury (2010) *HM Treasury Spending Review 2010.* London: Crown Copyright.

Weber, M. (1968) *Economy and society: An outline of interpretive sociology.* New York: Bedminster Press.

FIVE

Normalisation of youth austerity through entertainment: critically addressing media representations of youth marginality in Britain

Shane Blackman and Ruth Rogers

Introduction

This chapter focuses on how newspaper headlines and reality TV programmes exploit forms of popular culture such as successful television series to convey a political and moral message that reinforces the marginality of young adults in society. Critically, we call upon the 'returned gaze' of youth positioned in austerity, to show how young people are pushed to the edges of society by populist representations of social crisis but remain the mechanism used by both government and media to exert control. The second part of the chapter addresses two zones of media representations: where young adults are projected as scroungers and marginalised through mockery, defining them as a burden rather than an asset for society

'Sacrificial lambs' and a 'smart tongue': young adult austerity through the lens of entertainment

Initially we will examine whether young adults in popular factual TV entertainment can be described as 'sacrificial lambs'. We identify a convergence between newspaper representations of what Loic Wacquant (2008) has called 'advanced marginality' with the growth of reality television programmes such as *Benefits Street* (screened on 6 January 2014, Channel Four). In contrast, to previous depictions of youth poverty, such as the drama documentary *Cathy Come Home* by Ken Loach in 1966 where the portrayal evokes empathy, much of the new image of youth poverty is delivered with little sympathy (Paterson et al, 2015). The critical attention created by *Benefits Street* has overshadowed previous programmes that combined both documentary and TV reality styles of production. *Mail Online* (21 January 2014) reported: 'Benefits Street's parade of scroungers and drug addicts give Channel 4 its highest ratings since 2012'.

The rise of popular factual entertainment according to Corner (2000) is related to the commercial opportunities created through a deregulated television broadcasting environment, seeking to capture new audiences. For Beattie (2004, pp198-99) it is not merely that TV reality programmes are cheap in terms of production costs; he notes that popular light entertainment is increasingly replacing critical inquiry with personal confession, where the emphasis is on 'emotion and the display of subjective feelings'.

In the UK, before *Benefits Street*, on 29 November 2006, the BBC produced Brian Wood's *Evicted*, a documentary in six parts following the personal stories of Charlotte, 13, Chloe, 7, and Sarah, 15. *Evicted* has more in common with Ken Loach's (2016) new film *I, Daniel Blake*, as it follows three young girls and their families into homelessness, unpleasant hotel rooms, and temporary accommodation hostels. Although it conforms to Corner's (1995, pp28-9) idea of 'intensive subjectivity', *Evicted* has the power of being a raw emotional programme. It was the winner of the 2007 BAFTA for best documentary, and in 2007 there was an *Evicted Update*. Lucy Mangan in *The Guardian* reported (29 November 2007) that: 'a year on, happy endings were scarce for the *Evicted* girls'.

It is possible to see degrees of similarity between *Evicted* and *Poor Kids*, shown on BBC One on 7 June 2011 in three parts. The programme focuses on 3.5 million children living in poverty in the UK. We see eight-year-old Courtney from Bradford, 10-year-old Paige in Glasgow, and 11-year-old Sam and his 16-year-old sister Kayleigh from Leicester. Steve, father of Sam and Kayleigh, lives apart from them after having a heart attack. The *Daily Mirror* (6 June 2011) reports: 'it seems desperately unfair that Kayleigh was driven to take her own life, simply for being poor'. For these young people, there are no holidays – only coldness, skipping meals, no spare change, few if any new clothes or toys, and they are surrounded by mould. Angie Sammons (9 June 2011), writing in *Liverpool Confidential*, states that watching these young people: "Their integrity, their acceptance of their lot, and their complete trust and faith in their well meaning but disenfranchised parents, was humbling". In *Poor Kids*, young people are central stage, the film has an ethnographic feel, as they reveal their honesty. BBC News (12 June 2011) reported positively on 'Leicester family's overwhelming response to *Poor Kids*'.

In contrast, the impact of *Benefits Street* has been the generation a new raft of similar programmes, including: *Benefits and Proud* (2014, Channel 5); *Undercover Benefit Cheats* (four episodes, 12 August 2015, Channel 5); *On Benefits* (2016, Channel 5); *Benefits by the Sea, Jaywick* (2016, Channel 5); and *The Great British Benefits Handout* (2016, Channel 5). A key difference concerning TV reality programmes including *Benefits Street* is that the tabloid media coverage of individual people under conditions of low income is such that they are described as 'reality TV stars'. The label 'TV star', applied to ordinary people on low or no income, keeps viewers and participants on a knife-edge of subjective experience. As a viewer, you are encouraged to empathise with some and then to see others with disgust and loathing.

As a result, TV presenter Paul O'Grady was critical of the Channel 4 series *Benefits Street*. Talking on the BBC programme *The One Show* (14 January 2014), he stated: "These people are the sacrificial lambs on the altar of light entertainment and they have gone willingly: a smart tongue has got them to say all sorts and it is a very unfair representation of unemployment in this country".

The leader of Hull City Council, Steve Brady, affirms O'Grady's understanding, in the *Hull Daily Mail* (18 June 2014). After viewing *Benefits Britain: Life on the Dole*, Brady stated that: "These TV programmes on individuals are really using them in quite a cruel way really, because they don't even realise they are being ridiculed. It is quite sad to watch. It showed people wasting their lives."

Another BBC programme, *The Scheme* (18 May 2010), was a BAFTA-award winning documentary series and had a focus on drug and drink problems in Kilmarnock. However, BBC News (30 June 2011) reported that SNP MSP Willie Coffey said the programme had dangerously exposed people already at risk: "for nothing more than public entertainment. It was tabloid TV at its worst – local people were kidded and conned by this venture."

Further accusations of the poor being set up as an 'amusement' were made by Mark Sweeney in *The Guardian* (28 May 2015), commenting on the BBC's *Britain's Hardest Workers: Inside the low wage economy* (first series began 8 September 2016), which sets 25 of the UK's lowest-paid workers against each other to win cash prizes. Several newspapers (*Independent* 29 May 2015; *Daily Express* 28 May 2015; and *The Guardian* (28 May 2015) reported this programme as '*Benefit Street* meets *The Hunger Games*', arguing that it was degrading TV entertainment, which is a misplaced social experiment. Commenting on the BBC's *Britain's Hardest Workers*, Phil Harrison in *The Guardian* (Harrison, 22 August 2016) concludes: 'As life begins to imitate art, the show implies that the basement level of the UK job market now conforms pretty much exactly to the template of the competitive reality show'.

Imogen Taylor (2013) maintains that these programmes capture the so-called pleasure of voyeurism; here the lens of austerity is turned on the vulnerable and could be described as 'live sociology' without theory (Back, 2012). The apparent fun of looking at others who are struggling, whereby they become entertainment, was challenged according to BBC News (8 January 2014), which reported: '*Benefits Street* series sparks hundreds of complaints' for its negative portrayal of benefit claimants and the depiction of criminal activity.

Parodies and crafted evidence: questioning TV and newspaper representations of youth marginality

One of the success stories of British comedy is its ability to critique the political order, but it may also reinforce the status quo through cruel laughter (Kamm and Neumann, 2016). We identify that the tabloid media have repeatedly employed the success of these TV programme character identities as a means of negatively labelling young adults in Britain. For example, the character-based comedy programme *Little Britain* (BBC One, 2005–07), with its fictional young chav mum figure of Vicky Pollard, has received a host of awards. The deliberate merging of narratives from reality and fiction within newspaper headlines not only exaggerated parodies but also short-circuits critical thinking. *The Sun* (10 February 2009) used a photograph of Vicky Pollard to claim: 'BRITAIN is producing a generation of "super chavs"'. Jones (2011, p128) notes that Vicky Pollard, while capturing the popular imagination for fun focused on the grotesque, also fired up the vicious imaginations of the right wing. For example, a key figure for Jones (2011, p125) is the 'right-wing journalist Richard Littlejohn', the *Daily Mail* columnist who speaks of the London rioters in the following terms:

> 'We're talking about a wolfpack of feral inner-city waifs and strays who spend their time smoking dope, drinking lager and playing Grand Theft Auto on their stolen PlayStations. The soundtrack of their lives comprises wealthy, bling-laden rappers, surrounded by near-naked booty, singing about smacking bitches and killing cops.' (Littlejohn, 12 August 2011)

Littlejohn crafts an appeal to an exaggerated common sense. This is an example of what Howard Becker (1963, p148) called a moral entrepreneur whose 'crusade is fervent and righteous, often self righteous'. The use of forms of popular culture such as television programmes, films, computer games and popular music, can be described as the normalisation of austerity through entertainment. For example:

- *Daily Star* (11 November 2010): 'Anarchy in the UK';
- *The Telegraph* (9 August 2011): 'Carry on Looting!';
- *Mail Online* (12 September 2012) '"I don't give a f★★★ what people think": Jobless mother-of-four who pockets £1,100 handouts on "Shameless estate" claims BBC deliberately made her look worse in documentary';
- *Mail Online* (7 August 2013): 'Serial thief dubbed the real-life Vicky Pollard is finally jailed for crime spree against shop staff';
- *The Sun* (10 October 2013): 'Through the Benefit Keyhole';
- *The Star* (11 December 2014): 'Shameless';
- *The Sun* (19 March 2016): 'Shameless benefits cheat invented THIRTEEN children to net £10k in handouts'.

The use of TV-mediated representation of young adults in poverty as a dominant image by newspapers disguises young people's real lives as they are pushed into the margins of society. Shildrick et al (2012, p82) argue that the media representation of youth poverty was at odds with young people's understanding of their 'churning around' between low pay and insecurity. Newspaper headlines recast inequality and poverty as a form of entertainment, so that the misery and despair of marginality are mediated through these popular representations. The use of reference points, such as 'Carry on', 'Shameless' or 'Vicky Pollard', from within popular culture are subjective. This not only raises the question of the accuracy and evidence being brought forward by newspapers, but it also suggests a deliberate distortion of social reality through narratives derived from fictional popular culture (Windle, 2010). There is a parallel between the selective nature of media representations and the strategies that policy makers use as evidence, according to MacCoun and Reuter (2008, p1), because there is a dependency on 'implicit rules' and these 'rules of evidence usually remain unspoken'.

Stevens and Measham (2014, p1229), speaking in relation to the development of drug policy, argue: 'Politicians sometimes choose to ignore the recommendations of independent experts, despite their pledges of allegiance to evidence-based policy'. It would appear that evidence is used to justify one decision and then ignored in another, suggesting that morality or politics rather than evidence may play a key role in policy development.

Therefore, the media and political use of evidence-based material are not always founded on systematic review, but through selective and secretive think tanks which, for Monbiot (2011), are engaged in the manufacture of ignorance to appease their funders. For Slater (2011, p111) such crafted data buffer 'politicians and their audience from viable alternatives and inoculates them against the critique of autonomous scholarship'. For example, in the aftermath of the London riots in 2011, Boris Johnson was reported by Nicholas Watt in *The Guardian* (9 August 2011) as stating: "It is time that people who are engaged in looting and violence stopped hearing economic and sociological justifications ..."

Also, the then Prime Minister David Cameron (2011) argued that the "riots were not about poverty", they were "about behaviour". This analysis is apparent in Iain Duncan Smith's Social Justice Policy Group 2006 and his focus on young people through the use of terms like dysfunction and dad-lessness, which resembles Charles Murray's development of the 'underclass' thesis (MacDonald, 1997).

In contrast, Kevin O'Sullivan (18 January 2014), *Sunday Mirror* journalist, takes a critical stance, stating that *Benefits Street* as a "carefully edited portrait of underclass hell is entertaining – but has little value as a social document". For Tracey Jenson (2014, p3), Iain Duncan Smith's 'War on Welfare': 'reinvents an imagined "underclass" for the purpose of welfare reform which is set to immiserate the most marginalised and precarious families in Britain'.

The speaking eye of youth marginality: the 'fourth look'

In this section, we look at one particular image used by newspapers. It is a photograph by Kerim Okten of a young adult male against a backdrop of burning vehicles in the urban streets of Hackney, London. It was taken and used as part of the news coverage of the London riots in 2011. This representation is featured as the central photographic image on four tabloid newspapers: *The Sun, The Star, The Daily Mail, the Daily Express*, and also the *i* (owned by *The Independent*) and the *Guardian*; it featured again in *The Sun* as a small insert on a front page. Within news media it is quite unusual for the exact same image to be repeated across newspapers. However, there were differences in terms of headlines and subheadings, for example:

- *The Daily Express*: 'FLAMING MORONS: Thugs and thieves Terrorise Britain's Streets' (9 August 2011);
- *Daily Mail*: 'THE ANARCHY SPREADS'; front page *Daily Mail* Comment: 'To blame the cuts is immoral and cynical. This is criminality pure and simple' (9 August 2011);
- *The Sun*: 'Anarchy. Riots spread across London, Birmingham hit by looting, 215 arrests, PM jets back' (9 August 2011);
- *The Daily Star*: 'Anarchy IN THE UK. PM dashes back as riot terror spreads' (9 August 2011);
- *The Guardian*: 'London riots escalate as police battle for control. Full-scale alert as violence spreads across capital, Disorder breaks out in Birmingham city centre';
- *i Independent*: 'Out of Control: Riots reach crisis point' (9 August 2011).

In the photograph, the young man in a grey tracksuit is masked and his hands are inside black gloves. He is wearing an Adidas tracksuit worth about £20 and his Adidas Superstars are valued at approximately £67. He looks sharp; he is pictured moving and represents an image of an everyday working-class style icon. In relation to the headings used in each paper, the key words applied in the accounts that surround him are as follows: *war, mindless, thugs, thieves, terrorise, yobs, rampage, masked, morons* and *sickened*. Unlike the other young people featured in the newspapers' coverage, who are dramatically involved in different forms of disturbances, the figure in the grey tracksuit is not engaged in looting, fighting or violence. He remains aloof. What makes this one picture different from all the other representations is that the camera looks directly into the eyes of the figure and he is looking back at us as much as we are looking at him. In film theory, this is known as the 'fourth look', defined as the returned gaze (Willemen, 1993). What we see is the speaking eye of the youth looking back. We see an expression of youthful power and resistance. It is seen as threatening, as it is clear from his posture that he is strong, determined and unhindered. The stylistic representation of the grey tracksuit makes him appear 'cool' as an ordinary teenager. Also, through the use of the mask he becomes identified as an iconic rebel or 'bandit' engaged in a struggle (Hobsbawm, 1969). For Kelsey (2015, p257), these representations of the youthful hooded figure set a context for suppression of certain explanations of young people's deprivation, but such representations later become repoliticised by both government and media as examples of the problems in society, which require punishment via benefit reduction.

Another issue concerns whether the young male is black, as the picture suggests he is not from a white ethnic group, but this remains unclear. The newspaper headlines seek to make the connection between the words used – destruction and violence – and the image, but language fails to do this, as the figure is alone and not part of any riot or disturbance. He is part of the spectacle; there is an attempt to make him into a monster through images of fire and smoke plus use of terms such as 'war zone' and 'guerrilla war'. Thus it is the violence of the headlines that surround the figure which seek to make him the object of fear and danger. But with the returned gaze, the viewer becomes subject to the figure's gaze. As deLong (2012, p104) suggests, the viewer has seen the *fourth look* – it is time for us 'to run in horror'.

Two zones of media representations: 'scroungers' and mockery

In our analysis of newspaper headlines and reality television programmes, we identified two interlocking zones of media representation where young adults feature as a social problem in society. The two zones are: young adults as scroungers; and young people addressed through mockery. The emphasis is on young adults as unproductive and irresponsible, setting the reader up to see young adults as a burden on society, while reinforcing their marginality.

Young adults as scroungers

'Poverty porn' has emerged as a term nationally and internationally used within both media and academic studies on chronic or absolute poverty, but it has a contradictory twist, as Collin (2009, p3) observes, in that it promotes popular stereotypes instrumentally breeding a culture of voyeurism and human destitution. The reality of living on a low wage was a key part of *The Scheme* about young adults in local authority housing in Kilmarnock, Scotland.

Graham (22 June 2011) in *The Guardian* argues that the people in this programme are 'reduced to comic figures of derision'. She asserts that: 'the show is exploitative poverty porn'. The idea of poverty porn is that it refers to the media's presentation of 'moral theatre' as entertainment, which causes both anger or outrage, rather than generating sympathy, where people's intimate lives are laid bare under incisive scrutiny opening up the personal for dissection and judgement.

The Sun newspaper pursues this style when reporting: 'Help us stop £1.5bn benefits scroungers'. Jenna Sloan (12 August 2010) examines a young Kent couple, Jamie and Chris, who are pictured smiling with their two young children, with phrases including 'feckless', 'slash', 'sick', 'wasted', 'shame', 'shambolic', 'handouts', 'cannot be bothered' and 'we live nicely on benefits'. The tone of aggressive blame and hatred towards this young couple intensifies when they are compared with Andy Rolf, a volunteer Territorial Army soldier fighting in Afghanistan 'with Our Boys', who works in construction to support his large family. Abigail Scott Paul (2013, p2), addressing poverty porn, suggests that: 'programmes only served to reinforce how people in poverty are objectified on TV for the gratification of others'. Thus within newspapers we identify extreme use of hostile language directed at claimants, but in TV reality programmes moral judgement is mediated by a controlling voiceover, which oozes an apparent superiority.

A recurring figure in the tabloid newspapers and on reality television between 2015 and 2016 has been 18-year-old Travis Simpkins from Sheffield. Travis first appeared in February 2015, when he was 18, on the reality television programme *Benefits Britain: Life on the Dole* (Season 2, episode 6). Just before Travis appeared on television, the *Daily Mail* promoted the television show with the headline: 'How to get famous in Britain: Scrounger, 18, stars in benefit documentary because he thinks it'll make him as big as White Dee – and get his teeth fixed into the bargain' (*Mail Online*, 16 February 2015). Travis is not only portrayed as a scrounger (similar to Stephanie, Dean, Josh, Titch and Danielle, to be discussed later), but he is represented in a mocking way, in that he is portrayed as a joke and an object to be laughed at. For example, his desire to get his teeth fixed and 'make it' as a reality TV star is effectively mocked (*Mail Online*, 16 February 2015), as is his claim that 'realistically, I think I will actually be a millionaire' (*Benefits Britain*, 2015).

The *Benefits Britain* episode featuring Travis begins with the voiceover stating: 'In *Benefits Britain*, some of the welfare cuts are beginning to bite. But some of the 18–30 brigade *aren't* that bothered' (emphasis in original). The show then cuts to Travis as he walks through a council estate: "I don't think a job would be a good idea for me yet, cos I've just turned 18. You don't want to grow up yet when you get to my age." Later, Travis explains how he does want a job, but for him "the sky's the limit" (the camera then cuts to Travis's feet to show him wearing odd socks). Later, Travis has a job interview as a charity fundraiser. However, he becomes nervous and leaves as soon as he realises how many people are on the interview panel. The story of Travis ends with him sitting on the sofa with two friends following his aborted interview drinking Red Bull and vodka: "I can assure you now, I will *not* be applying for another job, [laughs], because they might get fed up with me ADHD so, I can't put up with it. And it's as *simple as that* [laughs]".

On 28 June 2016, Travis reappeared in the media after the EU referendum and following the resignation of the British Prime Minister, David Cameron. It was reported in the *Plymouth Herald* with the headline: 'A self-confessed "benefits scrounger" has spoken of his dreams to become Prime Minister – with plans to legalise weed and unite the country'. *The Sun* (27 June 2016) ran the same story, with the headline: 'Move over, Boris! This 19-year-old benefits scrounger who made his own girlfriend homeless wants to be the next Prime Minister (and yes, his main policy is to increase benefits)'. The same day, the *Daily Star* also ran the headline: '"I'd smash it as PM" Benefits scrounger would hand out more dole money and free boob jobs' (*Daily Star*, 25 June 2016). These are all headlines that define Travis on the basis of mockery.

Another character appearing in the same episode of *Benefits Britain* was a 25-year-old single mum of two, Stephanie, also portrayed as a scrounger. The mocking voiceover introduces Stephanie with the comment: "At 2 and 4, the kids can be a bit of a handful. *Thankfully*, Stephanie gets £300 a week from taxpayers to help bring them up." She is pictured, with lots of tattoos, smoking a cigarette and wearing lots of jewellery. Stephanie says she will get a part-time job when her children go to school, with the voiceover stating: "Until then, Stephanie will *just* have to put up with being a benefits mum. On the equivalent of a £20 grand a year salary." The emphasis on tattoos and jewellery is meant to evoke anger in the viewer: that Stephanie should be buying the 'correct thing' not luxuries.

Further portrayals of so-called young benefit 'scroungers' include 19-year-old Dean from Essex. In the same episode of *Benefits Britain*, Dean is first pictured standing outside a cashpoint counting £20 notes from his benefit money. Dean states for the camera: "A Jobcentre's a Jobcentre at the end of the day. It's basically free money [laughs]." Dean is later quoted as saying: "Eventually I'd like to get a job, it's just … when I can find one". The mocking voiceover comments: "Dean left school 3 years ago and still hasn't found a job. But *he's* not bothered. He still lives at home with mum." Dean states: "I send most of my time in my bedroom, watch tv, listen to music, go on instagram, go on snapchat, bbm, twitter, take selfies". The mocking voiceover follows up with: "He also likes his bed, in fact he doesn't even leave it to speak to his mum. To get his £60 a week in benefits, Dean is forced to leave his bed."

The TV portrayal of Britain's unemployed as lazy, rude scroungers has also been seen in newspaper reports:

- *Daily Express* headlines include: 'War on scroungers' (28 August 2011) and 'Madness of Britain's handout culture: Scroungers rake in £85,000 a year from benefits' (14 May 2014).
- The *Sunday Times* reported on how: Young 'too unskilled to work' (13 June 2015).
- In a more critical stance on this portrayal, *The Guardian* ran an article on 'Lazy, drunken, promiscuous, rude ... why the UK loves to hate young white men' (19 December 2015).
- In 2013, in the *Daily Mirror*, David Cameron was criticised for the 'lazy stereotyping' of Britain's young people and blaming them for not having jobs (28 October 2013).

Young people addressed through mockery

Towards the end of the previous section, an emergent factor was the use of mockery against young adults within TV reality programmes through the use of voiceover commentary. Our argument is that a convergence can be identified between reality television programmes and newspaper representation, focused on young people not doing what is described as the 'correct thing'. For example, the *Daily Express* headline on 21 December 2012 reads: 'NO BENEFITS FOR BEER AND DRUGS', stating further: 'Benefits should not be spent on luxuries' or to 'buy alcohol and cigarettes'. This tabloid headline and narrative from the *Daily Express* is a template for subsequent newspaper headlines affirming the idea that people who claimed benefits: 'were scroungers, sponging off the state'.

Not doing the 'correct things' also applies to young mothers. For example, the *Daily Express* (2 February 2015) headline reads: 'Feckless mother left two young children home alone while she went drink-driving with baby'. The issue of not spending money on the 'correct things' is also reported by the *Mail Online* (7 March 2016) in *Benefits by the Sea: Jaywick*: 'Pregnant heroin addict and a woman who prefers to spend her cash on tattoos not food: new benefits documentary is set to shock Britain'.

Both newspapers and TV reality programmes identify young adults engaged in 'deviant leisure', that is forms of low-level criminality, which are not merely reckless but also demonstrate their irresponsibility.

In relation to drug use, Blackman (2011, p105) argues: 'One common feature of British media reporting is to present intoxication through the inverted use of the metaphor of youth "being the best" at getting "wrecked"'. For example:

- *Mail Online* (14 November 2008): 'Welcome to Britain, land of the rising scum. ... We've cornered the market on welfare layabouts. Drug addicts and feral gangs';
- *Mail Online* (7 May 2012): 'Booze Britain: Young women in North East fined for drunkenness more than anyone else in the country';
- *Daily Mirror* (29 November 2013): 'Britain's girls are the second worst teenage boozers in the WORLD';
- *The Telegraph* (13 May 2014): 'Britain's binge drinking levels are among the highest in the world';
- *Mail Online* (23 November 2015): 'Female of the species is becoming more like the male ... when it comes to booze: Alarming rise in women drinking alcohol say experts';
- *Daily Mirror* (28 July 2016): 'Brits killed by illegal drugs hits highest level since records began'.

Here we see that the personal tragedy of victims is displaced into inverted false praise through parody. Stating that British young adults are the 'highest' or 'second worst' casts young people as society's 'mock heroes' – that is, worthy of admiration, where the 'bad' is celebrated, which later becomes evidence of young adult irresponsibility.

In TV popular factual entertainment, mockery takes the form of an authoritative voice-over. For example, *Benefits Britain*, broadcast in 2015, set in Hastings, features a young 24-year-old man, nicknamed 'Manik'. The episode opens with Manik leaning against a wall on his mobile phone and the scene includes his conversation:

Manik: 'No, I didn't say that. She said to me that you said that I said to you that say, yeah bang, this is what's going on. And another thing, yeah right ...'

Voiceover: 'Manik's 24. He's been trying to get a job for 3 years, but ... He's got a bit of a dodgy past.'

Manik: 'I've been in care, I've been in gangs, and I used to drink, smoke drugs, love fighting.'

Voiceover: 'And he also loves tattoos. Manik lives in a flat with a mate, paid for by benefits. And he gets 56 quid a week in handouts ... With no job on the horizon, Manik's only hope now, is making it big as a rapper.'

The media narratives of Manik and other claimants for 'not doing the correct thing' become generalised to others by a focus on personal tragedy and regret, which are packaged under the issue of whether young adults can be trusted.

Another example can found in the BBC series *Saints and Scroungers*, with eight episodes from 2009 until 2012. Here the claimants' voices are projected as being central to the 'gritty' message of the programme. However, the false dichotomy in the *Saints* and the *Sinners* is that the *Saints* are confirmed as buying all the 'correct things' and the *Sinners* are shamed for false benefit claims and buying inappropriate items, such as too many televisions.

Also, we identify the easy narrative within the media representations, where a change of title to *Benefits and Proud* (Channel 5) seeks to predetermine the viewer to mock and have little sympathy for people who claim benefit. The project of a 'culture of worklessness' as casual evidence of crime and deviance (MacDonald et al, 2014) fuels a pervasive sense that everyone on benefits is lazy, deviant and playing the benefits system (Tyler, 2013).

Further, mockery is present in *Benefits Britain*, which explores the lives of three young friends: Josh, Danielle and Titch, who are in their early 20s and live together in a council-paid bedsit. Having just moved to Blackpool to: "start their new benefits life", Josh explains how difficult it is to survive on £57 a week: "You gotta do what you gotta to survive. Obviously I'd go out and shoplift if I had to." The scene then immediately cuts to a completely different character attempting to kick a door down, which draws an implicit association between Josh and violent vandalism. Titch then goes on to explain: "I can't get a job cos of my criminal record. At the end of the day, yeah, you gotta do what you gotta do to get through. The only way you're going to do that is by hustling, which is, 9 times out of 10 it's illegal." The voiceover cuts in with a similar mocking tone to that in the earlier portrayal of Travis: "And the 22-year-old would know. He's just come out of his seventh stretch inside. And when he hasn't got the cash, he's still pretty nimble with his fingers." The scene then cuts to him shoplifting a pair of gloves from *Poundland* for Danielle. The mocking voiceover explains: "The boys have criminal records as long as your arm".

We also identify a gender division in the representation of young adult women on low income and claiming benefit, mocked through their body shape and sexuality, for example:

- the young woman in *The Sun* (22 February 2014) headline 'BENEFITS MADE ME 23st';
- the *Daily Express* (27 April 2015) headline: 'EXPOSED: Meet the 32-stone woman who claims £18,000 in benefits as she's too fat to work', focusing on Rochelle, a young women of 21, who is unemployed and said she put on the weight due to "boredom".

The newspaper makes the connections between obesity and benefits, where the female body is seen with abhorrence and disgust, as expressed by journalist Katie Hopkins from the *Daily Mail* (Hopkins, 22 December 2015):

> But I've had enough of seeing your girlie bits clapping in the breeze as you lie on the pavement, Spanx rolled around your knees. Enough of playsuits, rammed up the dark crevasse of Summer, enough of the body con dress rolled up under the armpits of Nicole, who is semi-conscious eating a kebab.

This style of journalism positions young women as hypersexual. For example, the *Mail Online* (25 May 2016) reports on Channel 5 documentary *On Benefits*: 'Single mother on benefits uses her £20K-a-year handouts to fund her dreams of becoming a plus-size burlesque dancer called Chazabelle Royale'. We see visuals of Charlene Taylor, aged 20, mother of one, size 16, as she states "I can't help it if my stomach doesn't fit in my knickers right" and practises her burlesque act in her council house bedroom and garden. The newspaper mockingly reports that Charlene recently spent £500 on a professional photo-shoot to boost her Facebook page, 'which at the time of writing had 94 fans – with "nice, sexy shots"'.

On 21 April 2016, *The Sun* reports on Suzi, a young woman who features on Channel 5's *On Benefits: Life on the Dole*: '*On Benefits*: Sequel to Too Fat To Work features 22-stone woman who claims she can't work ... but still does unpaid extra jobs'. *The Sun* repeats the argument that young people on benefits are not supposed to buy luxuries; they are meant to buy the correct thing, stating: 'Suzi also spent over £100 getting a new wardrobe for her "showbiz" lifestyle'.

In these examples, both Charlene and Suzi are presented as a challenge to male sexual domination (Braziel and LeBesco, 2001). They confront the feminine ideal and are not only seen as violating socially prescribed sexual roles, but also the camera lingers voyeuristically on their (mockingly) large shape to suggest a lack of sexual inhibition.

Conclusion

In this chapter, we have sought to demonstrate that the serious social issue of youth marginality within contemporary TV reality programmes has been reduced to a form of entertainment. The tabloid newspaper coverage of austerity among young adults has been conducted as an intensive media campaign of 'hatred', where the goal is to 'shop benefit cheats' labelled as 'scroungers'.

There is some opposition to the authoritarian narrative of youth marginality projected by government and media shown through the notion of the 'fourth look'. However, this resistance becomes exploited as evidence for further punitive policies or promotion of respectable fears (Korte and Regard, 2014). The depoliticisation of youth marginality takes its most extreme form where the voices of young people are used against themselves as a form of self-stigmatisation, which are then used by government to increase sanctions on their benefits.

Through the use of media headlines and popular factual entertainment such as TV reality programmes, we have identified two strategies that promote the marginalisation of young people in society: first, through the mockery of young people; and second, they are judged as not doing the 'correct thing'. Here, viewers and readers do not have to empathise with young people who are struggling, and thus no guilt is experienced.

Both tabloid newspapers and TV reality programmes construct young adults who claim benefits as 'scum', a burden on society and totally untrustworthy (Nayak and Kehily, 2014). Thus, young people lose their agency, because both media and government have identified that society cannot trust them – and also assert that young people cannot even be trusted by themselves. This circular policy agenda means that young people are continually being defined as deficient.

References

Back, L. (2012) 'Live sociology: social research and its futures', in Back, L. and Puwar, N. (eds) Live Methods, *Sociological Review*, 60: 18–39.
BBC News (12.6.2011) 'Leicester family's 'overwhelming' response to Poor Kids'.www.bbc.co.uk/news/uk-england-leicestershire-13703928

BBC News (30. 6. 2011) 'MSPs brand BBC's The Scheme "tabloid TV"', http://www.bbc.co.uk/news/uk-scotland-13975325

BBC News (8.1.2014) 'Benefits Street series sparks hundreds of complaints'. http://www.bbc.co.uk/news/entertainment-arts-25653477

BBC *The One Show* (14.1.2014) Interview with Paul O'Grady.

Beattie, K. (2004) *Documentary Screens*. London. Palgrave.

Becker, H. S. (1963) *Outsiders*. New York: Free Press.

Blackman, S. (2011) 'Rituals of intoxication: young people, drugs, risk and leisure', in Bramham, P. and Wagg, S. (ed.) *The new politics of leisure and pleasure*, London: Palgrave. (97-118)

Cameron, D. (2011) PM's speech on the fightback after the riots, https://www.gov.uk/government/speeches/pms-speech-on-the-fightback-after-the-riots

Collin, M. (2009) 'What is poverty porn and why does it matter for development?', *Aid though*, 1 July. www.aidthough.org/?=69

Corner, J. (1995) *Television form and public address*. London. Edward Arnold.

Corner, J. (2000) 'What can we say about documentary?', *Media, Culture and Society*, 22.5: 681688.

Daily Express (9.8.2011) 'FLAMING MORONS: Thugs and thieves Terrorise Britain's Streets', www.express.co.uk/news/uk/263843/Flaming-morons-UK-riots-in-pictures

Daily Express (28.8.2011) 'War on scroungers', www.express.co.uk/news/uk/267673/War-on-scroungers

Daily Express (21.12.2012) 'NO BENEFITS FOR BEER AND DRUGS', www.express.co.uk/news/uk/366303/No-benefits-for-beer-and-drugs

Daily Express (14.5.2014) 'Madness of Britain's handout culture', www.express.co.uk/news/uk/475772/Madness-of-Britain-s-handout-culture-Scroungers-rake-in-85-000-a-year-from-benefits

Daily Express (2.2.2015) 'Feckless mother', www.express.co.uk/news/uk/555674/Lancashire-mother-went-drunk-driving-with-baby-and-left-two-children-home-alone-at-3am

Daily Express (27.4.2015) 'EXPOSED: Meet the 32-stone woman who claims £18,000 in benefits', http://www.express.co.uk/news/uk/568907/Benefits-and-Bypasses-Channel-Five-32-stone-woman

Daily Mail (9.8.2011) 'THE ANARCHY SPREADS', www.charlesapple.com/2011/08/the-london-riots-on-tuesdays-u-k-front-pages/

Daily Mirror (6.6.2011) 'Our children don't deserve a life of poverty', www.mirror.co.uk/news/uk-news/our-children-dont-deserve-a-life-of-poverty-133034

Daily Mirror (28.10.2013) 'Lazy stereotyping' of Britain's young people', www.mirror.co.uk/news/uk-news/david-cameron-blasted-lazy-stereotyping-2651345

Daily Mirror (29.11.2013) 'Britain's girls are the second worst teenage boozers in the WORLD', www.mirror.co.uk/news/uk-news/binge-drinking-british-girls-second-2866305

Daily Mirror (28.7.2016) 'Brits killed by illegal drugs hits highest level since records began', www.mirror.co.uk/news/uk-news/brits-killed-illegal-drugs-hits-8513803

Daily Star (11.11. 2010) 'Anarchy in the UK', www.dailystar.co.uk/news/latest-news/162433/Anarchy-in-the-UK

Daily Star (25.6.2016) '"I'd smash it as PM" Benefits scrounger would hand out more dole money and free boobjobs', www.dailystar.co.uk/news/latest-news/525516/Travis-Simpkins-benefits-scrounger-Prime-Minister-boob-jobs-benefits-money-UK

deLong, A. (2012) *Mesmerism, Medusa, and the muse.* Plymouth. Lexington Books.

Fergusson, R. (2016) *Young people, welfare and crime.* Bristol: Policy Press.

Graham, J. (22.6.2011)' Is The Scheme packed with shameless stereotypes?' www.theguardian.com/tv-and-radio/tvandradioblog/2011/jun/22/bbc-the-scheme-shameless-stereotypes

Harrison, P. (22,8.2016) 'Britain's Hardest Workers: the most gobsmacking reality TV show to date', The *Guardian* www.theguardian.com/tv-and-radio/2016/aug/22/britains-hardest-workers-the-most-gobsmacking-reality-tv-show-to-date

Hobsbawm, E. (1969) *Bandits.* London: Weidenfield and Nicolson.

Hopkins, K. (22.12.2015) 'I know it's warm out, girls, but this really isn't cool!', www.dailymail.co.uk/news/article-3370433/I-know-s-warm-girls-really-isn-t-cool-KATIE-HOPKINS-Britain-s-drunk-young-women-need-cover-calm-else.html

Hull Daily Mail (18.6.2014) 'Benefits Britain: Life On The Dole "is TV at its worst" – Hull City Council leader Steve Brady', www.hulldailymail.co.uk/benefits-britain-life-dole-tv-worst-8211-hull/story-21253594-detail/story.html

i *Independent (9.8.2011)* 'Out of Control: Riots reach crisis point', www.charlesapple.com/2011/08/the-london-riots-on-tuesdays-u-k-front-pages/

Independent (29. 5. 2015) '"Benefits Street" meets "The Hunger Games" is a new low for the BBC', http://www.independent.co.uk/voices/comment/10285586.html

Jenson, T. (2014) 'Welfare common-sense, poverty porn and doxosophy', *Sociological Research Online*, 19 (3): 3, www.socresonline.org.uk/19/3/3.html

Jones, O. (2011) *Chavs*, London. Verso.

Kamm, J. and Neumann, B (2016) (eds) *British TV comedies: Cultural concepts, contexts and cntroversies*. London.Macmillan.

Kelsey, D. (2015) 'Defining the 'sick society': Discourses of class and morality in British, right wing newspapers during the 2011 England riots',*Capital and Class*, 39(2), 243-264.

Korte, B. and Regard, F. (2014) (eds) *Narrating poverty and precarity in Britain*, Berlin.deGruyter.

Littlejohn, R. (2011) 'The politics of envy was bound to end up in flames', *Daily Mail,* 12 August, www.dailymail.co.uk/debate/article-2025021/UK-riots-2011-The-politics-envy-bound-end-flames.html

Loach, K. (1966) *Cathy Come Home*. BBC television.

Loach, K. (2016) *I, Daniel Blake*.Wild Bunch, Why Not Productions.

MacCoun, R. J. and Reuter, P. (2008) 'The implicit rules of evidence-based drug policy: a U.S. perspective'. *Journal of Drug Policy*, 19: 231-232.

MacDonald, R. (1997) (ed) *Youth, the 'underclass' and social exclusion*. London: Routledge.

MacDonald, R., Shildrick, T. and Furlong, A. (2014) "Benefit Street' and the myth of workless communities', *Sociological Research Online*, 19 (3): 1, www.socresonline.org.uk/19/3/1.html

Mail Online (14.11.2008) 'Welcome to Britain, land of the rising scum. ... We've cornered the market on welfare layabouts. Drug addicts and feral gangs', http://www.dailymail.co.uk/news/article-1085518/*RICHARD-LITTLEJOHN-Welcome-Britain-land-rising-scum-.html*

Mail Online (7.5.2012) 'Booze Britain: Young women in North East fined for drunkenness more than anyone else in the country. ,www.dailymail.co.uk/news/article-2140657/Booze-Britain-Young-women-North-East-fined-drunkenness-country.html

Mail Online (12.9.2012) 'I don't give a f★★★ what people think', www.dailymail.co.uk/news/article-2201847/Trouble-Estate-Residents-say-broadcaster-town-look-like-Shameless.html

Mail Online (7. 8. 2013) 'Serial thief dubbed the real-life Vicky Pollard is finally jailed for crime spree against shop staff', www.dailymail.co.uk/news/article-2385906/Real-life-Vicky-Pollard-Jade-Underwood-jailed-crime-spree.html

Mail Online (21.1.2014) '*Benefits Street's* parade of scroungers', www.dailymail.co.uk/news/article-2543261/Benefits-Streets-parade-scroungers-drug-addicts-Channel-4-highest-ratings-2012.html

Mail Online (16.2.2015) 'How to get famous in Britain', www.dailymail.co.uk/news/article-2955542/How-famous-Britain-Scrounger-18-stars-benefits-documentary-thinks-ll-make-big-White-Dee-teeth-fixed-bargain.html

Mail Online (23.11.2015) 'Female of the species is becoming more like the male.... when it comes to booze: Alarming rise in women drinking alcohol say experts', www.dailymail.co.uk/health/article-3330734/Female-species-like-male-comes-booze-Alarming-rise-women-drinking-alcohol-say-experts.html

Mail Online (7.3.2016) 'Pregnant heroin addict', www.dailymail.co.uk/news/article-3480234/Pregnant-heroin-addict-woman-prefers-spend-cash-tattoos-not-food-New-benefits-documentary-set-shock-Britain.html

Mail Online (25. 5.2016) 'Single mother on benefits uses her £20K-a-year handouts', www.dailymail.co.uk/femail/article-3608489/Single-mother-benefits-dreams-new-life-burlesque-dancer.html

Mangan, L. (29.11.2007) 'Evicted Update', *The Guardian*. www.theguardian.com/culture/tvandradioblog/2007/nov/29/lastnightstvevictedupdate

Monbiot, G. (2011) 'Think of a tank', *The Guardian*, 12 September, www.monbiot.com/2011/09/12/think-of-a-tank/

Nayak, A. and Kehily, M.J. (2008) *Gender, youth and culture*. London. Palgrave.

O'Sullivan, K. (18.1.2014) 'Benefits Street is a big fat shameless show', www.mirror.co.uk/tv/tv-previews/kevin-osullivan-benefits-street-big-3035752

Paterson, L. Coffey-Glover, L. and Peplow, D. (2015) 'Negotiating stance within discourses of class: Reactions to Benefits Street', *Discourse and Society*, 27, 2: 195-214.

Plymouth Herald (28.6.2016) 'Benefits Britain teen', www.plymouthherald.co.uk/benefits-britain-teen-i-ll-help-poor-in-plymouth-if-you-vote-me-for-prime-minister/story-29451675-detail/story.html

Sammons, A. (9.6.2011) 'Poor Kids', *Liverpool Confidential*. http://old. liverpoolconfidential.co.uk/Entertainment/TV-and-Film-Reviews/ TV-Review-Poor-Kids-BBC1

Scott Paul, A (2013) 'Poverty porn? Who benefits from documentaries on Recession Britain?' www.jrf.org.uk/blog/2013/08/poverty-porn-who-benefits-britain

Shildrick, T., MacDonald, R., Webster C. and Garthwaite, K. (2012) *Poverty and insecurity: Life in low-pay, No-pay Britain*. Bristol: Policy Press.

Slater, T. (2011) 'From 'criminality' to marginality: rioting against a broken states', *Human Geography*, 4,3: 106–115.

Sloan, J. (12.8.2010), 'Help us stop £1.5bn benefits scroungers', *The Sun*, www.thesun.co.uk/sol/homepage/feature/3091717/The -Sun-declares-war-on-Britains-benefit -culture.html

Stevens, A. and Measham, F. (2014) 'The 'drug policy ratchet': why do sanctions for new psychoactive drugs typically only go up?', *Addiction* 109(8):1226–32.

Sunday Times (13.6.2015) 'Young "too unskilled to work"', www. thesundaytimes.co.uk/sto/news/uk_news/article1568571.ece

The Guardian (9.8.2011) 'London riots escalate as police battle for control', www.theguardian.com/uk/2011/aug/08/london-riots-escalate-police-battle

The Guardian (19.12.2015) 'Lazy, drunken, promiscuous, rude ...', www.theguardian.com/uk-news/2015/dec/19/young-white-men-uk-most-hated-social-group-public-attitudes

The Sun (9.8.2011) 'Anarchy. Riots spread across London, Birmingham hit by looting, 215 arrests, PM jets back', www.charlesapple. com/2011/08/the-london-riots-on-tuesdays-u-k-front-pages/

The Sun (22.2.2014) 'BENEFITS MADE ME 23st', www.twitter. com/skynews/status/436987333938655233

The Sun (19.3.2016) 'Shameless benefits cheat invented THIRTEEN children to net £10k in handouts', www.thesun.co.uk/sol/ homepage/news/7012977/Shameless-benefits-cheat-invented-THIRTEEN-children-to-net-10k-in-handouts.html

The Sun (21.4.2016) 'On Benefits', www.thesun.co.uk/archives/ news/1139710/on-benefits-sequel-to-too-fat-to-work-features-22-stone-woman-who-claims-she-cant-work-but-still-does-unpaid-extra-jobs

The Sun (27.6.2016) 'Move Over Boris!', www.thesun.co.uk/ living/1348464/this-19-year-old-benefits-scrounger-who-made-his-own-girlfriend-homeless-wants-to-be-the-next-prime-minister-and-yes-his-main-policy-is-to-increase-benefits

Telegraph (9. 8.2011) 'Carry on Looting!', www.twitter.com/cliffordstott/status/762609957762134016

Telegraph (13.5.2014) 'Britain's binge drinking levels are among the highest in the world', www.telegraph.co.uk/news/health/news/10825449/Britains-binge-drinking-levels-are-among-the-highest-in-the-world.html

Tyler, I. (2013) *Revolting subjects: Social abjection and resistance in neoliberal Britain*. London. Zed Books.

Wacquant, L. (2008) *Urban outcasts*. Cambridge. Polity Press.

Watt, N. (9.8.2011) 'Was this Boris Johnson's Hurricane Katrina moment?', www.theguardian.com/politics/2011/aug/09/boris-johnson-katrina-moment-holiday

Willeman, P. (1986) 'Voyeurism, the look and Dwoskin', in Rosen, P. (ed) *Narrative, apparatus, ideology: A film theory reader*. New York. Columbia University Press: 210-18.

Willemen, P. (1993) *Looks and frictions: Essays in cultural studies and film theory*, London. British Film Institute.

Windle, J. (2010) '"Anyone can make it, but there can only be one winner": modelling neoliberal learning and work on reality television', *Critical Studies in Education*. 51(3): 251–63.

Part two:
Intersections of youth marginality: class, gender, ethnicity and education

SIX

Pramface girls? Early motherhood, marginalisation and the management of stigma

Mary Jane Kehily

Introduction

This chapter examines how marginalised working-class youth, in particular teenage mothers, come to be represented through such labels as 'chavette' and 'pramface' in a reconfiguration of class-based inequalities in the UK (Haywood and Yar, 2006; Jones, 2011; Adams and Raisborough, 2011; Skeggs and Loveday, 2012; Young, 2012). The chapter explores the deeply affective nature of these representations, how they leak out into everyday life and come to adhere to particular bodies and spaces (Goffman, 1963; Hall, 1980).

A contribution of the chapter is to move beyond the familiar terrain of textual deconstruction, to further consider how working-class young women manage social class stigma and might themselves speak back to these markers of abjection (Back, 2007). It is suggested that young motherhood needs to be understood within the context of what is happening to motherhood at a broader societal level. The chapter illustrates how, in the contemporary context, differences between women may be polarised and compounded by the experience of becoming a mother. Significantly, the chapter considers the ways in which social differences between women may be played out in the cultural sphere of representations and practices of consumption (Byrne, 2006). An overarching theme of the chapter discusses the ways in which motherhood has become a site of new social divisions between women, concluding that while the stubborn markers of class disparagement cannot easily be displaced, paying attention to how they might be understood and evaluated within local youth circuits offers nuanced readings that may resonate more closely with working-class experience.

The chapter is based on data derived from a five-year ESRC-funded project, beginning in 2005, exploring the transition to motherhood among a diverse sample of 62 first-time mothers in two contrasting locations (metropolitan and new town) in the South East of England documented in *Making modern mothers* (Thomson et al, 2011).[1] *Making modern mothers* explores what it means to become a mother in 'new times' and how this can be understood as a moment of identity change, characterised by age and socioeconomic status. Noting how the increasing participation of women in higher education and the labour force since 1945 has transformed the shape and meaning of women's biographies (Lewis, 1992; Crompton, 2006), the study examines the uneven nature of change as reduced social mobility and widening inequalities between women are reflected in a movement towards later motherhood for the majority and early motherhood for a minority. Lewis comments on the widening gap between the 'teenage unmarried mother, unable to escape from dependence on state benefit and the professional woman in her thirties, married to another professional, having her first child and able to pay for a nanny' (Lewis, 1992: 10) as a distinctive feature of women's lives in late modernity. This phenomenon appears to run against the grain of second-wave feminist ideas of the 1970s, which promoted motherhood as a potential site of solidarity between women, requiring social recognition from the state and the active support of men in the home, workplace and locality.

Historically, in the post-war period, the UK has had the highest rates of teenage pregnancy in Europe, leading to policy and public health concerns with age replacing earlier concerns around illegitimacy and marriage as markers of autonomy and respectability (Arai, 2009). The most obvious manifestation of motherhood as a site of new social divisions between women has been the intensive public focus on teenage pregnancy as a *social problem* (Social Exclusion Unit, 1999; McDermott and Graham, 2005; Macvarish, 2010; Department for Education, 2012). While there is some evidence that pregnancy rates are falling in England and Wales (Office for National Statistics, 2015), in the field of popular representation, early motherhood retains its associations with disaffection from education, lack of opportunity, poor socioeconomic circumstances and excessive sexuality, compressed colloquially in the term 'pramface'.

The study drew upon longitudinal qualitative methods and cultural analysis to generate intergenerational case studies that focused on the changing identities of women as they become mothers for the first time. The study sought to address the following research questions:

- What does motherhood mean to first-time mothers?
- What are the intergenerational narratives concerning motherhood?
- How does becoming a mother change women's identities?
- How have women of different generations imaged and practised motherhood?
- What part do men play in influencing women's expectations and experiences of motherhood?

This chapter focuses on a particular subset of 10 teenage mothers, aged 15-19 years, accessed through a charity funded by the local council to provide parenting classes and support groups for pregnant teenagers and young mothers. Individual interviews aimed to understand young motherhood from the perspective of young women themselves, in order to explore their relationship to contemporary representations of motherhood in a changing maternal landscape. A photo–elicitation exercise, used as part of the interview schedule, invited women to comment on representations of pregnancy in popular culture. This method offered valuable insights into how the project of pregnancy and early motherhood can incite particular emotions that young women speak back to, as they narrate personal accounts of conception and impending motherhood in the context of a social climate in which their fertility is cast as a problem.

Embodying motherhood

This section focuses on the ways in which first-time pregnancy is embodied and lived by women themselves. Consideration is given to the resources women may draw upon to think about and imagine themselves as new mother, such as representations of pregnancy and motherhood to be found in women's magazines, advertisements and popular culture more generally. Our findings suggest that *all* women were invested in motherhood as a moment of profound identity change. In broad terms, birth can be seen as an intergenerational act, reconfiguring relationships within the family.

Age emerged as the 'master category' through which normative notions of mothering can be constituted. In the representational sphere of pregnancy magazines and women's magazines more generally, pregnancy is promoted as a beautiful big adventure. In popular culture, the maternal subject is encoded as a woman with choice in her life: aged between 25 and 35, heterosexual, in employment and in a relationship. By contrast, representations of young mothers draw upon popular pathologies of teenage pregnancy within a societal context in which youthful citizenship is premised upon economic productivity and embodied forms of social capital.

The 'pramface' girl can be seen as a recent and distinctive class-cultural formation that exists as both a media construct and a reconfiguration of enduring class-based social divisions, fuelled by historical conceptualisations of an undeserving poor and an underclass (Pearson, 1983). Pramface girls assume an embodied style of feminine excess, denoting an overly abundant and unruly sexuality (Skeggs, 1997, 2004). Comedic characterisations such as Vicky Pollard in the TV show *Little Britain* embody an aggressive caricature of working-class femininity as a drinking, shoplifting and fighting young mother in the maelstrom of a laughably troubled life. Pramface girls emerge as figures of parody and moral rebuke, contemporary folk devils (Cohen, 1972; Tyler and Bennett, 2010), who invoke an affective register associated with feelings of shame and stigma.

Young motherhood can be seen as a particularly feminised route to poverty, marked by the determining prospect of an early exit from full-time education and limited employment opportunities. While early motherhood remains a largely 'working class affair' (Walkerdine et al, 2001), in the contemporary era it is an arena in which socioeconomic differences between women are defined and compounded by distinct practices of childrearing (Clarke, 2004; Byrne, 2006; Tyler, 2008). Thomson et al (2011) found age to be the 'master category' in shaping the maternal experience. For women in their late 20s to mid-30s, new motherhood is discursively constructed as the apex of feminine achievement and a celebration of romantic coupledom for women who have put education and career first. Pregnancy magazines, for example, celebrate the increased visibility of pregnancy and the confidence of mature motherhood, colloquially termed 'yummy mummy'. While older mothers are depicted as hosting pink champagne baby showers, spilling over with designer accessories, a recurrent theme in young women's accounts is a shift in consumer identity from 'teen' to 'new-mother-with-responsibilities'. For teenage mothers, pregnancy signalled the end of childhood and childish selfishness. As Zoe (aged 17) articulates:

> Zoe: 'I should be going out clubbing and enjoying myself and working and spending all my money on myself and on clothes, and obviously you can't 'cos you've got someone else to think about ...'

Young mothers responded to their change in status with new consumer practices: cutting back on 'going out' and fashion wear, to focus on the baby rather than themselves (Ponsford, 2011). As a bourgeois feminine ideal, the 'yummy mummy' sticks together the cumulative affects of class, whiteness and heterosexuality and translates this into an object of desire and aspiration, visibly displayed in the sphere of consumption. In contrast, the experiences of young working-class mothers involved managing and consuming with limited resources, preparing for motherhood on a small budget, while continuing to live with parents and to seek state benefit.

Managing the bump, managing stigma

Young mothers, having their first child between 15 and 20 years, demonstrated an acute awareness of how their pregnancy was viewed by others. In the wider context, where normatively appropriate behaviour resides in expectations of delayed pregnancy, teenage mothers-to-be can be made to look and feel aberrant. For them, the bump was not associated with the embodied display and celebrity status promoted by pregnancy magazines. Rather, the pregnant tummy was a potential source of *shame*, the locus of attention and judgement (Yardley, 2008). Here Zoe (aged 17) recites the 'funny' looks and comments that follow her around:

> Zoe: 'Some people look at you funny because you're young and you've got a bump … two ladies were sitting on the bus the other day talking about how young people were getting pregnant and how it was a disgrace and all this lot! And I wanted to say something, but I couldn't because I didn't want to be rude … [At the parenting class] some girls cover their bump and some girls don't. I usually do but sometimes my tops do rise and I think that's what they were shocked about 'cos some of my tummy was hanging out.'

Aware of the 'shock value' generated by being young and pregnant, and without saying anything herself, Zoe's protruding tummy prompts comment from others. Young mothers remarked on feeling 'self conscious' and out of place in public settings, aware that their tummy invited negative appraisal. There were times in the parenting class when this 'shock value' could be capitalised upon. The 'tummy flash' was most in evidence in moments of conflict with staff at the parenting classes, where it acted as a gesture of defiance, a 'what-you-gonna-do-about-it' flash of resistance designed to unsettle adults around them. Exposing the pregnant tummy in this context was a non-verbal, affective response that challenged adult authority and simultaneously acted as an embodied statement that they are visibly pregnant and should not be subjected to stress. The bump as marker of shame could then be inverted in moments of protest, in which teenage girls assert themselves as young mothers-to-be on a transition to adulthood.

For older women in the sample, the health risks related to a delayed pregnancy meant that some aspects of early motherhood could secretly be desired. Young mothers had an abundance of embodied resources associated with youthfulness – enhanced health, energy, elasticity and renewal – that gave them a certain physical capital. These embodied resources, it could be argued, enable young mothers to cope with the demands of motherhood and assert their 'natural' right to be pregnant. Zoe is attuned to these differences and offers a counterpoint to contemporary 'age-appropriate' discourses of first-time motherhood:

> Zoe: 'What's the difference between having a baby now and having a baby when you're older? There's still the [absence of] knowledge, you can't change the fact that you're gonna have a baby for the first time. No matter how old you are it's the same set of issues, you know, sleepless nights, breastfeeding, changing the baby and you're not gonna know any different because you're 17 or you're 30. Older people don't think like that. They judge you because you're young and having a baby ... I love being pregnant. I absolutely love it. I'd go through it again and again.'

In claiming new motherhood as a near *universal* experience, Zoe demonstrates her command of the knowledge necessary for her new role. Keen to assert that youth should not be a barrier to motherhood, she has enjoyed the embodied experience of pregnancy and is prepared for the transition to parenthood. In a study undertaken in Australia of young mothers from refugee backgrounds, McMichael (2013) has shown how early pregnancy may be unplanned but it is not unwanted. For those with few material resources this is not necessarily unusual. Since becoming pregnant, Zoe's parents had thrown her out of the family home, and her boyfriend had split up with her. Despite these hardships, Zoe's love of pregnancy and desire to repeat it ('again and again') shone through, intimating that she, at least, has managed some forms of stigma.

Other young women in the study found ways of managing stigma and performing respectability through practices of consumption. In an effort to make limited resources go a long way, many young women developed a finely tuned pecuniary knowledge, investing in a stylisation of themselves as well-informed and experienced shoppers. By making particular consumer choices, young mothers-to-be demonstrated their capacity to care and their readiness to mother. While chav culture is associated with the 'bling' of excessive and conspicuous consumption (Tyler, 2008, 2010), early motherhood signalled the end of selfish and self-centred spending and the beginning of responsible adulthood, where baby comes first. This was expressed in terms of the small but significant changes in consumer practices that marked a shift in personal priorities:

> Cody: 'I feel like I've changed already, I've sort of become more responsible and just little things like not spending so much money in a day and putting off getting a manicure and stuff like that. I know it sounds silly but little things just make you think, you're not going to be able to do that when the baby comes.'

> Zoe: 'I feel like I've got my thinking cap on where it's made me grow up all of a sudden. Before I was rubbish with money and now I have to budget ... It [pregnancy] does make you rethink everything 'cos you can't be selfish knowing you've got a little baby and its needs are more important than your needs are.'

A haunting feature of young women's accounts is the need to claim their status as good mothers through consumption. There is an insistence on buying everything new to showcase a fitness for motherhood. Often accompanied by a disdain for second-hand or hand-me-down baby things that, for them, would be tainted by prior use and may risk an association with poverty, the danger of looking poor and, by inference, a lack of care for your child:

> Farah: 'Mum said we can get second hand but I said to her and I'm saying to everyone, this is my first [laughs] baby, I'm not having second hand or car boot things. Second hand is like using someone else's things. I don't like it ... I want my OWN baby stuff.'

Particular efforts were made to save for more expensive items, such as buggies, prams and cots:

> Mumtaz: 'I'm gonna buy the nicest pram, my pram has to be wicked. I don't wanna be walking down the street with a bad pram. Don't want people to think, you know, I can't provide for my baby. Oh my God, of course I can provide for my baby.'

When purchasing prams and buggies, young mothers were drawn to the more expensive, top-of-the-range products, such as the Bugaboo range. A popular and fashionable manufacturer with endorsements from celebrity mothers and 'yummy mummies', the up-market status of the brand was sealed by an appearance on the television series *Footballer's Wives*. Bugaboo advertises its products as, 'multi-terrain' and flexible pushchairs that glide over all surfaces with frog-like suspension and consummate ease. Appealing to parents who 'live life on the fly', Bugaboo claims, 'It's not about where you are but where you are going' (www.bugaboo.com). In the use of promotional material, in which products take on the properties of a car rather than a baby carriage, Bugaboo may strike a chord with young mothers who do not own cars and have no other means of transport.

Young women's consumer preference may indicate a knowingness in relation to the stigma of early motherhood as well as offering a strategy for managing the stigma through the visibility of consumer goods bought to demonstrate their ability to mother and to provide for their child. In choosing expensive buggies, young women demonstrate an awareness of their locality and, consequently, their place within it. Investing in a high-end buggy can be seen as a confident act, facilitating a way of being in the world in which young mothers feel equipped to traverse the environment around and beyond their neighbourhood. Mother, baby and buggy can become intrepid adventurers, able to navigate the all-weather conditions they encounter.

Cleansing spoilt identities

The proliferation of representations of working-class youth as chavs and pramface girls can be seen as a ubiquitous and seemingly enduring feature of class cultural formations in the UK (Lawler, 2005). Further it appears that certain (non-)working-class bodies – notably those of unemployed teenage mothers – have become primary sites for the projection of disgust. This disfigurement speaks to wider concerns about social divisions in late modernity that has seen an increased polarisation between rich and poor, and thickening demarcations between the 'rough' and the 'respectable'. Moreover, these relations intersect with contemporary ideals of gender, ethnicity and sexuality that serve to further displace working-class youth as peripheral, while simultaneously bringing middle-class norms and values centre-stage.

While the pramface girl widely recognised figures of defilement, the concern of the chapter is to consider whether young women themselves recognise these representations or come to identify or resist them in any way. The interest was with how young women might manage the negative accumulation of affects that surround and come to interpolate them and how, if at all, they might speak back to these mediated hailing devices and amplified representations. In short, how are these projections assimilated, rejected and negotiated by young women themselves?

Notably, the young women in this study show agency and affiliation, appearing as articulate and knowing subjects of how they and others are represented. This suggests that future studies could do much more to engage with working-class people themselves, rather than relying on the hyper-real mediated depictions which abound, and in turn serve to construct them as 'other'. Connecting media representations with their 'objects' of hate (or humour) not only invokes more compelling forms of deconstruction, but also elicits the potential to return the gaze back upon these technologies of judgement. By looking beyond these ubiquitous mediations and exploring the life-worlds of young people, a more complex, subterranean social class dialogue can be seen taking place.

To this effect, the 'spoiled identities' (Goffman, 1963) of pramface can be differently figured, when composed alongside the counter-articulations and affective understandings derived from marginalised working-class communities. This is seen in the recasting of motherhood as a quasi-universal experience for women that seeks to render age irrelevant and the negative affect attributed to the 'teenage mum' redundant. These responses provide sharper insight into the struggle for representation as an activity that is open to contestation and always in process. In doing so, we can trace the intensities of feeling that bring into being these subjectivities as societal figures of abjection and abhorrence. It is also possible to glimpse the emotional disconnect that young people may feel in relation to the production of monstrous others (seen, for example, when Katie Price's books regularly top bestseller lists and working-class figures on reality game shows are championed by a youthful audience).

The discursive cleansing of spoiled identities is an attempt to make hygienic what is publicly regarded as toxic. Here, the seemingly fixed taxonomies of class disparagement that settle on the marked bodies of lower working-class youth can momentarily be rendered into sliding signifiers. By making slippery the 'lumpen' categories of class, young people can be seen as active subjects who contest, resist and struggle to overturn widely held representations that cast them as stigmatised others. Inevitably, such readings may displace, though not entirely remove, the feelings of stigma and abjection from a broader signifying chain of meaning that renders lower working-class youth unequivocally monolithic, impassive and sub-human (Campbell, 1993). While this slippage is partial, incomplete and forever subject to the power of dominant media representations, it reveals the value of eliciting the perspectives of marginalised youth to reconfigure social norms and hollow out at least some of the markings of stigma.

Note

[1] The project team: Rachel Thomson, Mary Jane Kehily, Lucy Hadfield, Sue Sharpe. We are grateful for the support of the Economic and Social Research Council, grant RES-148-25-0057.

References

Adams, M. and Raisborough, J. (2011) 'The self-control ethos and the "chav": Unpacking cultural representations for the white working class', *Culture & Psychology*, 17, 1: 81-97.

Arai, L. (2009) *Teenage pregnancy: The making and unmaking of a problem*. Bristol: Policy Press.

Back, L. (2007) *The art of listening*. London: Routledge.

Byrne, B. (2006) *White lives*. London: Routledge.

Campbell, B. (1993) *Goliath: Britain's dangerous places*. London: Methuen.

Clarke. A. (2004) 'Maternity and materiality: Becoming a mother in consumer culture', in J. Taylor, L. Laynes and D. Wozniak (eds) *Consuming motherhood*. New Brunswick, NJ: Rutgers University Press.

Cohen, S. (1972) *Folk devils and moral panics*. London: Paladin.

Crompton, R. (2006) *Employment and the family: The reconfiguration of work and family life in contemporary societies*. Oxford: Oxford University Press.

Department for Education (2012) *Teenage pregnancy: Past successes – future challenges*, independent report. London: Teenage Pregnancy Independent Advisory Group.

Goffman, E. (1963) *Spoiled identities: Notes on the management of stigma.* Simon and Schuster.

Hall, S. (1980) 'Encoding/decoding', in S. Hall, A. Lowe and P. Willis (eds) *Culture, media, language.* London: Hutchinson.

Haywood, K. and Yar, M. (2006) 'The "chav" phenomenon: Consumption, media and the construction of a new underclass', *Crime, Media, Culture,* 2, 1: 9-28.

Jones, O. (2011) *Chav: The demonization of the working-class.* London: Verso.

Lawler, S. (2005) 'Disgusted subjects: The making of middle-class identities', *The Sociological Review,* 53, 3, 429-46.

Lewis, J. (1992) *Women in Britain since 1945.* Oxford: Blackwell.

Macvarish, J. (2010) 'The effect of "risk-thinking" on the contemporary construction of teenage motherhood', *Health, Risk and Society,* 12, 4, 313-22.

McDermott, E. and Graham, H. (2005) 'Resilient young mothering: Social inequalities, late modernity and the "problem" of "teenage" motherhood', *Journal of Youth Studies,* 8, 1, 59-79.

McMichael, C. (2013) 'Unplanned but not unwanted? Teen pregnancy and parenthood among young people with refugee backgrounds', *Journal of Youth Studies,* 16, 5: 663-78.

Pearson, G. (1983) *Hooligan: A history of respectable fears.* Basingstoke: Macmillan.

Ponsford, R. (2011) 'Consumption, resilience and respectability amongst young mothers in Bristol', *Journal of Youth Studies,* 14, 5, 541-60.

Reay, D. (2004) 'Mostly roughs and toughs': Social class, race and representation in inner-city schooling', *Sociology,* 35, 8: 1005-23.

Skeggs, B. (1997) *Formations of class and gender: Becoming respectable.* London: Sage.

Skeggs, B. (2004) *Class, self, culture.* London: Routledge.

Skeggs, B. and Loveday, V. (2012) 'Struggles for value: Value practices, injustices, judgment, affect and the idea of class', *The British Journal of Sociology,* 63, 3: 472-90.

Social Exclusion Unit (1999) *Teenage pregnancy,* Cm 4342 (http://dera. ioe.ac.uk/15086/1/teenage-pregnancy.pdf).

Thomson, R., Kehily, M. J., Hadfield, L. and Sharpe, S. (2011) *Making modern mothers.* Bristol: Policy Press.

Tyler, I. (2008) 'Chav mum, chav scum: Class disgust in contemporary Britain', *Feminist Media Studies,* 8, 4, 17-34.

Tyler, I. and Bennett, B. (2010) 'Celebrity chav: fame, femininity and social class', *European Journal of Cultural Studies,* 13, 3, 375-93.

Walkerdine V., Lucey, H. and Melody, J. (2001) *Growing up girl*. Basingstoke: Palgrave.

Yardley, E. (2008) 'Teenage mothers experience of stigma', *Journal of Youth Studies*, 11, 6, 671–84.

Young, R. (2012) 'Can neds (or chavs) be non-delinquent, educated or even middle-class? Contrasting empirical findings and cultural stereotypes', *Sociology*, 41, 6: 1114–60.

SEVEN

Leisure lives on the margins: (re)imagining youth in Glasgow's East End

Susan Batchelor, Lisa Whittaker, Alistair Fraser and Leona Li Ngai Ling

Introduction

Compared to previous generations, young people today have increased resources to engage in leisure, as well as a greater range of activities from which to choose. Changing patterns of education and employment may have extended the period during which young people are dependent on their family and the state, but they have also increased the period in which young people are able to prioritise their social interests and have comparatively high levels of discretionary spending (Roberts, 2014). As a result, some sociologists have argued that the relationship between youth leisure and 'old' social divisions, such as class and place, have weakened (for example, Bennett, 2000; Miles, 2000; Muggleton, 2000) and that the leisure interests and activities of young people across the world have converged (Best and Kellner, 2003) as a result of the growth of globalised consumer industries and digital media.

There is also, however, a growing body of research which suggests that young people's leisure experiences continue to be shaped by local, place-based opportunity structures (Nayak, 2003; Pilkington and Johnson, 2003; O'Connor, 2005; Nilan and Feixa, 2006). In other words, while there is some evidence of convergence in young people's leisure interests, actual engagement in so-called 'global youth culture' remains stratified by structural factors (Ball et al, 2000), including neighbourhood of residence (Shildrick, 2006). Young people from marginalised communities, for example, are often 'leisure poor' due to a combination of financial constraints and lack of local provision (MacDonald and Marsh, 2005; Byrne et al, 2006).

The following chapter explores experiences of leisure among marginalised youth in the East End of Glasgow. The data presented, drawn from qualitative interviews and focus groups with young people aged 15 to 25 years, highlight the relative immobility of young people's leisure lives, which are primarily located in and around the family home. Declining participation in street-based leisure is attributed to increasing surveillance and social control, by parents and police, but also to wider processes of market-led regeneration and the commercialisation of urban amenities. Against a backdrop of labour market restructuring and state funding cuts, young people in the East End lack the financial means necessary to participate fully in commercialised leisure lifestyles. Some cope with this by retreating into the private sphere, hanging out with friends at home and online; others, however, adopt creative strategies to enable them to engage in commercialised leisure, albeit in marginal ways.

Youth leisure, class and place

Youth leisure has long been a source of public and political concern, in the UK and elsewhere. Traditionally this concern has focused on young people's presence in public space, and their potential for engaging in delinquent and disorderly activities. As Shildrick and MacDonald (2006) acknowledge, 'street-corner socializing' is a longstanding and enduring feature of working-class culture, dating as far back as the 1800s (Davies, 1992). Middle-class communities, by contrast, have tended to favour more structured leisure activities (Hendry et al, 1993). As a result, anxieties about street-based youth are not about youth in general, but about working-class youth, who are represented as more of a threat to social order and therefore as more in need of surveillance and social control (Muncie, 2014). Indeed, much of the academic research on how working-class young people spend their spare time tends to focus on 'risky' behaviour and criminality, rather than 'ordinary' experiences of leisure (MacDonald, 2011). This then serves to legitimate various forms of state intervention. As a range of both historical and contemporary scholarship has shown, working-class young people are more rigorously policed than their middle-class counterparts (Goldson, 2013; Jackson and Bartie, 2014), and those living in marginalised communities are disproportionately subject to place-based enforcement strategies such as child curfews (Waiton, 2001) and dispersal orders (Crawford and Lister, 2007).

In the late 1950s and the 1960s, anxieties about youth centred on the affluent teenager and the threat posed by new commercial forms of leisure provision, such as coffee bars and dance halls (Abrams, 1961; Jephcott, 1967; Jackson, 2008). The commercialisation of leisure remains a central theme within contemporary debates, with academic attention focusing particularly on the contribution of the growing consumer industry to processes of individualisation (Furlong and Cartmel, 2007). It has been suggested that, whereas in previous generations identity was primarily shaped in occupational settings, in the contemporary period 'identity revolves around leisure' (Kellner, 1992, p153), especially the consumption of symbolic goods and lifestyles. Much of this consumption takes place within city centre spaces, which have been transformed into cosmopolitan destinations for shopping and leisure. In particular, in the postindustrial period, the UK has witnessed the growth of a booming night-time economy, a development driven largely by the commercial interests of the alcohol industry and targeted predominantly at a 'young adult' market (Chatterton and Hollands, 2003; Winlow and Hall, 2006). This means that young people are able to participate in a 'supermarket' of 'scenes', 'neotribes' and 'lifestyles', providing they have the necessary material and cultural resources (MacDonald and Shildrick, 2007). Young unemployed people, or those who on account of their 'flawed' consumption choices do not display the 'correct' signifiers of style, are often excluded from commercial leisure spaces – just as they are moved on or 'dispersed' in public space.

A much more contemporary concern relating to youth leisure, space and place relates to the advance of information and communications technology (ICT) and its impact on young people's social participation and wellbeing. Research has pointed to a growth in the numbers of young people accessing the internet to play games and watch television, and the rise of new forms of sociability as young people retreat to their bedrooms to communicate with peers via social media (Lincoln, 2012; Livingstone, 2007). This shift towards home-based leisure has implications for young people's health, with concerns being raised about the link between screen-based, sedentary pursuits and obesity, but also cyber-bullying, poor self-image, self-harm and social withdrawal (Livingstone et al, 2012). While access to the internet was once the preserve of the well-off, recent research indicates that the vast majority of young people in the UK now have access to a smart phone or a home computer (Office for National Statistics, 2015) and that marginalised youth are media- and technologically savvy. Research with young homeless people, for example, suggests that ICT has the potential to make marginalised youth feel more connected and included, and can improve engagement, as well as helping them to move away from street-based identities (Karabanow and Naylor, 2010; Rice and Barman-Adhikarin, 2014).

(Re)imagining youth in Glasgow's East End

The research reported here was undertaken as part of a wider comparative study of youth leisure in Glasgow and Hong Kong. Adopting a qualitative case study approach, the *(Re)Imagining Youth* project sought to explore the leisure values, attitudes and habits of young people in these two geographically disparate cities in order to interrogate contemporary debates relating to youth, globalisation and social change (Bachelor et al, forthcoming; Fraser et al, forthcoming).[1] The data presented here is drawn from the Glasgow fieldsite, Dennistoun, a residential neighbourhood located in the East End of the city.

In many ways, Glasgow's East End epitomises the kind of structural marginality depicted by Loic Wacquant in his study of *Urban outcasts* (2008). Typical of many post-industrial areas in the UK, the area is known largely for its high rates of poverty and unemployment, poor health and low mortality, and is often stigmatised as a breeding ground for welfare dependency and violent gang culture (Gray and Mooney, 2011; Fraser, 2015; Mooney et al, 2015b). Much of the district falls within the 15% 'most deprived' data zones in Scotland (Scottish Government, 2012), containing high levels of vacant or derelict land and deteriorating social housing (Clark and Kearns, 2013).[2] Dennistoun itself, however, is more socioeconomically mixed, incorporating pockets of severe deprivation (Scottish Government, 2012), high levels of child poverty (HMRC, 2016) and young people not in education, employment or training (Scottish Government, 2012), alongside a growing population of middle-class students and artists, attracted to the relatively affordable housing market and the proximity to Glasgow city centre.

Data collection in Dennistoun included: eight focus groups with 42 young people; and 22 interviews with 23 young people; alongside a number of targeted ethnographic observations. Young people were accessed via local youth organisations, schools and colleges, as well as via employers and employment agencies, criminal justice agencies and social work. These access points were chosen to try to ensure coverage and diversity across key variables, including age, gender and work/study status. The resultant sample (focus groups and interviews combined) contained broadly comparable numbers of school pupils, college students, university students, employed and unemployed young people. All of the university students combined full-time education with part-time employment, usually in the service sector, as did two thirds of the college students. All of the employed young people worked in entry-level, low-paid, insecure jobs, despite having completed college diplomas or university degrees. Two thirds of the young people currently looking for work were college or university graduates. The majority could broadly be described as 'working class'.

While, as a group, our sample do not represent the most socially deprived or excluded young people, insofar as a majority were engaged in some form of education or employment, their lives were constrained in various ways by their precarious labour market position. Glasgow currently has the highest rate of youth unemployment in Scotland, and one of the highest figures in the UK for young people 'not in employment, education or training' in the UK (Hudson et al, 2012). Yet unemployment is not the only – or indeed the main – problem that young people in Glasgow face. The shift to a service-based economy has been accompanied by a decline in full-time work (Cumbers et al, 2009), and indeed many of our participants were working on part-time and/or zero-hours contracts. Difficulties brought on by unemployment and underemployment were a prominent theme in our discussions, as were difficulties of combining full-time study with part-time work. These patterns had clear consequences for young people's leisure, not only in terms of financial constraints, but also in terms of spatial and temporal constraints. For some participants, 'free time' was viewed as something of a curse – spent in a constant round of jobcentre appointments and searches for work. For others, the difficulty was lack of 'free' time, due to combination of coursework commitments, antisocial hours, long commutes to work or university, and the blurring boundaries between work and leisure.

Reputation, risk and retreat

Spatial immobility was a key theme in the Glasgow data, linked in part to young people's place attachment and attendant anxieties about territorialism and violence, but also – importantly – their marginal status in relation to commercialised leisure. As stated earlier, much of the literature on young people and leisure highlights the significance of the street as a site for leisure, particularly for working-class youth who often lack access to space for sociality at home and do not have the financial resources required to access commercial venues. While very few of the *(Re)Imagining Youth* participants said that they currently spent time 'hanging about' in their neighbourhood, many had done so previously, during their early to mid-teens:

'When you're a kid you don't have a lot of money and you cannae dae the things you want to do, so you just need to find anything to amuse yourself […] like, just out on the street. Me and ma pals, we would just think of somewhere we could go and just walk there. Like the skate park, we used to just go there and spend all day there.'

Unsurprisingly, these formerly street-orientated young people tended to report high levels of neighbourhood affinity and identity, and often said that the best thing about their local area was the people who lived there. Most had extensive family and peer networks living close by, often within the surrounding streets. The following comments were fairly typical in this regard:

'I like staying here and I wouldnae move. It would feel weird going somewhere else. This is just what I know. […] All my family are quite close, when we were growing up all my cousins were there and that was all my pals. I didn't need any pals because I had my cousins. […] Everyone knows everyone, especially when you're in the pubs now you're older, that's how you get to know people as well, so you get used to the faces and you feel safer. Like, if something were to happen someone would know who you are.'

This preference for familiar faces and places played an important role in shaping young people's opportunities for leisure, insofar as it meant that participants tended to limit themselves to the opportunities that were available (hyper-)locally. While most of the young people said that they were happy to go into the city centre to access leisure opportunities, they were often reluctant to consider other opportunities within the East End that were outwith their immediate locale, unless they had existing contacts there. This reluctance to venture into neighbouring areas of the East End was often attributed to territorialism and the perceived threat of violence.

Participants tended to have a very finely grained knowledge of their own particular neighbourhood, which they sometimes constructed as comprising just a few streets, marked out by boundaries that were usually invisible to a researcher's eye (see also Fraser, 2015). They were also often careful to distinguish their own area from other so-called 'bad' areas, for example disputing whether particular districts were part of the 'real' Dennistoun and recounting stories about 'other' areas with a reputation for gang violence or sectarianism, as in the following example:

> '[Area B], it's quite — It's a really heavily segregated area. Like the biggest kind of thing in Glasgow is the whole Celtic, Rangers sectarian thing, and in [Area B] it's like a really, really, really, really, really heavily Rangers stronghold base. [...] If you aren't that kind of person in that place, then you are by definition different, and that can be really difficult, and it is really difficult growing up, because everybody there, that's just kind of what their life is.'

Again, when referring to their younger years, participants told us about activities or facilities that they couldn't access in neighbouring areas due to the threat of violence, and reflected on the impact that territorial and sectarian issues had on parental surveillance and control. For example, one young person explained how, as a child, he was unable to attend birthday parties in Area B because they were held in the Grand Orange Lodge and his Roman Catholic parents refused to take him. Another young person related a story about her younger brother being 'jumped' on a bridge by a group of young men from a neighbouring area, 'just because they recognised him as somebody from Duke Street'. Subsequent to this she and her siblings were told to take the long route home: 'even though it was quicker and quieter to go round that way they would always say "Go up to Duke Street, because there is people there and it's a bit safer"'.

Despite such stories, there was a sense that divisions were declining in the East End and that gang fighting was rapidly becoming 'a thing of the past'. Indeed, there appeared to be a decline in young people congregating on the street in general, according to both our interview-based and observational data. As stated earlier, none of the young people we spoke to said that they currently spent time socialising outdoors in the neighbourhood, which despite their age surprised us.

Studies of youth leisure commonly identify an age-related transition from 'casual' to 'commercial' leisure during mid- to late adolescence (Hendry et al, 1993; Chatterton and Hollands, 2003), while research with 'socially excluded' or marginalised youth has shown how some young people persist in street-based socialising into their early 20s (MacDonald and Marsh, 2005; Shildrick, 2006; MacDonald and Shildrick, 2007). Our participants were able to offer examples of other young people who: 'at 21/22 still go up a side street, up a lane, stand there and drink and a' that'. In the main, however, they said that such groups were in the minority, and that both they and their younger relations were much more likely to be found indoors, usually online:

> Tony: I normally just sit playing the computer, go round and see one of my mates. That's basically all I dae.

> Dylan: Just lounging about the house playing the computer all day [...]

> Rylan: Nowadays kids don't really go out, kids that are younger. Like I've got two wee cousins and they stay in and play their PlayStation and play their iPad rather than play football or meet their mates.

> Tony: See when you're walking through the streets, when do you ever see boys out playing football on the street? Or lassies oot like playing skipping ropes or runnin' aboot with prams and stuff or balls?

> Rylan: See at the summer now, you'd be lucky if you seen two people oot. They're all in the hoose.

> Tony: It's just deid.

Private spaces, including participants' own homes and the homes of friends and family members, featured prominently in discussions across the sample. Most free time at home was spent 'just chilling', watching YouTube or Netflix, playing computer games, or just hanging out. Hanging out sometimes involved 'being alone together', with different family members all on their respective devices, or 'sharing online', usually (but not exclusively) with locally based peers. Indeed, the primary function of ICT for young people in our study was building and maintaining local friendships through the creation of shared spaces and shared time. However, ICT also facilitated engagement with wider youth and consumer culture, as well as allowing young people to develop their professional profiles and portfolios.

Regeneration, commercialisation and exclusion

While young people were generally positive about living in Dennistoun and its environs, they highlighted a lack of accessible leisure spaces in the neighbourhood, including informal public spaces and low-cost commercialised venues. Local parks, for example, were considered run-down and unsafe, with little provision for older teenagers. Signs prohibiting ball games and bike riding were prominently displayed throughout the fieldsite, and young people were regularly 'moved on' if they tried to congregate in the park or the street. As one participant recounted, referring to his teenage years:

> 'There was never anything to do. You always wanted to go out and play fitba or stuff like that, but there was nothing there. And when you tried to go and play fitba, maybe out on the street, the polis would come and stop you and say, "Look, you've got to move, there's nae ball games allowed here". Then you'd go and sit at the end of the street, the way we're sitting the noo, talking to your mates and they'd still say, "Look, you have to move". But it doesn't matter where you went, you were getting harassed all the time. They would just say, 'Move on, just move'. But where are you gonnae go?'

During our observations in the East End, we were struck by the number of play parks and sports facilities, including 5-a-side pitches and basketball courts, that were fenced off from young people, either because they had been abandoned or because entry required a fee. Following austerity measures, many local authority and third sector facilities were operating on reduced hours, with restricted populations (younger children as opposed to teenagers, for example).

Local commercial provision was also deemed to be unsuitable and unsatisfactory by participants, as indicated in the following excerpt:

> 'There should be better stuff tae dae but there's nothing. There's only a bookies, a hairdressers and a shop. I cannae believe the amount of bookies they open up, pawn shops. There's a football pitch but they try and charge you to go and play on it. It's no even the fact that they charge you, it's the fact they charge you about seven quid per person for an hour! I mean, whit?! Seven quid an hour to play a game of fitba?!'

There were signs that the landscape of leisure was changing in the East End, however, due in large part to repeated regeneration efforts, most recently those associated with the Glasgow 2014 Commonwealth Games (Paton et al, 2012). While several participants were positive about the impact of the Games on their everyday lives – some had gained part-time work or volunteering experience, for example, while others enjoyed free tickets or improved transport links – others were more critical of the Games' 'legacy':

> 'Noo its left and it's not affordable for people to access some of the buildings and venues. They're good to look at, but they don't get used. They said they're leaving a legacy, but what kind of a legacy is left behind for people? Some of the young people I work with were very involved in it, part of the opening and closing ceremony, they got to meet the athletes and they had a great experience, which was good. But some other young people that I work with were getting searched in their own streets.'

This mixed picture is in line with the findings from other Games-related research, which has highlighted community concerns about urban governance practices and the limitations of a market-led approach to regeneration (Mooney et al, 2015a; Clark et al, 2016). As intimated earlier, the new leisure facilities, particularly the Sir Chris Hoy Velodrome, were regarded as too expensive for young people to access and therefore as of no material benefit to the local community: 'They're brilliant if you're an athlete [...] if you've got the right bike. But who needs it? Who's going to pay 55 pound to join?'

Lack of money was a key barrier to participation in commercial leisure for many of our participants, the majority of whom were employed part-time, if employed at all. As one young man explained: 'Everything is money nowadays, so if you think about going oot on a night, if you are thinking about just hanging out, you need money'. The high costs associated with new 'craft' breweries and 'hipster' barbecue joints appearing in gentrified areas of Dennistoun made some participants feel excluded, creating divisions between 'local' young people and newly resident (predominantly middle-class) students and artists:

> 'There's a lot of regeneration, that's kind of been the buzzword of the last couple of years in Glasgow, and there are so many like — It's just a really trendy place. Like Duke

Street, Dennistoun, all this kind of modernisation, I think it's cool and such, but I don't really — It's nothing that I really take part in, just because it costs a lot of money and I don't have a lot of money, so I can't really engage in it, but it's just — [...] I don't know, it's kind of like that whole exclusion thing. I mean, it's like seven quid for a burger or something. Like I know people have got to set their prices and that, but it still feels like a form of exclusion.'

That is not to say that young people did not participate in commercial leisure, but rather that they tended to treat it as a 'luxury', 'saving it for special occasions'. Or they employed creative strategies to 'do it on the cheap', for example planning their drinks out to make them last a whole evening. Going 'up the town, window shopping' was a popular activity among young people, both young men and young women, largely because it allowed them to participate in predominant patterns of youth leisure without having to spend any money. This 'flawed consumerism' (Bauman, 1998) did not go unchallenged, however. Young people who did not exhibit 'appropriate' cultural identities through their choice of clothing or footwear, for example, were often denied access to pubs and clubs, and sometimes shops. They were also 'moved on' by staff in cafes and bars for lingering too long over a drink, which may have been shared between two or three young people.

Conclusion

While leisure is often associated with freedom and choice, our data demonstrate some of the ways in which young people's leisure continues to be regulated by social, spatial and cultural factors. In line with previous research, it shows that the local neighbourhood in which young people reside structures their access to material resources, including leisure space. Unlike previous studies, however, we found limited evidence of young people simply hanging about the streets where they live. Rather, a central finding of the study was the significance of home-based leisure and the centrality of ICT to youth leisure lives. ICT enables marginalised young people to feel more connected, both to their neighbourhood peers and to wider commercial youth culture, yet it can also reinforce leisure time immobility and isolation.

While place-based attachments remain central to sense of self, and preferred leisure activities still involve collective sociality, our evidence suggests a growth in individualised forms of leisure among marginalised youth. Processes of urban regulation and regeneration have effectively excluded young people from public space, restricting traditional patterns of teenage leisure participation. State funding cuts and the commercialisation of urban amenities have also narrowed the opportunities available for older young people, who are located on the fringes of the labour market. Against this backdrop, participants' retreat to the private sphere is interpreted less as an active engagement in global youth culture and more as a response to material inequalities. Though recent social transformations have provided new opportunities for youth leisure, the leisure lives of young people on the margins remain restricted.

Notes

[1] ESRC Project Code: ES/K010409/1. A detailed description of the research is available on the *(Re)Imagining Youth* website: www.reimaginingyouth. wordpress.com

[2] The proportion of people in income deprivation is 25% (n=43,595), 86% higher than the Scottish average, and the proportion of working-age people who are employment deprived is 22% (n=26,625), 77% higher than average (Scottish Government, 2012).

References

Abrams (1961) *Teenage consumer spending in 1959*. London: Institute of Practitioners in Advertising.

Ball, S J., Maguire, M. and Macrae, S. (2000) *Choice, pathways and transitions Post-16*. London: Routledge.

Batchelor, S., Fraser, A., Ling, L. and Whittaker, L. (forthcoming) '(Re)Politicising youth: from Scotland's Indyref to Hong Kong's Umbrella Movement' in S. Pickard and J. Bessant (eds) *Youth politics in crisis: New forms of political participation in the austerity era*. London: Palgrave.

Bauman, Z. (1998) *Work, consumerism and the new poor*. Buckingham: Open University Press.

Bennett, A. (2000) *Popular music and youth culture: Music, identity and place*. Basingstoke: Macmillan .

Best, A. and Kellner, D. (2003) 'Contemporary youth and the postmodern adventure', *Review of Education, Pedagogy, and Cultural Studies*, 25: 75-93.

Byrne, T., Nixon, E., Mayock, P. and Whyte, J. (2006) *Free time and leisure needs of young people living in marginalised communities*. Dublin: Combat Poverty.

Chatterton, P. and Hollands, R. (2003) *Urban nightscapes. Youth cultures, pleasure spaces and corporate power*. London: Routledge.

Clark, J. and Kearns, A. (2013) *Go Well in Glasgow's East End: Baseline Community Survey*. Glasgow: Glasgow Centre for Population Health.

Clark, J., Kearns, A. and Cleland, C. (2016) 'Spatial scale, time and process in mega-events: The complexity of host community perspectives on neighbourhood change', *Cities*. 53: 87-97.

Crawford, A. and Lister, S. (2007) *The use and impact of dispersal orders: Sticking plasters and wake-up calls*. Bristol: Policy Press.

Cumbers, A., Helms, G. and Keenan, M. (2009) *Beyond aspiration: Young people and decent work in the de-industrialised city*. Glasgow: University of Glasgow.

Davies, A. (1992) *Leisure, gender and poverty*. Buckingham: Open University Press.

Fraser, A. (2015) *Urban legends: Gang identity in the post-industrial city*. Oxford: Oxford University Press.

Fraser, A., Batchelor, S., Ling, L. and Whittaker, L. (forthcoming) 'City as lens: (Re)imagining youth in Glasgow and Hong Kong', *Young: The Nordic Journal of Youth Research*.

Furlong, A. and Cartmel, F. (2007) *Young people and social change: New perspectives* (2nd edn). Buckingham: Open University Press.

Goldson (2013) 'Youth and policing', in B. Goldson (ed) *Dictionary of youth justice*. London: Routledge.

Gray, N. and Mooney, G. (2011) 'Glasgow's new urban frontier: 'Civilizing' the population of "Glasgow East"', *City*, 15, 1: 4-24.

Hendry, L. B., Schucksmith, J., Love, J. and Glendinning, A. (1993) *Young people's leisure and lifestyles*. London: Routledge.

HMRC (2016) *Personal Tax Credits Statistics: Children in low income families local measure (Scotland)*. London: HMRC.

Hudson, N., Liddell, G. and Nicol, S. (2012) *Youth unemployment: Key facts*. Edinburgh: Scottish Parliament.

Jackson, L. (2008) 'The "coffee club menace": policing youth, leisure and sexuality in post-war Manchester', *Cultural and Social History*, 5, 3: 289-308.

Jackson, L.A. and Bartie, A. (2014) *Policing youth: Britain 1945–70*. Oxford: Oxford University Press.

Jephcott, P. (1967) *Time of one's own*. Edinburgh and London: Oliver and Boyd.

Karabanow, J. and Naylor, T. (2010) 'Being hooked-up: exploring the experiences of street youth with ICT', in E. Looker (ed.) *Digital diversity: Youth, equity, and information technology*. Waterloo: Wilfred Laurier.

Kellner, D. (1992) 'Popular culture and the construction of postmodern identities' in L. Scott and J. Friedman (eds) *Modernity and identity*. Oxford: Blackwell.

Lincoln, S. (2012) *Youth culture and private space*. Basingstoke: Palgrave.

Livingstone, S. (2007) 'From family television to bedroom culture: Young people's media at home' in E. Devereux (ed.) *Media Studies*. London: Sage.

Livingstone, S., Haddon, L. and Görzig, A. (eds) (2012) *Children, risk and safety on the internet*. Bristol: Policy Press.

MacDonald, R. (2011) 'Youth transitions, unemployment and underemployment: Plus ça change, plus c'est la même chose?', *Journal of Sociology*, 47, 4: 427–44.

MacDonald, R. and Marsh, J. (2005) *Disconnected youth? Growing up in Britain's poor neighbourhoods*. London: Palgrave.

MacDonald, R. and Shildrick, T. (2007) 'Street corner society: Leisure careers, youth (sub)culture and social exclusion', *Leisure Studies*, 26, 3: 339–55.

Miles, S. (2000) *Youth lifestyles in a changing world*. Buckingham: Open University Press.

Mooney, G., McCall, V. and Paton, K. (2015a) 'Exploring the use of large sporting events in the post-crash, post-welfare city', *Local Economy*, 30, 8: 910–24.

Mooney, G., McCall, V. and Paton, K. (2015b) 'Poverty, territorial stigmatisation and social insecurities as social harms', *Scottish Justice Matters*, 3, 3: 27–8.

Muggleton, D. (2000) *Inside subculture: The postmodern meaning of style*. Oxford: Berg.

Muncie, J. (2014) *Youth and crime* (4th edn). London: Sage.

Nayak, A. (2003) *Race, Place and globalization: Youth cultures in a changing world*. Oxford: Berg.

Nilan, P. and Feixa, C. (eds) (2006) *Global youth? Hybrid identities, plural worlds*. London: Routledge.

O'Connor, P. (2005) 'Local embeddedness in a global world: Young people's accounts', *Young* 13: 9–26.

Office for National Statistics (2015) *Internet access: Households and individuals 2015*. London: HMSO.

Paton, K., Mooney, G. and McKee, K. (2012) 'Class, citizenship and regeneration: Glasgow and the Commonwealth Games 2014', *Antipode*, 44, 4: 1470–89.

Pilkington, H. and Johnson, R. (2003) 'Peripheral youth: Relations of identity and power in global/local context', *European Journal of Cultural Studies*, 6, 3: 259–85.

Rice, E. and Barman-Adhikarin, A. (2014) 'Internet and social media use as a resource among homeless youth', *Journal of Computer-Mediated Communication*, 19, 2: 232–47.

Roberts, K. (2014) 'Youth and leisure experiences: youth cultures and social change in Britain since the early twentieth century', in S. Elkington and S.J. Gammon (eds) *Contemporary Perspectives in Leisure*. London: Routledge.

Scottish Government (2012) *Scottish Index of Multiple Deprivation 2012*. Edinburgh: Scottish Government.

Shildrick, T. (2006) 'Youth culture, subculture and the importance of neighbourhood', *Young: The Nordic Journal of Youth Research*, 14, 1: 61–74.

Shildrick, T. and MacDonald, R. (2006) 'In defence of subculture: Young people, leisure and social divisions', *Journal of Youth Studies*, 9, 2: 125–40.

Wacquant, L.J.D. (2008) *Urban outcasts: A comparative sociology of advanced marginality*. London: Polity Press.

Waiton, S. (2001) *Scared of the kids? Curfews, crime and the regulation of young people*. Sheffield: Sheffield Hallam University.

Winlow, S. and Hall, S. (2006) *Violent night: Urban leisure and contemporary culture*. Oxford: Berg.

EIGHT

Asylum rejected: 'appeal rights exhausted' Afghan care leavers facing return

Kim Robinson and Lucy Williams

Introduction and context

This chapter starts from the core assumption that social workers and support staff have a duty of care to work with *all* marginalised young people, regardless of their family background, citizenship or immigration status. However, our experience of the care system for unaccompanied asylum-seeking children (UASC) indicates that various systemic failures have created challenges for these young people over and above those of other young people in care. For example, unaccompanied asylum-seeking children receive only temporary protection (until they are 18), varying degrees of support (as evidenced by the use of foster care versus independent housing) and limited access to mainstream education. Unaccompanied asylum-seeking children in the UK are supported within children's services rather than within the asylum support service. As such, they become the responsibility of the local authority for their port of entry and, in contrast to adults, they have not been dispersed around the UK. There are plans in place to transfer cases from the 'entry' local authorities supporting large numbers of young asylum seekers, but at the time of writing (May 2016) this had not yet begun.

This chapter reports on research conducted in Kent, with young men from Afghanistan. These young people make up the second largest nationality of unaccompanied asylum-seeking children in the county and are commonly targeted for removal post-18. Kent local authority has responsibility for a large number of unaccompanied asylum-seeking children, as it includes the Port of Dover, a main crossing route from France.

Local authorities are unsurprisingly reluctant to publicise up-to-date figures for the young asylum seekers they support. However, in April

2016, Kent announced that it was supporting 'about 830' and that 'the continuing duty of care to support those who had reached their 18th birthday brought the number nearer to 1,400' (BBC News, April 2016). In terms of more exact numbers, data do show that across the UK, 3,043 unaccompanied asylum-seeking children entered the care system in 2015, 656 of whom were from Afghanistan (Home Office, 2016).

Our data are drawn from our evaluation of a return initiative, the 'Positive Futures' Project, which proposed a return package enhanced with extra training and skills to encourage young 'appeal rights exhausted'[1] Afghan care leavers to return to Afghanistan (Robinson and Williams, 2014). During the course of the evaluation, we spoke to 12 individual 'appeal rights exhausted' care leavers, eight caseworkers working directly with 'appeal rights exhausted' care leavers, 12 members of the steering group, including representatives of the Home Office, Immigration Enforcement, project staff and four experts with experience working with 'appeal rights exhausted' Afghan care leavers. In addition, we have drawn on the findings from interviews with a further six young people who took part in a study carried out for Mind in Bexley (Williams, 2016). Both research projects were approved by the School of Social Policy and Social Research's Ethics Committee at the University of Kent.

Data from the research suggest that the immigration status of these vulnerable young people undermines the support provided by social workers and increases their marginalisation and inequality of opportunity. All 18 of the young people in our study had their asylum claims considered 'unfounded', were classified as 'appeal rights exhausted' and faced return to Afghanistan.

This chapter explores three areas of concern that, we argue, have had a negative impact on the care that young people receive from social workers:

• The first relates to legal processes and the lack of legal representation.
• The second relates to age assessment, which fixes bureaucratic processes to a date of birth that has, arguably, been determined arbitrarily.
• The third area is uncertainty of future and the threat of a forced return to countries of origin.

While these concerns affect all young asylum seekers, they are particularly pertinent in the case of Afghan youth. This chapter explores these issues in turn, as well as providing a discussion of the young people's strengths and high levels of resilience and determination to succeed (Bogen and Marlowe, 2015). Before discussing these areas, however, we briefly outline the literature on social work best practice with unaccompanied asylum-seeking children.

Social work practice with unaccompanied asylum-seeking children

Social work has been actively engaged with the concerns facing unaccompanied asylum-seeking children from an early date (Cemlyn and Briskman, 2003; Bhabha, 2004; Hayes and Humphries, 2004; Kohli and Mitchell, 2007). There is now a substantial international literature on analysing the issues and challenges of providing care and building trust with this vulnerable group. Indeed, the literature has focused on the experiences of children arriving in Kent specifically (Matthews, 2011, 2012) and the UK more generally. It highlights what has been termed as the bewildering system they face (Crawley, 2010; Sigona and Hughes, 2012; Chase and Allsopp, 2013; Bloch et al, 2014). Social work has engaged with topics including:

- the practice of listening to and engaging with young people (Crawley, 2011; Kohli, 2006);
- the organisational challenges of practice in local authority settings (Crawley, 2010; Wade, 2011);
- the conduct and ethics of age assessments (Cemlyn and Nye, 2012);
- dominant discourses of racism (Masocha and Simpson, 2011, 2012);
- key social work practice concerns relating to pathway planning and assessment (Wade, 2011; Kohli, 2011).

There is also a body of literature focusing on best social work practice (Kelly and Bokhari, 2012; Robinson, 2013), which argues for more robust and humane methods of working with children. We argue that these approaches are critical in order to safeguard the rights, mental health and wellbeing of children (Akister et al, 2010; McFarlane et al, 2011; Fazel et al, 2012).

The detention of children continues to be a key issue internationally, with ongoing campaigns to release them and their families (Dennis, 2012; Australian Human Rights Commission, 2014). In addition, specific campaigns and advocacy reports raise awareness of unaccompanied asylum-seeking children issues challenging local authority care provision and Home Office practices (Crawley, 2010; Pinter, 2012a, 2012b; Brighter Futures, 2013).

In the UK, much of this literature has been developed in the context of increasingly punitive migration controls and with reference to the inherent tension between the Children Act 1989 and the various immigration legislation and instruments that undermine legal protection for children (Bhabha and Crock, 2007; Bianchini, 2011; Finch, 2012; Human Rights Watch, 2012; UNHCR, 2014). Agencies promoting the rights of young people have highlighted concerns regarding what they see as the abuse of human rights and high levels of destitution facing unaccompanied asylum-seeking children (Pinter, 2012a, 2012b; Joint Committee on Human Rights, 2013; Vine, 2013). These abuses of rights are exacerbated for 'appeal rights exhausted' care leavers, as they face losing all support, including access to housing, income and social workers once they turn 18.

While the Children (Leaving Care) Act 2000 extended the responsibilities of local authorities as corporate parents to indigenous care leavers beyond the age of 18 (Grimshaw et al, 2014), this level of support has not been extended to asylum-seeking young people who have also been in the care system. The Children (Leaving Care) Act 2000 and the Children and Families Act 2014 were enacted to protect care leavers, but in the case of refugees, and indeed other migrant care leavers, rights and entitlements are withdrawn when temporary leave ends.

Drawing from our interviews with young people, this chapter now discusses in greater detail the systemic problems contributing to the marginalisation of unaccompanied asylum-seeking children in the care system. To conclude, we consider options for how social workers and social care providers could further support young people facing these challenges.

The creation of marginalisation: systemic challenges

As noted earlier, researchers have identified a wide range of issues facing unaccompanied asylum-seeking children in the UK. These issues include the fact that support is often determined by the ages of unaccompanied asylum-seeking children, many of whom do not know their date of birth. An additional issue is the withdrawal of support to care leavers post-18. Unaccompanied asylum-seeking children are granted discretionary leave to remain in the UK on arrival, which entitles them to support and to employment, but only until they reach 18 or are granted Refugee status or Leave to Remain on some other grounds.

The processes by which young people are refused asylum and made ineligible for leaving care provisions have been well documented (Wade, 2011; Wright, 2012). A report by the Office of the Children's Commissioner explicitly examines two areas of policy: the representation of unaccompanied asylum-seeking children cases and their transition into adulthood (Matthews, 2014). It finds both areas poorly conducted and managed. Warren and York (2014) highlighted the lack of effective legal representation, after reviewing the cases of 20 young people refused asylum.

We argue that the UK care system is unable to protect young people from destitution, detention and deportation post-18. Systemic problems compound the disruption, bereavement, loss and potentially trauma-inducing events that unaccompanied asylum-seeking children have suffered during their journey or in their countries of origin. As a consequence, young people turning 18 are often unprepared for futures in either the UK or in their countries of origin.

Age assessment

The political context that surrounds the care of unaccompanied asylum-seeking children enmeshes immigration control in care decisions. One clear example of this is the emphasis placed on age assessments, by which social workers or other experts assign an age and a date of birth to young people lacking verifiable identity documents. Many young people arrive not knowing their date of birth according to Western traditions, and even when they do carry papers from their countries of origin, these may not be accepted. Age assessment determines the services that young people are entitled to and, ultimately, the date when they will become subject to removal (Bianchini, 2011). Post-18, and if they are deemed to be 'appeal rights exhausted', the local authority in which they are resident may carry out a formal Human Rights assessment. However, if they are found to be ineligible for further support, they will become destitute and subject to adult immigration controls. As adults, they may be eligible for accommodation outside the areas they have grown up in,[2] but may also have to report regularly to immigration authorities, and may be subject to electronic tagging, or face detention and potentially forced removal.

Age assessment processes inscribe the young person into care and immigration systems, but allow them little opportunity to challenge their assessed age. Young people describe the process of age assessment as confusing, confrontational and demonstrating that they are not trusted. Our interviews with young people describe the process as upsetting and potentially traumatising in its own right:

> P7: 'I was 15 when I came but Social Services, they didn't believe most of the guys – they told them about their age they wouldn't believe – they had their own way of assessing our age. Each person had their own Social Worker and they would asses my age based on the times I had travelled and had been living – I didn't remember the exact times or years so it wasn't accurate and he just assessed my age as 17. That was a big mistake from him which cost me, you know, cost me dearly to be honest, cost me a lot – imagine if you are assessed 2 years older and you don't not have the experience of a 17 year-old you are only 15 – in life you struggle with things.'

In Kent, age assessments are carried out on approximately 50% of unaccompanied asylum-seeking children (personal communication) and, as the process takes between three and six months, it delays the young people's entry into normal life in the UK. Before the age assessment is completed, young people stay in residential care, and from there they move on to foster families (if they are under 16) or into supported independent housing. Age assessments place young people into asylum and immigration categories, which create significant and enduring inequalities within the unaccompanied asylum-seeking children population and between unaccompanied asylum-seeking children young people and others in care.

Legal processes and the lack of legal representation

Our interviews with young people also described both the lack of sufficient *and* effective legal aid. Young people were being refused legal aid and representation, because their cases were considered to have failed the 'merits test' needed to obtain Legal Aid Agency funding. Reduced access to legal aid since the Legal Aid, Sentencing and Punishment of Offenders Act 2012 has also meant that there are fewer solicitors offering services. For example, from our research with various voluntary sector groups within Kent, it was estimated that there were over 100 young refugees without any legal representation. They have to rely on their solicitors, but may be anxious that they are not committed to working on their behalf. The opacity of a complex system leaves them expecting to be let down:

P7: 'I had all my hope on him as he was fighting for me with the system to have my asylum granted and obviously he wasn't working – I can say this now but back then I didn't know – he wasn't working as much [as] he should have been, he just brushed me off as I think he does for most cases.'

The lack of legal representation means that young people may have to represent themselves in courts alone, however vulnerable they may feel. Appearing in court is frightening for anyone, and both P4 and P6 describe feeling that the odds were stacked against them:

P4: 'We don't know about these things official things we don't know – how can you expect a person to respond ... for me it was doubly difficult – even though I knew the language it was a new thing and normally new things are scary especially when your life is hanging ... if you are not ready you are going to make a mess and its going to go against you – if you are ready everything will be sorted – if I went to Court now the same Court – it would be total different situation. But when I went at that time, I was ill I was mentally messed up basically.'

P6: 'Going to Court is so difficult – they ask questions, questions, question for decision, decision – decision is coming ... refused. I have been six or seven times I think so or more than that ...'

Uncertain futures and the threat of a forced return

The young people we interviewed, all denied international protection as refugees, highlighted their limited options: to accept 'voluntary' return to countries that they fled from as children or to continue challenging refusal and to try to establish a right to remain in the UK. We know from our work with young Afghans (Robinson and Williams, 2014, 2015a, 2015b) and from other reports (Gladwell and Elwyn, 2012) that young Afghan care leavers are extremely reluctant to return, so the second option is most likely.

Refusing to return means living under the threat of destitution, detention and deportation, and is a kind of war of attrition with the Home Office. Two young people in this situation told us:

'I know that, I've been in detention, I know that every single day about this thing [voluntary return], they can give some money and you can go back to Afghanistan to live there – what am I going to do with that money if I haven't got family? If I go somewhere and they see me they might kill me as well. I've got problem with that people as well – if they find me out they are not give me a chance. Its not right!'

'Those people they are not going to listen to you, they are going to shoot you. Its not like England talking easy you know!'

The individual struggles of young people are part of an increasingly punitive welfare environment, which limits support workers' resources to help as well as young people's agency and capacity to help themselves. Living in destitution while trying to establish a case to remain wears young people down, but they are clear that remaining in the UK, even without support, is better than returning:

P7: 'Nobody would want to have this life on a daily basis … for a year or two years its alright you can live with that but in the meantime things were getting tougher on asylum seekers and when David Cameron he restricted from every angle and its not easy to live … you see other people doing what they want and having what they wish – its makes you feel like you have been separated from a group of people who are doing good and you are not allowed to do what the rest are doing.'

Across the EU, governments are emphasising voluntary return as a solution for asylum seekers whose claims have been rejected. Some of these schemes provide some material support for reintegration and are intended to allow migrants to return with dignity and with small funds to assist their reintegration. The voluntary nature of 'voluntary' return is often disputed in cases when migrants would prefer to stay but are obliged to return, and it is telling that very few young Afghans have taken up the offer of the programmes (Robinson and Williams, 2014). Young people fear returning to a dangerous and unfamiliar environment, where they have little chance of a future. They are not interested in money or reintegration support packages. Absconding and living below the state's radar seems to be a viable option for some young people.

Discussion: options for young people post-18

The trajectory of young refugees is described by Ravi Kohli (2011) as a journey towards safety, belonging and success all the while under the shadow of temporary admission and enforced return to country of origin. Young people seeking asylum alone are clearly a vulnerable group for many reasons. They have lost their families and their communities and lack strong social support networks. In addition, many lack caring relationships with adults, have limited access to services and may live in poverty (Smyth et al, 2015).

Existing evidence from this research and other studies of young Afghans presents a clear picture that young care leavers do not want to return and will continue to fight to stay in the UK. Many cannot imagine a future in Afghanistan, and the continuing state of unrest evidenced from multiple sources, including Facebook and social media, makes return unpalatable if not a frightening prospect. The recent report by Gladwell et al (2016) describes the often harrowing experiences of young people forcibly returned to Afghanistan.

Karen Wells (2011) has shown that many young people do have loose social networks that connect them back to countries of origin and to migrant communities, but they are still likely to be considered as outsiders in Afghanistan. Being seen to return empty-handed is a particular problem, as there are cultural expectations that sons will provide for their families, especially if the family invested in getting them out of the country in the first place. Generalised insecurity and poverty in Afghanistan are also reported as problems for young people who have grown up in safety and relative affluence, and the perceived westernisation of returnees may also cause them problems. Gladwell et al (2016) refer to the assumption that returnees are wealthy (and therefore worth kidnapping) or involved with foreign agencies and/ or ideologically aligned with the West. Schuster and Majidi's research (2013 and developed in 2014) identifies three factors that inhibit sustainable return once removed to Afghanistan. These are: deep economic loss; the lack of transnational ties; and the shame of failure compounded by community suspicions of 'contamination'. Schuster and Majidi (2014) show how the stigma of deportation was particularly pronounced when deportees had been returned from longer distances – that is from Western countries rather than from Pakistan or Iran.

There are few educational opportunities for returnees in Afghanistan, and finding employment in Kabul is difficult without family connections and/or advanced skills (Gladwell et al, 2016). Literacy in Dari and Pashtu was also important, and an informant in Kabul stated that 'a returnee has to be above and beyond a young person who has been to high school and college here' (Gladwell and Elwyn, 2012, section 6.7).

The long-term outcomes for returnees are as yet unknown, but it is already clear that many returnees leave Afghanistan to seek safety elsewhere (Schuster and Majidi, 2014) and the prospect of onward migration is always an option – and one that is not prevented by assisted voluntary return.

Conclusion

Our work with young people focused on those facing return to countries of origin. They represent a specific group, whose experience cannot be generalised to all unaccompanied asylum-seeking children, but which represents a scenario (rejected as asylum seekers and facing detention, destitution and deportation from adulthood) that is a possible outcome for any unaccompanied asylum-seeking children entering the system.

Our work showed that social workers do not – and arguably cannot – prepare young people for this outcome, as the system is so contingent and variable. Social workers cannot know which of the young people they support will remain in the UK, and know little of their lives before they arrived. Drawing on young people's narratives, their experience and recollection of 'home' is conflicted, but they see their future as being in the UK despite their often unsatisfactory experience of education, support and care since their arrival.

Good services for unaccompanied asylum-seeking children are those that work with young people in care to deal with traumatic experiences and work to connect their past experiences with their futures. The pasts of too many children in care go unrecognised and unresolved. Addressing this requires ongoing support in supervision, training and development of social work teams, to enable them to challenge the dominant immigration discourses (Masocha and Simpson, 2011). Social workers must be mindful of the danger of collusion (Briskman et al, 2011; Bogen and Marlowe, 2015) and of how best to frame active advocacy (Nelson et al, 2014). We have written elsewhere about the need for better preparation of the workforce to address the needs of young people, and how supervision in services can enable social workers to critique their practice and promote self-care (Robinson, 2013). Cross-disciplinary working – collaborating with a wide range of experts, such as legal representatives, mental health and wellbeing specialists, interpreters, cultural and country experts – to support young people is another key strategy to address isolation and bewilderment at this complex system. It also enables us to address policy and practice and to focus on social justice.

Finally, we need to look at ways of promoting young people's strengths, resilience and inclusion. In so doing, we challenge the dominant discourse that leads social workers, as others, to focus on risk rather than need (Bogen and Marlowe, 2015; Masocha, 2015). This is particularly important in current times, where the media focus can be misleading about radicalisation and can ignore the need for inclusion, rather than further promoting marginalisation. There must be a greater investment in education for young people as a key mechanism for promoting this understanding and fully engaging with young people's need for security and a sense of belonging to both the UK and their countries of origin.

Note

[1] 'Appeal rights exhausted' migrants, often known as ARE, have been refused asylum or any form of temporary protection. Their leave to remain has expired and they have exhausted all appeals on their current case.

[2] Through what is known as 'Section 4' (section 4(1) of the 1999 Immigration and Asylum Act), though this is becoming increasingly difficult to obtain: https://www.gov.uk/government/uploads/system/uploads/attachment_data/file/513619/Asylum_Support_Section_4_Policy_and_Process.pdf

References

Akister, J., Owens, M. and Goodyer, I. M. (2010) 'Leaving care and mental health: outcomes for children in out-of-home care during the transition to adulthood', *Health Research Policy and Systems*, 8: 10. www.ncbi.nlm.nih.gov/pmc/articles/PMC2890536/

Australian Human Rights Commission (2014) *The Forgotten Children: National Inquiry into Children in Immigration Detention*. https://www.humanrights.gov.au/sites/default/files/document/publication/forgotten_children_2014.pdf

BBC News (2016) 'Kent County Council call to share refugee children "burden"', 13 April. www.bbc.co.uk/news/uk-england-kent-36036833

Bhabha, J. (2004) 'Seeking asylum alone: treatment of separated and trafficked children in need of refugee protection', *International Migration*, 42, 1: 141-8.

Bhabha, J. and Crock, M. (2007) *Seeking asylum alone: A comparative study, Australia, UK and the US*. NSW: Themis Press.

Bianchini, K. (2011) 'Unaccompanied asylum-seeker children: Flawed processes and protection gaps in the UK', *Forced Migration Review*, 37: 52-3.

Bloch, A., Sigona, N. and Zetter, R. (2014) *Sans papiers: The social and economic lives of young undocumented migrants*. London: Pluto Press.

Bogen, R. and Marlowe, J. (2015) 'Asylum discourse in New Zealand: moral panic and a culture of indifference', *Australian Social Work*. DOI:10.1080/0312407X.2015.1076869, 17 September.

Brighter Futures (2013) *The Cost of Waiting*. London: Praxis/ Brighter Futures. www.brighterfutureslondon.co.uk/wp-content/ uploads/2013/07/The-Cost-of-Waiting-ALL-1UP-Web.pdf

Briskman, L., Zion, D. and Loff, B. (2012) 'Care or Collusion in Asylum Seeker Detention', *Ethics and Social Welfare*, 6, 1: 37-55.

Cemlyn, S. and Briskman, L. (2003) 'Asylum, children's rights and social work', *Child & Family Social Work*, 8, 3: 163-78.

Cemlyn, S. and Nye, M. (2012) 'Asylum seeker young people: Social work value conflicts in negotiating age assessment in the UK', *International Social Work*, 55, 5: 675-88.

Chase, E. and Allsopp, J. (2013) 'Future citizens of the world? The contested futures of independent young migrants in Europe', *Refugee Studies Centre Working Paper*, Series 97, Barnett Papers, Social Research, Working Paper 13-05. www.rsc.ox.ac.uk/files/ publications/working-paper-series/wp97-future-citizens-of-the- world-2013.pdf

Crawley, H. (2010) *Chance or choice? Understanding why asylum seekers come to the UK*. London: Refugee Council. www.refugeecouncil.org. uk/assets/0001/5702/rcchance.pdf

Crawley, H. (2011) '"Asexual, apolitical beings": the interpretation of children's identities and experiences in the UK asylum system', *Journal of Ethnic and Migration Studies*, 37, 8: 1117-1184.

Dennis, J. (2012) *Not a minor offence: Unaccompanied children locked up as part of the asylum system*. Refugee Council. www.refugeecouncil. org.uk/assets/0002/5945/Not_a_minor_offence_2012.pdf

Fazel, M., Reed, R. V., Panter-Brick, C. and Stein, A. (2012) 'Mental health of displaced and refugee children resettled in high-income countries: risk and protective factors', *The Lancet*, 379: 266-82.

Finch, N. (2012) 'Return of separated children to country of origin' in E. Kelly and F. Bokhari (eds) *Safeguarding children from abroad: Refugees, asylum-seeking and trafficked in the UK*. London: Jessica Kingsley Publishers, 119–34.

Gladwell, C., Bowerman, E., Norman, B. and Ghafoor, A. (2016) *After return: Documenting the experiences of young people forcibly removed to Afghanistan*. Refugee Support Network. http://www.refugeesupportnetwork.org/resources/after-return (Accessed 23/2/17)

Gladwell, C. and Elwyn, H. (2012) *Broken futures: Young Afghan asylum seekers in the UK and in their country of origin*. UNHCR New Issues In Refugee Research, 246. http://www.refworld.org/docid/5142dc952.html (Accessed 23/2/17)

Grimshaw, R., Roberts, R., Bebbington, P., Dowling, M. and Hougham, C. (2014) 'Reducing poverty: from evidence to strategy', *Institutional care and poverty: Evidence and policy review*. Joseph Rowntree Foundation Institutional and Centre for Crime and Justice Studies. www.crimeandjustice.org.uk/sites/crimeandjustice.org.uk/files/Institutional%20Care%20and%20Poverty%20Report%20August%202014.pdf

Hayes, D. and Humphries, B. (eds) (2004) *Social work, immigration and asylum: Debates, dilemmas and ethical issues for social work and social care practice*. Jessica Kingsley.

Home Office (2016) *National statistics: Asylum*. www.gov.uk/government/publications/immigration-statistics-october-to-december-2015/asylum

Human Rights Watch (2012) *Caught in a net: Unaccompanied migrant children in Europe*. www.hrw.org/sites/default/files/HRW_CRD_migrant_brcohure_low.pdf

Joint Committee on Human Rights (2013) *Human rights of unaccompanied children and young people in the UK – First report of session 2013–14*. London: TSO. www.publications.parliament.uk/pa/jt201314/jtselect/jtrights/9/9.pdf

Kelly, E. and Bokhari, F. (eds) (2012) *Safeguarding children from abroad: Refugees, asylum-seeking and trafficked in the UK*. London: Jessica Kingsley Publishers.

Kohli, R.K.S. (2006) 'The sound of silence: listening to what unaccompanied asylum-seeking children say and do not say', *British Journal of Social Work*, 36: 707–21.

Kohli, R.K.S. (2011) 'Working to ensure safety, belonging and success for unaccompanied asylum-seeking children', *Child Abuse Review*, 20: 311–23.

Kohli, R.K.S. and Mitchell, F. (eds) (2007) *Working with unaccompanied asylum-seeking children: Issues for policy and practice*. Palgrave Macmillan.

Masocha, S. (2015) 'Construction of the "other" in social workers' discourses of asylum seekers', *Journal of Social Work*, 15, 6: 569–85.

Masocha, S. and Simpson, M.K. (2011) 'Xenoracism: Towards a critical understanding of the construction of asylum seekers and its implications for social work practice', *Practice*, 23, 1: 5–18.

Masocha, S. and Simpson, M.K. (2012) 'Developing mental health social work for asylum seekers: A proposed model for practice', *Journal of Social Work*, 12, 423–43.

Matthews, A. (2011) *Landing in Kent: The experience of unaccompanied children arriving in the UK*. London: Office of the Children's Commissioner. www.childrenscommissioner.gov.uk/sites/default/files/publications/Landing_in_Kent_-_The_experience_of_unaccompanied_children_arriving_in_the_UK.pdf

Matthews, A. (2012) *Landing in Dover*. London: Office of the Children's Commissioner. www.oijj.org/sites/default/files/documental_9683_en.pdf

Matthews, A. (2014) *'What's going to happen tomorrow?' Unaccompanied children refused asylum*. London: Office of the Children's Commissioner. https://www.childrenscommissioner.gov.uk/sites/default/files/publications/What's%20going%20to%20happen%20tomorrow.pdf

McFarlane, C. A., Kaplan, I. and Lawrence, J. A. (2011) 'Psychosocial indicators of wellbeing for resettled refugee children and youth: conceptual and developmental directions', *Child Indicators Research*, 4: 647–77.

Nelson, D., Price, E. and Zubrzycki, J. (2014) 'Integrating human rights and trauma frameworks in social work with people from refugee backgrounds', *Australian Social Work*, 67, 4: 567–81.

Pinter, I. (2012a) *Into the unknown: Children's journeys through the asylum process*. London: The Children's Society. https://www.childrenssociety.org.uk/sites/default/files/tcs/into-the-unknown--childrens-journeys-through-the-asylum-process--the-childrens-society.pdf

Pinter, I. (2012b) *'I don't feel human': Experiences of destitution among young refugees and migrants*. London: The Children's Society. https://www.childrenssociety.org.uk/sites/default/files/tcs/research_docs/thechildrenssociety_idontfeelhuman_final.pdf

Robinson, K. (2013) 'Voices from the front line: social work with refugees and asylum seekers in Australia and the UK', *British Journal of Social Work*, 44, 6: 1602–20.

Robinson, K. and Williams, L. (2014) *Positive futures – A pilot project to develop and test a model to assist appeal rights exhausted care leavers to consider assisted voluntary return*. The South East Strategic Partnership for Migration (SESPM). www.secouncils.gov.uk/wp-content/uploads/2012/04/Positive-Futures-Evaluation-Report-Final-18-Aug.pdf

Robinson, K. and Williams, L. (2015a) 'Leaving care: unaccompanied asylum-seeking young Afghans facing return', *Refuge*, 31, 2: 85-94. http://refuge.journals.yorku.ca/index.php/refuge/article/view/40312/36354

Robinson, K. and Williams, L. (2015b) 'Young Afghans facing return', *Forced Migration Review*, 50: 60-1. www.fmreview.org/en/dayton20.pdf

Schuster, L. and Majidi, N. (2013) 'What happens post-deportation? The experience of deported Afghans', *Migration Studies*, 1, 2: 221-40.

Schuster, L. and Majidi, N. (2014) 'Deportation stigma and re-migration', *Journal of Ethnic and Migration Studies*, 41, 4: 635-52.

Sigona, N. and Hughes, V. (2012) *No way out, no way in. Irregular migrant children and families in the UK*. COMPAS: Centre on Migration, Policy and Society, University of Oxford. https://www.compas.ox.ac.uk/media/PR-2012-Undocumented_Migrant_Children.pdf

Smyth, B., Shannon, M. and Dolan, P. (2015) 'Transcending borders: Social support and resilience, the case of separated children', *Transnational Social Review*, 5, 3: 274-95.

UNHCR (2014) *Unaccompanied and separated asylum-seeking and refugee children turning eighteen: What to celebrate?*, https://www.coe.int/t/dg4/youth/Source/Resources/Documents/2014_UNHCR_and_Council_of_Europe_Report_Transition_Adulthood.pdf

Vine, J. (2013) *An inspection into the Handling of asylum applications made by unaccompanied children*. London: Independent Chief Inspector of Borders and Immigration. http://icinspector.independent.gov.uk/wp-content/uploads/2013/10/An-Inspection-into-the-Handling-of-Asylum-Applications-Made-by-Unaccompanied-Children-FINAL.pdf

Wade, J. (2011) 'Preparation and transition planning for unaccompanied asylum-seeking young people: A review of evidence in England', *Children and Youth Services Review*, 33: 2424-30.

Warren, R. and York, S. (2014) *How children become 'failed asylum seekers'*, Kent Law Clinic, University of Kent. https://www.kent.ac.uk/law/clinic/how_children_become_failed_asylum-seekers.pdf (Accessed 23/2/17)

Wells, K. (2011) 'The strength of weak ties: the social networks of young separated asylum seekers and refugees in London', *Children's Geographies*, 9, 3-4: 319-29.

Williams, L. (2016) *The mental wellbeing of young former unaccompanied asylum-seeking children in East Kent – Final Report*. Bexley: Mind.

Wright, F. (2012) 'Social work practice with unaccompanied asylum-seeking young people facing removal', *British Journal of Social Work*, 44, 4: 1027-44.

NINE

Responses to the marginalisation of Roma young people in education in an age of austerity in the United Kingdom

Jenny van Krieken Robson

Introduction

'Fear, loathing and prejudice in Blunkett's back yard: A deeply disturbing dispatch as the ex-Labour Home Secretary warns of race riots over the Roma influx in Sheffield' (Reid, 2013) is representative of media headlines in 2013 about the arrival of Roma people in Sheffield. Such events were reported as if they were commonplace; this resonated with the frequent media representations of English Gypsies as the 'other' (Bhopal and Myers, 2008) and earlier media reports of racism experienced by Roma in Northern Ireland in 2009. 'Romanian gypsies beware beware. Loyalist C18 are coming to beat you like a baiting bear' (McDonald, 2009) read the headlines, as they repeated a text circulated widely through social media. McVeigh (2009) argues that the media narrative about the experiences of Roma remains uncontested and consistent. I further suggest that such a discourse circulated in the media locates Roma as problematic, and is visible in education contexts where practitioners engage with Roma young people.

This chapter reports on research (Robson, 2012) emerging from the dilemmas of teachers and family workers as they worked in schools to include Roma young people in the United Kingdom (UK). The fieldwork took place between 2009 and 2011; at the end of this period, a newly elected Coalition government implemented a policy of austerity that led to significant reductions in public expenditure at a local level, with the consequence of services for children and families being 'eradicated, reorganised or pared down as a result' (O'Hara, 2014, p3). This study explored how the experiences of *inequality* and *marginality* for Roma young people were understood by teachers and family workers as they worked in this changing environment. It concludes with a discussion of what might shape a response that has the potential to reduce inequality and address injustice for Roma young people; in times of austerity, actions to address inequality and discrimination may not be constrained by the available resources.

A lived experience of inequality: perspectives from the literature

Roma young people and their families moved throughout Europe (including to the UK) from countries newly formed following the collapse of the communist regimes (for example the Czech Republic and Slovakia). Initially, families came as asylum seekers to the UK and then as migrants following the enlargement of the European Union in 2004 and 2007 (European Dialogue, 2009a). In the UK, the phrase 'Gypsy, Roma and Traveller' is frequently used in academic research in education and in education policy to describe all Gypsy and Traveller people, as well as Roma from Eastern Europe (Wilkin et al, 2009). The term 'Gypsy, Roma and Traveller' is often abbreviated in education policy and practice to the label 'GRT' so that audiences are potentially unaware of its meaning. The uncritical use of 'GRT' communicates an impression of homogeneity, instead of emphasising the diversity and complexity of background, origins and experiences of young people (Robson, 2012). Externally defined categories that arise through the need to fix identity are problematic; Belton (2010, p42) argues that such identities can be 'permanent and unchanging' and can lead to discrimination. Labels such as 'GRT' potentially mask the lived experience of Roma young people as they arrive in the UK.

The experience of inequality, marginality and discrimination for Roma as they migrate across the Europe Union is well documented; research has found that Roma are often stereotyped as societal problems and may find themselves even more marginalised in EU member states than in their country of origin (Fundamental Rights Agency, 2009). A 2014 study (Fundamental Rights Agency, 2014) of Roma education across 11 EU states (excluding the UK) found that Roma young people are subject to systemic segregation within education either in mainstream provision or through inappropriate placement in special schools. Roma young people (and their families) arriving in the UK do so having been marginalised within education in their country of origin. An earlier review of research in the wider European context (European Union Monitoring Centre, 2006) identified the intersection of a range of factors that influenced the inequality in education provision and outcomes experienced by Roma young people; factors include direct and systemic discrimination, compounded by poverty, poor access to services and marginalisation.

Earlier research into the lives of Roma young people in London found that they experienced racism, discrimination and prejudice in education when they first arrive in the UK (Ureche et al, 2005). Similarly, a more recent study found that Roma in the UK were viewed as having varied and complex needs, compounded by the presence of poverty and the experience of entrenched discrimination (Brown at al, 2013).

Some studies provide a more hopeful picture. For example, a survey found that Roma children and young people previously enrolled in segregated or special schools in their country of origin had made the transition to mainstream schools in the UK (European Dialogue, 2009b). Similarly, a study found that although 85% of Roma young people interviewed had been placed in special or segregated schools in their countries of origin, only a minority were considered to have special educational needs when they arrived in UK schools (Fremlova and Ureche, 2011). Their needs were such that they could be met within mainstream – and not specialist – provision. The same study found that a large majority of the Roma young people interviewed had experienced racist bullying and verbal abuse in school in their country of origin. However, in seven out of the eight UK localities in this study, Roma young people reported that they were not experiencing racism in their UK schools (Fremlova and Ureche, 2011). These findings suggest that Roma children and young people in the UK are not victims of structural and systemic discrimination within education found in other European states. However, the question remains as to how the prevalent societal discourse that locates Roma people as problematic impacts on their experience of education.

Using case study as a methodology, this research study explored the responses of education practitioners working in two towns (one urban and one coastal) in the south east of England. Case study was appropriate, as the phenomenon being studied – the ways in which teachers and family workers (hereafter referred to as 'practitioners') understood and responded to the inequality experienced by Roma young people – was inseparable from the context (Yin, 2003). Furthermore, case study gave visibility to the diverse and sometimes contradictory views held by practitioners about young Roma people (Stake, 1995, 2005). Foucault's (1980) theoretical perspective on discourse is central to this study; he argues that relationships of power are implemented through the 'production, accumulation, circulation and functioning of a discourse' (p90). Foucault's discourse theory provides a framework for analysis of the researcher's observation as a participant and practitioners' accounts of their work with Roma young people.

The study arose from the researcher's observations of the dilemmas experienced by practitioners in secondary schools and the community, as they responded to incidents where Roma young people experienced inequality and discrimination. Such dilemmas can be related to Mills's (1959) description of the 'personal troubles of the milieu', where issues arise in the self and in the local environment and in the 'public issues of the social structure'; where issues arise from the values and life of institutions or in the public realm. Through analysis of the dilemmas faced by teachers, family workers and young people, the experiences of *inequality* and *marginality* for Roma became visible in the local and wider social structures.

Marginality of Roma young people

There was a prevailing and hegemonic discourse about Roma operating in the schools and the wider community. This discourse emerged as fragments from the analysis of data collected through interviews and participant observation. Such fragments revealed a discourse that was 'established, consolidated and implemented' (Foucault, 1980, p90) to create 'relationships of power which permeate, characterise and constitute the social body' (Foucault, 1980, p90) in the research setting.

The discourse was complex, dynamic and multifaceted. It began with a denial of Roma identity; practitioners believed they were migrants from Slovakia or Romania and this inhibited consideration of the history or the legacy of discrimination. The young people were frequently referred to as the 'Romanians' even in situations where they described themselves as Roma or where they provided identity that evidenced they came from another European country. The status of their families as migrants and their purpose in coming to the UK was questioned. Roma young people were perceived as a burden and as a drain on resources, as shown in the following extracts from interviews with practitioners in the setting:

> 'Resentment! Teachers say that the Roma children take up a lot of their time, they set up a support system and the child does not turn up. The teachers say they are not

attending. The children tend to move a lot, there is a lot of wasted time.'

'Roma were viewed by practitioners as an additional burden and there were lots of discussions about the number of children and questions about the resources. So accepting the children into the class often became a discussion about the resources.'

'It is a whole picture – it is to do with the media. There are negative images about the Roma. It also mirrors what they hear from other services (e.g. benefit frauds). A lot of people believe that Roma are living off their taxes – it starts as a personal view and now it is across the whole service.'

'People don't want to change they don't want to address these needs because they say in a few years time they will be gone – they would have moved on.'

These accounts illustrate the resistance and resentment to meeting needs of young people or understanding the reasons why young people may be hesitant to engage with support structures. Responses by some practitioners appeared conditional upon both the availability of additional resources and evidence that individual young people had been victims of discrimination in their countries of origin. Narratives about Roma young people promoted a version of the truth (that is, 'living off taxes'), and these were circulated uncritically within the schools and wider community. Bauman's (1997) perspective on the 'stranger' supports an understanding of the ways in which this discourse of marginality operated; he argues that such phenomena are an essential, and often manufactured, element within the postmodern society:

> What makes people strangers and therefore vexing, unnerving, off putting and otherwise a problem is – let us repeat – their tendency to befog and eclipse boundary lines which ought to be clearly seen. (Bauman, 1997, p25)

Roma young people became the 'stranger' through a cumulative discourse that questioned their status and purpose as migrants and suggested that their needs were too complex to be met by the school. This sustained a belief that additional resources are required to meet their needs, and when resources are unavailable, their needs cannot be met. This discourse establishes relationships of power (Foucault, 1980) in the setting that characterises Roma young people as a problematic group (Robson, 2012). Through the circulation of narratives that reported Roma young people as having low attendance at school, they became feared 'strangers', who may contribute to a school's low ranking in performance tables or in inspection. Practitioners attributed the actual or risk of the school's poor performance in the statutory inspection to the Roma. Young people positioned in this way become the 'vagabond' in Bauman's postmodern society; the focus for legitimised negativity, where 'unspoken fears, secret self-deprecations and guilt too awesome to be thought of are dumped' (Bauman, 1997, p25). This discourse operated in ways that resisted the arrival and acceptance of Roma young people within the school community, and where the response of 'no action' by practitioners was legitimised on the basis that Roma young people would stay a short time before returning to their country of origin.

McVeigh's (1997, 2008) theory of 'sedentarism' provides further insight into this discourse of marginality. Sedentarism can be understood as a 'system of ideas and practices which serves to normalise and reproduce sedentary models of existence and pathologise and repress nomadic modes of existence' (McVeigh, 1997, p9). As a position, it privileges ideas and practices embedded within established and static communities. Furthermore, McVeigh (1997, p9) suggests that sedentarism can be enacted through intentional or unintentional practices that construct being 'sedentary' as the only possible mode of existence in society. In this way, sedentarism serves to characterise new or different phenomena as the other – and to be feared.

In the research setting, Roma young people were constructed as problematic; it was suggested by practitioners that the support structures in the school could not anticipate or respond to their needs arising from nomadism. The narrative operating in the setting validated the belief that Roma families were short-term visitors in the locality. This discourse operated in ways that placed Roma young people on the margins within education settings; *it failed to acknowledge or respond to their experiences* and cumulated through the *convergence and intersection* of multiple negative discourses operating in the setting, for example migration, living on benefits, sedentarism, burden on resources, poor attenders, not being victims of discrimination. This resonates with Ureche et al's (2005) study, which found that Roma young people experienced racism, discrimination and prejudice in education.

Moving from sustaining to resisting the dominant discourse about Roma

Some practitioners sustained and replicated the hegemonic discourse about Roma young people in their work. They adopted a 'funded approach to the work' (Robson, 2012) and promoted the view that addressing Roma disadvantage could only be achieved through additionally funded project work. A study (Brown et al, 2013) highlighted the reliance in the UK on specialist posts and separately funded provision to meet the needs of Roma families. The same study found in a survey of local authorities that 60% of respondents viewed low levels of funding as a barrier to successful work with Roma.

At a time of 'austerity', the announcement in 2010 of a reduction of 19% in public expenditure (HM Treasury, 2010), and the removal of dedicated funding to promote the educational achievement of Gypsy, Roma and Traveller children (Foster and Norton, 2012), contributed to a view that schools did not have the resources to meet the needs of Roma young people. This reinforced the belief that the funding intended for all young people in the school was not available for the Roma.

A further practice that extended this discourse was the perception that Roma young people need specialist support, as their needs are considered to be so great that they cannot be met by teachers or other practitioners in schools. This reinforced the view that teachers require specialist knowledge to include Roma young people in the learning environment and positioned Roma young people as problematic. Similarly, Bhopal and Myers (2008, p49), in their account of the formation of Gypsy identities, argue that practices operating among practitioners working with Gypsy children remain uncontested, and that this reinforces an attitude that Gypsy children are the responsibility of specialists. In an earlier study, Bhopal (2004) found that some schools relinquished responsibility for the problems they associate with Gypsy children. This resonated with my findings that Roma young people were viewed as being on the margin of teachers' and family workers' practice.

This sense of professional helplessness was validated by a powerful discourse that positioned Roma young people beyond the reach of practitioners' skills and resources. Earlier studies (European Union Monitoring Centre, 2006) found that teachers are not able to identify the underlying causes of Roma children's low achievement and this hindered their ability to form an appropriate response. Furthermore, in the wider European context, programmes to address the education inequalities experienced by Roma young people are frequently structured as targeted (sometimes segregated) projects, supported by short-term funding (European Commission, 2010). In this way, institutional structures act to validate, cumulate and replicate a discourse that positions Roma young people on the margins of education.

Some practitioners were aware of how relationships of power constituted and permeated the social body of their practice (Foucault, 1980). They resisted the hegemonic discourse about Roma that was operating in schools. By listening to and learning from the experiences of Roma young people, they identified actions realisable in their own practice that would address the inequality of Roma young people in education. Practitioners became aware of how local education policies discriminated against Roma young people, despite having the stated aim of enabling access to school. In accounts of their work, some practitioners questioned whether policies were responsive to the needs of Roma. For example, as the following extracts from interviews with practitioners in the setting show:

> 'The Roma families do not know the systems here and these families who arrive mid-term they do not know how to access the services. A lot of children slip through the net – the schools tend not to support the families particularly primary and secondary transfer. The literature they send home is in English.'

> 'Sometimes we have had cases where the families have been offered two or three different schools for their children. ... Absolutely ludicrous when you start to think about the families who culturally do not feel it is appropriate for children to travel very far away from them anyway and they have not got the money to send their children on buses to school and the actual practicalities of getting three children into three different schools.'

Practitioners recognised that the impact of school admission policies and practices was to 'normalise and reproduce sedentary models of existence' (McVeigh, 1997, p9) and, in this way, the arrangements for admission to school compounded the inequality and marginality experienced by Roma. Responding to cultural issues may lead practitioners and their institutions to make changes in practice (Save the Children, 2001). Through this process, some practitioners developed new approaches outside the established practices in their institutions, although many practitioners felt compelled to work within existing policies rather than explore alternative solutions.

By focusing on the universality of young people's needs, some practitioners sought to reposition Roma alongside all young people in their setting. They introduced a humanitarian dialogue that emphasised themes of safety and wellbeing. In this way, they initiated discussions that dispelled myths about Roma young people's needs as different from those of other young people in the setting; this countered the discourse that constructed Roma as the 'stranger' or that Roma young people's needs could not be met from within the resources available in the school. Through this proactive approach, practitioners contested the view that the needs of Roma young people were so complex that they could only be met by teachers and family workers with 'expertise' about Roma. This challenges restrictive paradigms about work with Roma that may operate within practice settings. In an earlier study, Bhopal and Myers (2008) argued that there was an unchallenged approach by academics and professionals in work with Gypsy communities, and that this meant that 'new interpretations of Gypsy culture, engagements by the culture in new circumstances, or new approaches by the culture towards society are liable to be overlooked or ignored' (p43). By engaging in conversations about the needs of Roma young people as they accessed school in the UK, practitioners gave visibility to the marginalisation, discrimination and challenges that Roma faced in the new context.

Practitioners were aware of the negative discourse that operated about Roma young people. Schools discussed the suggestion that Roma young people had formed and remained in 'gangs'; by describing the friendship groups of Roma young people as 'gangs', practitioners extended the discourse that positioned the Roma as the 'other' or the 'stranger' and a phenomenon to be feared (Bauman, 1997). While some practitioners focused on the issues that the 'gangs' presented for the school (for example that some young people and teachers found this intimidating), others began to explore the underlying reasons why Roma young people remained together in a group (for example fear of racist abuse and isolation). Practitioners began to initiate dialogue and debate about the experience and legacy of discrimination for Roma, as shown in the following extracts from interviews with practitioners:

> 'People's personal views get in the way of their professionalism. Sometimes they are racist – it is improving. They don't realise it – they are just ignorant. It is their attitude ... they

cannot see the bigger picture and how they can help the families.'

'I think it is breaking barriers. I think teaching is about your belief system and your values system. Unless you are challenging that and you are getting people to question their own belief system, you are getting them to question prejudice and discrimination and to really look and unpeel the layers.'

Initially, practitioners adopted an approach of 'focusing on the facts', with a goal of educating their schools on the legacy of discrimination and on the discrimination faced by the Roma. I questioned the effectiveness of this approach, as the provision of information about discrimination against Roma in a wider European context did not challenge practitioners working in schools to reflect on their own attitudes and the situation of young people in the locality. For some practitioners, their responses to Roma young people appeared to be conditional on meeting individual young people and on hearing the narratives they gave about their experiences of injustice. It was only when practitioners moved beyond this approach of 'contact' with young people to engagement with the issues that they faced in the school and the locality that the connection was made to the wider systemic persecution and injustice that Roma people experienced as individuals and groups. Similarly, Osler and Starkey (2010) suggest that within human rights education, the exploration of others' narratives can 'resonate with the struggles of learners' (p143).

Conclusion: towards shaping a response to challenge the inequality experienced by Roma young people in times of austerity

This chapter began with an analysis of the entrenched discourse circulating in the media about Roma and the ways in which it remained uncontested. In the UK, Roma young people did not experience the structural and systemic segregation in education universally found in their countries of origin (Fremlova and Ureche, 2011). However, the hegemonic and negative discourse visible in schools in this study operated in ways that positioned Roma as a problematic group and influenced the response of education practitioners.

In times of austerity, the discourse established, consolidated and implemented relationships of power (Foucault, 1980); perceptions of Roma young people, their needs, the resources needed to meet their needs and the resources available in the school were shaped by the discourse. A version of the 'truth' about Roma young people permeated the schools, as some practitioners sought to justify an approach that both denied the legacy of discrimination experienced by Roma and explicitly established the needs of Roma young people as being too great to be met by the resources and skills available in the school. The power of the discourse constructed Roma families as 'strangers' and 'vagabonds' to be feared (Bauman, 1997); it consolidated views of sedentarism operating in the setting, by pathologising nomadic modes of existence (McVeigh, 2008). As a result, Roma young people were marginalised within education, and their lived experiences of discrimination remained hidden from practitioners' view.

Some practitioners pieced together fragments of the discourse through their experiences of working with Roma young people. Such experiences can be understood as 'ritual like' (they were linked to institutional processes such as policies or procedures), 'problematic' (they were troubling for practitioners and led to unresolved issues for Roma young people) and 'routine' (they occurred regularly) (Denzin, 1989, p33). Practitioners became aware of ways in which relationships of power were constituted and permeated the social body of their practice (Foucault, 1980). This new-found knowledge led to responses that both resisted the hegemonic discourse and established alternative discourse about Roma. Mills' (1959) framework of the 'personal troubles of the milieu' and the 'public issues of the social structure' supports an understanding of how practitioners engaged in this process.

Opportunities for dialogue and debate about their experiences in the 'milieu' enabled practitioners to problematise and explore the complexity of issues for Roma young people found within their own practice. This process gave visibility to the complex discourse and the intersection of such issues as racism and sedentarism, enabling them to be named in practice. Through engagement with the narratives of injustice told by Roma young people, practitioners connected the day-to-day experiences of discrimination visible in the 'milieu' with the legacy of systemic discriminatory practice prevalent in the 'public issues of the social structure'.

Osler and Zhu (2011) argue for the strengths of narratives as tools to give visibility to the voices and experience of marginalised people; in this way, they suggest that 'narratives fill the blind spots in the dominant discourse' (p231). By moving beyond a position of contact with young Roma and listening to their narratives, practitioners considered the issues for Roma informed by European, national and local perspectives (Robson, 2012).

Such opportunities have the potential to build alternative responses – shaped by new knowledge – to the persistent and prevailing inequality experienced by Roma young people. In this way, Roma young people can be repositioned from the margins to the centre of practice. This moves *beyond a view* that, in times of austerity and entrenched negative public discourse, actions to address discrimination and inequality for Roma are constrained by perceptions of available resources or a reliance on a funded approach to work.

References

Bauman, Z. (1997) *Postmodernity and its discontents*. Oxford: Blackwell.

Belton, B. (2010) 'Knowing Gypsies', in D. Le Bas and T. Acton (eds) *All change! Romani studies through Romani eyes*. Hatfield: University of Hertfordshire Press, 39–48.

Bhopal, K. (2004) 'Gypsy Travellers and education: Changing needs and changing perceptions', *British Journal of Educational Studies*, 52, 1: 47–64.

Bhopal, K. and Myers, M. (2008) *Insiders, outsiders and others*. Hatfield: University of Hertfordshire Press.

Brown, P., Scullion, L. and Martin, P. (2013) *Migrant Roma in the United Kingdom: Population size and experience of local authorities and partners*. Manchester: University of Salford.

Denzin, N.K. (1989) *Interpretative Biography*. London: Sage.

European Commission (2010) *Improving the tools for the social inclusion and non-discrimination of Roma in the EU: Summary and selected projects*. Brussels: European Commission.

European Dialogue (2009a) *New Roma communities in England: Strategic guide for directors and senior managers*. London: European Dialogue.

European Dialogue (2009b) *The movement of Roma from new EU Member States: A mapping survey of A2 and A8 Roma in England*. London: European Dialogue.

European Union Monitoring Centre (2006) *Roma and Travellers in public education: An overview of the situation in the EU member states*. Brussels: European Union Monitoring Centre.

Foster, B. and Norton, P. (2012) 'Educational equality for Gypsy, Roma and Traveller children and young people in the UK', *The Equal Rights Review*, 8, 85-112. www.equalrightstrust.org/ertdocumentbank/ERR8_Brian_Foster_and_Peter_Norton.pdf

Foucault, M. (1980) *Power and knowledge: Selected interviews and other writing 1972–1977*. London: Harvester Press.

Fremlova, L. and Ureche, H. (2011) *From segregation to inclusion. Roma pupils in the United Kingdom, a pilot research project.* Long Melford: Equality UK.

Fundamental Rights Agency (2009) *The situation of Roma EU citizens moving to and settling in other EU member states.* Brussels: European Union. http://ec.europa.eu/justice/discrimination/files/roma_situation_settling_eu_en.pdf

Fundamental Rights Agency (2014) *Education: The situation of Roma in 11 EU Member States.* Brussels: European Union. http://fra.europa.eu/sites/default/files/fra-2014_roma-survey_education_tk0113748enc.pdf

HM Treasury (2010) *Spending Review 2010.* London: The Stationery Office. https://www.gov.uk/government/uploads/system/uploads/attachment_data/file/203827/Spending_review_2010_executive_summary.pdf

McDonald, H. (2009) '"Romanian gypsies beware beware. Loyalist C18 are coming to beat you like a baiting bear"', *The Guardian*, 21 June. www.theguardian.com/world/2009/jun/21/race-northern-ireland-romanian-gypsies

McVeigh, R. (1997) 'Theorising sedentarism', in T. Acton (ed.) *Gypsy politics and Traveller identity.* Hatfield: University of Hertfordshire Press, 7–25.

McVeigh, R. (2008) 'The "final solution": reformism, ethnicity denial and the politics of anti-Travellerism in Ireland', *Social Policy and Society*, 7, 91–102.

McVeigh, R. (2009) 'First they came for the Gypsies', *Runnymede Quarterly Bulletin*, 359, 10–12.

Mills, C.W. (1959) (republished 2000) *The sociological imagination.* Oxford: Oxford University Press.

O'Hara, M. (2014) *Austerity bites: A journey to the sharp end of cuts in the UK.* Bristol: Policy Press.

Osler, A. and Starkey, H. (2010) *Teachers and human rights education.* Stoke on Trent: Trentham.

Osler, A. and Zhu, J. (2011) 'Narratives in teaching and research for justice and human rights', *Education, Citizenship and Social Justice*, 6, 3: 223–35.

Reid, S. (2013) 'Fear, loathing and prejudice in Blunkett's back yard: A deeply disturbing dispatch as the ex–Labour Home Secretary warns of race riots over the Roma influx in Sheffield', *The Mail on Sunday*, 15 November. www.dailymail.co.uk/news/article-2508120/Fear-loathing-prejudice-Blunketts-yard-A-deeply-disturbing-dispatch-ex-Labour-Home-Secretary-warns-race-riots-Roma-influx-Sheffield.html

Robson, J.V.K. (2012) 'Understanding practitioners' responses to inequality and breaches of human rights'. Unpublished PhD thesis. Canterbury: Canterbury Christ Church University.

Save the Children (2001) *Denied a future? The right to education of Roma/Gypsy Traveller children. Volume 2 (Western and Central Europe)*. London: Save the Children.

Stake, R.E. (1995) *The art of case study research*. London: Sage.

Stake, R.E. (2005) 'Qualitative case studies', in N.K. Denzin and Y. Lincoln (eds) *Strategies of qualitative inquiry*. London: Sage: 119-50.

Ureche, H., Manning, J. and Frank, M. (2005) *That's who I am: Experiences of young Romanian Roma in London*. London: The Children's Society.

Wilkin, A., Derrington, C. and Foster, B. (2009) *Improving the outcomes for Gypsy, Roma and Traveller pupils: Literature review*. Research Report No. DCSF-RR077. London: Department for Children, Schools and Families.

Yin, R.K. (2003) *Applications of case study research*. London: Sage.

TEN

Apprentice or student as alternatives to marginalisation?

Patrick Ainley

Introduction

The 2015 Conservative government confirmed the emphasis placed on apprenticeships by the 2010–15 Coalition, effectively dividing all English 18-plus year olds into two official categories – apprentices or students. Theresa May reaffirmed David Cameron's apprentice offer with an apprentice wage paid for by a levy on large employers that was both unexpected and resented by employers. Despite this, the combination of scrapping maintenance grants for undergraduates while raising their fees, plus a demographic fall in the number of 18–19 year olds and some pick-up in the economy, unrelenting advertising of apprenticeships has not stopped most 18-plus year olds who are qualified applying for higher education. They and their parents hope for secure, semi-professional employment, and are aware that those who fail to embark on the academic route – or who fail to complete it to graduation and often beyond – are at risk of marginalisation.

So the 'bubble' in student debt has continued to grow. However, changes in the youth labour market and in the wider economy undermine the policy goals of restarting social mobility through academic competition and of regenerating productive industry through 'German-style' apprenticeships.

These policies are 'magical solutions' to a real social problem – the reversal of limited upward social mobility in the mid-20th century into mass downward social mobility in the 21st (Bukodi et al, 2014; Roberts, 2015), and the fact that the latest applications of new technology obviate the need for apprentices and are proletarianising many professions, just as they have previously deskilled many trades (Braverman, 1974; Cooley, 1987 (republished 2016); Susskind and Susskind, 2015).

This chapter opposes the political and professional unanimity in favour of trying to rebuild the vocational route, with its possible complement of reintroducing grammar schools. It recalls past failures of vocationalism since the collapse of industrial apprenticeships in the 1970s to trace the substitution of education and training for employment as the UK economy opened to global competition in the 1980s. This has contributed not only to 'prolonging youth', but also to an ongoing process of social class reformation.

So it can be asserted that – following the prolonged recession from 2008 – rather than a permanently marginalised minority, a reconstituted reserve army of labour (Marx, 1971, pp642-55) has racheted up to include perhaps half of all employed people in insecure, unskilled, low-paid work. This reserve army includes many young people for at least some part of their lives, even when they are also students and/or apprentices, ducking and diving at two or three part-time jobs as well (see O'Leary, 2013). Their experience drives them to seek security, by running up a down-escalator of inflating academic qualifications.

However, the chapter does not respond by demanding 'the right to work' as part of an outdated post-war collectivised model of the labour market. Rather, it proposes that the entitlement to work and to learn about work – and not just to work – should be seen as part of a process of cultural and political emancipation. This recognises that technological change potentially enables a variety of occupations throughout an individual's working life to create a general educational entitlement for citizenship in a democratic and sustainable society. The perception of 'the problem' needs to change: it is not a 'youth problem' that young people have to overcome by acquiring 'skills' – actually qualifications, as most young people are overqualified but underemployed – rather, it is an economic problem, for which education can no longer be substituted as a solution.

Promises, promises: betraying a generation

Among the many promises made in the 2015 general election was this from David Cameron: 'Three million apprenticeships – that means three million more engineers, accountants and project managers' (Conservative Party, 2015). The *non sequitur* is blatantly delusional, if Cameron believed it, or it was misleadingly dishonest if he did not. Yet it is no more illusory than the promises made to university students that 'a good degree' guarantees the secure, professional jobs to which most aspire.

In fact, large numbers of boys follow neither of these two official routes, but leave school for unregulated, marginal employment. No one knows where, since the Careers Service has been privatised out of existence. These 'Lost Boys' – as they are widely referred to – are a survival of the *Status Zer0 youth* that Howard Williamson pointed to in relation to a so-called 'underclass' in 1997. Nearly 20 years later when, despite the raising of the 'participation age' to 18 in 2015, they did not show up in further education (FE) or higher education (HE), a minor moral panic followed, since women are now 60% of undergraduates, just as they are also the majority on apprenticeships. As a result, widening participation to young working-class men is to be added to the key indicators that will allow HE institutions to charge higher fees under the proposed Teaching Excellence Framework in the Higher Education and Research Bill that passed its second Commons reading in June 2016 (Department for Business, Innovation and Skills, 2016).

The 'Lost Boys' were also supposed to be mopped up by the expansion of apprenticeships funded by the levy on large employers that the Chancellor, George Osborne, unexpectedly announced in his 2015 autumn spending review. But this only provoked bitter recriminations from the employers' Confederation of British Industry because, as Martin Allen's ongoing research shows, many employers do not want or need apprenticeships, nor are they willing to fund them. Allen's work also shows that most apprenticeships continue to be low-skilled and what could be referred to as 'dead-end'. Of the approximately two million apprenticeships that have been created since 2010, the majority have been filled by adults, with many examples of existing employees being reclassified as apprentices to allow employers to access government subsidies. Two thirds of apprenticeships are only equivalent to GCSE, a level to which most young people are already qualified. Apprenticeships generally last only a year or less, and in most cases provide no employment guarantees and no opportunities to progress to a higher level, although they are supposed to do both. They are therefore not really apprenticeships at all but *Another Great Training Robbery* (Allen, 2016). This was confirmed by a damning Ofsted report at the end of 2015:

> Inspectors, observed for example, apprentices in the food production, retail and care sectors who were simply completing their apprenticeship by having existing low-level skills, such as making coffee, serving sandwiches or cleaning floors, accredited. While these activities are no doubt important to the everyday running of the businesses, as apprenticeships they do not add enough long-term value. (Ofsted, 2015, p4)

Unlike post-war apprenticeships, associated with heavy industrial manufacturing, the employment areas in today's post-industrial, largely service-sector labour market (where apprenticeships are most easily available) are in stereotypically feminine routine office work, low-skill retail or health and social care. There have been some changes so that, as Allen reports, by 2014 at least two thirds of starts were by people under 24, though only a quarter of these (120,000) were under 19 (Allen, 2016, p5). More young people also started Advanced level (A-level equivalent) schemes, even if numbers are low – just 35,000 starts in 2013/14, while the 15,000 Higher level apprenticeships, which can include higher education to degree level, is highly unlikely to create an 'alternative route to HE', as the Department for Business, Innovation and Skills claimed (2016, p7).

As it is, there are a few very good apprentice schemes that lead to well-paid and skilled careers, but these exceptions are massively oversubscribed and there continues to be concern about declining participation in the 'STEM' subjects: science, technology, engineering and maths. According to the Campaign for Science and Engineering (2015), the number of STEM apprenticeships had fallen from 70,100 in 2012 to 65,190 in 2013/14, with only 360 starts in science and maths in 2013/14. Even in the STEM areas, 60% of apprenticeships have continued to be at intermediate level and only 1% at higher level (Allen, 2016, p11). As Alison Wolf told *The Independent* (30 August 2015, quoted in Allen, 2016, p 11): 'What the government should be doing is concentrating on those high-value apprenticeships which teach vocational skills in manufacturing and engineering which historically Britain is bad at fostering. The danger is that money and resources is put into hitting a meaningless numerical target.'

Until now, the training of apprentices has been carried out by private providers, which then claimed government funding, but the new online levy of 0.5% of the wages bill of large employers (approximately 2% of all employers) will raise nearly £3 billion. Although potentially doubling apprenticeship funding, it cannot be regarded as a panacea, the main reason being the deregulated, low-skill labour market within which apprenticeships operate. Most apprentice training is therefore restricted to narrow, workplace-based National Vocational Qualifications, with functional skills included for those without A-C GCSE maths and English. FE colleges would be the obvious place to deliver additional education alongside work-based training, but they are being merged and closed under ongoing area reviews.

Not FE or HE but TE: tertiary education

Instead, FE students are being decanted into mass 'HE', or what Palfreyman and Tapper (2014, pv) call 'tertiary education (TE)'. As nearly all universities desperately compete to cram in students on whom their funding now depends as they pay more for less, institutions poach applicants from one another, creaming off those who originally applied for more 'middling' institutions but who can now trade up the hierarchy. From a young person's perspective, 'the student experience' that is subject to such intense management at all levels of learning, begins earlier and goes on longer as pupils-then-students face a series of hurdles that mark critical divergences onto one pathway or another. Without necessarily realising it, individuals can get locked into one or other of these tracks. Recovery from what later becomes evident is relegation to an inferior route (defined both by subject and by institution), while not impossible, then becomes increasingly difficult.

These points — and the pressure put on young people by family, teachers, peers and themselves — intensify in frequency throughout their educational careers: once every four years after initial testing in primary but then again on entry to secondary school, after retesting that government is imposing but teachers are resisting. Guided 'option choices' are then made after three years, followed by two years to the first critical cut-off point of five A-C GCSEs. Whether on the academic or vocational route from then on, on the one hand, modularised assessment avoids the trauma of end-of-course, "sudden-death" examinations, and such assessment is therefore being reduced in favour of old-style examinations. On the other, module tests break down the individual's scores into a running total (like US grade point averages), which there is incessant pressure to maintain. If these add up to three 'good' A-levels, options are open for application to the hierarchy of higher education.

Such is the competition between universities for students, recovery is still possible even at this late stage, since all degrees are officially equal. As long as you pass the first year, of course — if only with a 'fuck-it 40' pass-mark, as Cheeseman's undergraduate interviewees put it (Cheeseman, 2011; see also Ainley, 2008). Then you can leave behind the high point of the student experience, which is 'freshers', and return to 'the student bubble' for two more years of semester/module tests in order to hopefully gain more than 'a deadly Desmond' (2:2). Otherwise, you have lost your fee/loan investment and might as well have left at 18 for what employment you could find (see Cheeseman, 2011).

There is more risk of failure for those who can least afford to take it. A lack of confidence in their ability to 'hack it' afflicts students from poorer and minority backgrounds and limits their aspirations. They often choose to 'play safe' at seemingly less demanding and local, new universities with people like themselves. This is a powerful attractor up and down 'the endless chain of hierarchy and condescension that passes for a system [of higher education] in England' (Scott, 2015) and one which, moreover, is raddled with snobbery, sexism and racism. Students accept all this and their mounting debts with a resigned fatalism. For example, this comment from a survey on fees at a new university: 'The problem as I see it is that most young people know they are being "ripped off" but there is nothing we can really do about it'(quoted by Ainley, 2016, p65).

The odds on gaining a 2:1 or a first are good, however, since these are now achieved by approximately 70% of graduates (93% at Cambridge), as compared with approximately 20% of a much smaller cohort 30 years ago. They enable entry to usually only one-year Masters (regarded as virtually worthless on mainland Europe, and with two years generally required in the US), if not endless internships (Perlin, 2011). Even on this academic Royal Road, capped by a PhD (increasingly required to teach in HE), 'It doesn't matter how far you go in the English education system, they'll fail you in the end!', as former London schools' tsar Tim Brighouse said in one of his many *bon mots*.

The real 'student journey'

This is the real 'student journey' that is so much celebrated and regulated at universities. It is not so much an 'experience' as a process. So it is no wonder that references to schools as 'exam factories' proliferate (as in Hutchins for the NUT, 2015), or that during the 2011 student *Springtime* (Solomon and Palmieri, 2011), students associated with the autonomous Really Open University referred in their posters to their own Leeds University as a "sausage factory".

Young people are today subject to what Phil Cohen (1997, p284 and following) called the 'career code'. This had previously only been followed by a minority of grammar-school educated, traditionally middle-class youth, making an institutionalised transition from school to work and from living at home to living away by way of term-time residential HE on campus. This 'career code' has now been extended to, and largely accepted by, 'striving' parents and children, who think of themselves as 'hard-working people ... trying to do the right thing', as the then Prime Minister reiterated. Only a minority of 14-plus year olds are diverted to the once majority but always second-best 'vocation code' of 'apprenticeship'. As Cohen warned, 'this is not just the material effect of youth unemployment on school transitions; it is about changes in the codes of cultural reproduction' (Cohen, 1997, p233). It is another reason why vocational options are not so easily revived, especially in the absence of the employment to which they once led.

The 'career code' does impose coherence on young people's lives to make them comprehensible to their parents and themselves. Education becomes their occupation, but this is in some ways subsidiary to individuals' more personal concerns, as 'appropriate' behaviour is honed in the presentations that students are encouraged to perform throughout school, college and on into university; and also in the relentless presentation of self that is necessary for interviews and in CVs, as well as on Facebook. Insofar as these performances of 'interpersonal' and 'soft skills' have any retail value, it is in self-regulated and stereotypically feminine customer care.

Alienated learning

For education to all levels, this creates a situation where learning (increasingly reduced to training) becomes an end in itself. The result is alienating for teachers and students alike, as institutionalised education turns into its opposite, institutionalised 'stupification'. It forecloses possibilities of learning in pursuit of the next examination, which certifies mostly just the students' ability to pass on to the next stage. There is thus decreasing intrinsic interest or content in this institutionalised 'learning'. The end result is that students and teachers are forced by managers and inspectors to conform to a tyranny of transparency that spells out in every detail what will be required for quantified assessment. This task orientation seems deliberately designed to preclude thinking outside the tick-box and so, although teachers teach for longer and more intensively, their students study harder but learn less. As one student wrote in a final-year Education Studies project at the University of Greenwich more than 10 years ago:

'Students ... learn to connect their self-esteem and what they may achieve in life to their exam results ... Over-assessment has made subject knowledge and understanding a thing of the past as students are put through a routine year after year, practising what exactly to write and where in preparation for exams.' (quoted in Ainley, 2004)

In an historical and sociological context, such 'scholastic careers' can be said to have substituted for real ones in employment, acting in place of wage discipline as a means of social control over young people. Incidentally, this also reduces unemployment counts for the lengthening periods they are in the 'holding pens' of tertiary education and training, as Silva (2015, p 83) refers to the community colleges in the USA,

Throughout this extended time, institutionalised education functions as a giant sorting machine, rewarding through successive tests and examinations what it recognises as the largely literary accomplishments of those with more or less expensively acquired cultural capital. It thus pulls off 'the trick', as Bourdieu and Passeron called it in their 1964 report on French students, of appearing objective, while actually being biased towards the reproduction of privilege. Bourdieu entitled the epilogue he added to the English translation of this book 'The bamboozling of a generation' (originally *une generation abusée*').

It is ironic that, in what has been dubbed 'The Great British Class Fiasco' (Mills, 2013), Savage (2015) misappropriates Bourdieu, by giving equal weight to cultural and social capital as well as to economic capital, in making up his scale of seven classes – from an elite at the top to a 'precariat' at the bottom but with no necessary relation between them. Moreover, what Savage calls his 'multidimensional approach' to social class (Savage, 2015, p401) appeals to education researchers, among whom it is rapidly becoming a new orthodoxy. At least, they can claim to increase some pupils'/students' chances of upward social mobility, by compensating for their lack of economic capital by boosting their cultural capital, if not broadening their range of acquaintance to diversify their social capital. Hence, girls into engineering, visits to the opera for those on free school meals, inner-city youth on work placements in top City banks, and so on. So, 'educationalists' claim they are at least making the system a bit 'fairer' and are thereby advancing 'social justice' – equalising opportunities to be unequal, as Gove's version of 'grammar schooling for all' reworked Harold Wilson's 1964 description of comprehensives.

Yet, as Ken Roberts said: 'the best way to change mobility flows is to change the structure of opportunities itself'. He went on: 'virtually all policy-makers continue to act as if modest interventions in education and training will bring about significant redistribution of life-chances', ignoring the fact that, 'We are more likely to reduce unemployment rates among the least-qualified by reducing general unemployment than by providing the least-qualified with yet more education and training' (Roberts, 2001, pp223-4).

Conclusion

This chapter opposes the political and professional consensus in favour of attempting to rebuild the vocational route for those failed by the academic one. Repeated efforts to do this since the collapse of industrial apprenticeships in the 1970s confirm the substitution of education and training for employment. This has contributed not only to 'prolonging youth' but also to an ongoing process of social class reformation. This is reflected in widespread apprehensions of an 'Americanised' class structure, in which a new middle-working/working-middle class is divided from a marginalised so-called 'underclass', echoed in political pronouncements about hard-working – as opposed to (by implication) not hard-working – people. However, contrary to popular impressions reinforced by mainstream media, very few of this so-called 'underclass' are the same people plunged permanently into a 'culture of poverty'. Rather, as Shildrick et al (2010) confirmed in Glasgow and Teesside, most churn through part-time, insecure and low-paid jobs intermitted by spells of unemployment.

The reality is that – following the prolonged recession from 2008 – rather than a permanently marginalised minority, a reconstituted reserve army of labour has ratcheted up to include perhaps half of all employed people in permanently insecure, unskilled, often part-time and always low-paid jobs (Ainley, 2013). The ratchet will be notched up again by the further recession likely to be induced by Brexit. As Gamble (2009) remarked, following Marx, a reconstitution of the reserve army of labour is a key function of capitalist crisis.

During the economic crisis of the 1970s, it was manifested in what Finn (1987) called *Training Without Jobs*, succeeded today by what Ainley and Allen (2010) call 'education without jobs'. 'The pattern of cycling between low-paid work and unemployment was evident at the time of the UK's last recession [in the early 1990s]' (Clark and Heath, 2014: n.60, p258) and is now well established. Particularly, youth's marginalisation to a zero-hours, peripheral labour force, intermitted by prolonged stays in the holding pens of full-time education or training, would suggest that young people now contribute a significant part of this reconstituted reserve army, even if only for a period of their lives (Simmons et al, 2014). Spontaneous reaction against this marginalisation came with the nationwide 'riots' of 1981 and 2011. *The Guardian* (12 August 2012, quoted in Ainley and Allen, 2012) estimated that almost 80% of those up in court subsequently were under 25. Failed by an academic testing regime and dropping out of 'participation' from 14 on, the rioters no longer played by any rules.

Most young people, however, did not riot (Allen and Ainley, 2012) and are only too aware that to avoid relegation to the grey economy of irregular and insecure working, the more qualifications they have, the better their chances of employment. All young people and their parents should therefore be seen as 'active choosers' (Ball et al, 2000), not just those who are 'middle class' or more privileged. They and their parents also appreciate that earlier specialisation for narrow vocations are inappropriate, given the paucity of provision that this chapter reports. This was not appreciated by Education Secretary Nicky Morgan who, following Ofsted Chief Inspector Michael Wilshaw's caution against 'one size fits all' academic learning, criticised state schools for 'outdated snobbery' and promised a new law to ensure that they promote technical education and apprenticeships as real alternatives to university (reported in *The Independent* on 25 January 2016). People like Morgan and Wilshaw, together with the consensus of academic educationists who support them, are good at suggesting options for 'other people's children'. However, with so few alternatives available for young people, it is unsurprising that, despite the fees, most of those who are able try to progress to university, to improve their chances of more reliable employment. Schools can hardly be blamed for encouraging them, despite media pundits in the exemplar of a graduatised profession – journalism – where the fabled progress from tea-boy to editor has long disappeared and a degree qualification is needed even for National Council for the Training of Journalists or BBC apprentice training.

As stated in the introduction, the perception of 'the problem' needs to change. Instead of being one in which young people have to become much better prepared for 'employability' – either by an academic form of general education, or through government-backed, pseudowork placements, bogus apprenticeships and endless internships – it should be one in which an alternative economic framework of job creation allows sustainable employment opportunities to meet real human needs.

References

Ainley, P. (2004) For free universities: Caroline Benn's radical alternative for higher education' in M. Benn and C. Chitty (eds) *A tribute to Caroline Benn, education and democracy*, London Continuum, 2004

Ainley, P. (2008) *'Twenty years of schooling ...' Student reflections on their educational journeys*. London: Society for Research into Higher Education.

Ainley, P. (2013) 'Education and the reconstitution of social class in England', *Research in Post-Compulsory Education*, 18, 1-2: 46-60.

Ainley, P. (2016) *Betraying a generation: How education is failing young people*. Bristol: Policy Press.

Ainley, P. and Allen, M. (2010) *Lost generation? New strategies for youth and education*. London: Continuum.

Allen, M. (2016) *Another Great Training Robbery? Or a real alternative for young people? Apprenticeships at the start of the 21st century*. Rewritten and updated January 2016. Available as a free download from Radicaledbks.

Allen, M. and Ainley, P. (2012) 'Running from the riots – up a down-escalator in the middle of a class structure gone pear-shaped', contribution to *The riots one year on* Conference, 28 September, London: South Bank University.

Ball, S., Maguire, M. and Macrae, S. (2000) *Choices, pathways and transitions post-16*. London: RoutledgeFalmer.

Bourdieu, P. and Passeron, J.-C. (1964) *Les heretiers*. Paris: Editions de Minuit. Trans R. Nice (1972) as *The inheritors, French students and their relation to culture*. Chicago: University of Chicago Press.

Braverman, H. (1974) *Labour and monopoly capital: The degradation of work in the twentieth century*. New York: Monthly Review Press.

Bukodi, E., Goldthorpe, J., Waller, L. and Kuha, J. (2014) 'The mobility problem in Britain: New findings from the analysis of birth cohort data', *British Journal of Sociology*, 66, 1: 93-117.

Campaign for Science and Engineering (2015) http://sciencecampaign.org.uk/

Cheeseman, M. (2011) 'The pleasures of being a student at the University of Sheffield'. Sheffield: University of Sheffield, unpublished PhD thesis.

Clark, T. and Heath, A. (2014) *Hard times: Inequality, recession, aftermath*. London: Yale University Press.

Cohen, P. (1997) *Rethinking the youth question*. Basingstoke: Macmillan.

Conservative Party (2015) 'David Cameron – A Britain that gives every child the best start in life', posted on 2 February , http://press. conservatives.com/post/109906886845/david-cameron-a-britain-that-gives-every-child

Cooley, M. (1987) *Architect or Bee? The human price of technology.* London: Hogarth. (Republished 2016. Nottingham: Spokesman Books.)

Department for Business, Innovation and Skills (2016) *The Higher Education and Research Bill.* London: DBIS.

Finn, D. (1987) *Training without jobs: New deals and broken promises.* London: Macmillan.

Gamble, A. (2009) *The spectre at the reast: Capitalist crisis and the politics of recession.* Basingstoke: Palgrave Macmillan.

Hutchins, M. (2015) *Exam factories?*, London: NUT.

Lave, J. and McDermott, R. (2002) 'Estranged (labor) learning', *Outlines*, 1, 1: 19–48.

Marx, K. (1971) *Capital*, Volume 1. London: Allen and Unwin.

Mills, C. (2013) 'The Great British class fiasco: a comment on Savage et al', *Sociology*, 48, 3: 437–44, http://oxfordsociology.blogspot. co.uk/2013/04/the-great-british-class-fiasco.html

Ofsted (2015) *Apprenticeships: Developing skills for future prosperity.* https://www.gov.uk/government/publications/apprenticeships-developing-skills-for-future-prosperity

O'Leary, S. (2013) 'Dead Student Working', University of Greenwich unpublished undergraduate dissertation.

Palfreyman, D. and Tapper, T. (2014) *Reshaping the university: The rise of the regulated market in higher education.* Oxford: Oxford University Press.

Perlin, R. (2011) *Intern nation, How to earn nothing and learn little in the brave new economy.* London: Verso.

Roberts, K. (2001) *Class in modern Britain.* Basingstoke: Palgrave Macmillan.

Roberts, K. (2015) *Youth in transition, progression or regression.* Glasgow: Paper to annual conference British Sociology Association.

Savage, M. (2015) *Social class in the 21st century.* London: Penguin Random House.

Scott, P. (2015) *What is a university?.* Talk at premier of film 'At Berkeley'. London: Birkbeck College 27 February.

Shildrick, T., MacDonald, R., Webster, C. and Garthwaite, K. (2010) *The low-pay, no-pay cycle: Understanding recurrent poverty.* York: Joseph Rowntree Foundation.

Silva, J. (2015) *Coming up short: Working-class adulthood in an age of uncertainty.* Oxford University Press.

Simmons, R., Thompson, R. and Russell, L. (2014) *Education, work and social change: Young people and marginalization in post-industrial Britain.* Basingstoke: Palgrave Macmillan.

Solomon, C. and Palmieri, T. (eds) (2011) *Springtime: The new student rebellions.* London: Verso.

Susskind, R. and Susskind, D. (2015) *The future of the professions: How technology will transform the work of human experts.* Oxford: Blackwell.

Williamson, H. (1997) 'Status Zer0 youth and the "underclass": some considerations', in R. MacDonald (ed) *Youth, the 'underclass' and social exclusion.* London: Routledge.

ELEVEN

A school for our community: critically assessing discourses of marginality in the establishment of a free school

Claire Tupling

Introduction

Proposed in the 2010 Conservative Party election manifesto, 'free schools' were introduced in England following the 2010 Academies Act. Borrowing from the Swedish *fristående skolor* model (West, 2014), free schools are state-funded schools and independent of local authority control. Outside of local authority provision, free schools lay claim to be community focused. First, they are designed to be responsive to community demands for increased availability of 'good' schools, by providing schools where supply is not currently meeting demand. Second, they may be established by a range of organisations, including charities and businesses, as well as community and faith groups.

As such, free schools are positioned as being part of the 'Big Society' provision of local services (Morris, 2011), whereby the needs of localities are increasingly met through pluralist, community-based provision. Importantly, the potential of free schools to raise levels of educational attainment, particularly in the most deprived neighbourhoods, is celebrated in political discourses (Department for Education, 2013). For these reasons, free schools are positioned at the centre of communities, and local government is repositioned as being outside of the community, unrepresentative of community interests, and as having contributed to the failure of schools to address social inequalities.

Alternative discourses challenge the social justice claims made on behalf of free schools. While Green et al (2015) have observed that free schools are more likely to be located in neighbourhoods experiencing greater levels of deprivation, the pupils admitted to these schools may not be representative of these neighbourhoods. Rather than attracting pupils from the most deprived backgrounds, some researchers have observed that the intakes of free schools are likely to be characterised by segregation, as they are more likely to admit lower proportions of pupils in receipt of free school meals than do other, local authority, schools in their neighbourhoods (Morris, 2014, 2015; Walford, 2014). These findings raise an important question regarding which communities free schools can accurately claim to serve. Additionally, the positioning of free schools outside of local authority control raises questions surrounding who represents the community. As Hatcher (2011) contends, free schools are *less* democratic than local authority schools, despite the claims that free schools enable local communities to have more control of their local school provision. At the heart of these contested claims surrounding free schools is a problematic concept of *community* (Gerrard, 2013).

This chapter will, therefore, problematise the concept of *community* within the discourses of the establishment of one free school in Newtown (a pseudonym given to a real town in the North East of England). Newtown, as will be seen in more detail later, defines itself as a community, within a larger local authority area, from which it feels itself separate. However, the lack of available school places within the local community threatens the very existence of itself as community. Further, Newtown imagines itself as a separate community, and uses key free school application documents to express this.

Anderson (2006) discusses the ways in which language, in the form of print capitalism, lays a foundation for consciousness. The discourses contained in the 'print culture' relating to the establishment of this free school are examined in this chapter. Specifically, these include the approved free school application form and the consultation document, published during the 'pre-opening' phase, a year before the school eventually opened. Following the opening of the school, data relating to pupil premium are explored in consideration of claims that the free school will help to achieve aims of social justice. It is recognised that this represents one set of imaginary discourses, a partial picture of the views on community and schooling, and ones that do not reveal the experiences and views of parents and children who may be impacted by the creation of this new free school. Nevertheless, these discourses represent a powerful capital, constituting an official record of the rationale and the case for the establishment of a free school in Newtown.

Free schools, communities and new landscapes of schooling

The Academies Act 2010 made provisions for 'additional schools', otherwise known as 'free schools' (Academies Act, 2010). This policy initiative was very much borrowed from the Swedish *fristående skolor* model (Miller, 2011; West, 2014) whereby, in the 1990s, the Swedish government introduced a voucher system, enabling parents to choose from a range of schools. As Wiborg (2010) discusses, this led to an increase in independent schools that, while privately run, were publicly funded.

Forming the model for English free schools, the UK Coalition government invited applications from individuals or organisations interested in establishing free schools in England. Since the Academies Act 2010, free school applications have been invited, and approved in a series of 'waves'. As of spring 2016, the most recent applications for free schools have been submitted under 'wave' 10 (Department for Education, 2016b) and there are almost 400 open free schools, with others approved for opening in the forthcoming academic year.

Described by Goodwin (2011, p411) as the 'flagship education policy' of the Coalition government, free schools share a number a features; they are state-funded schools but independent of local authority control. Exempt from the National Curriculum, they may employ non-qualified teachers and are free to set their own pay and conditions. Importantly, in the context of parental choice and diverse provision, they may also set their own admission zones. Free schools may also be seen as 'start-up academies' (Hatcher, 2011, p485), sharing similarities to academies launched under the previous Labour administration, yet distinguishable from them in that they may be set up by parents, community groups, religious organisations or charities. Beyond these common features, free schools may differ in their curricula, the length of the school day and term times.

By introducing new providers into the schooling landscape, the emergence of free schools is arguably indicative of a 'reluctant state' (Ball, 2012) and, according to Lupton (2011), potentially the dismantling of state education. More recently, *Educational excellence everywhere* (Department for Education, 2016a) sets out the UK government's ambition for all schools in England to become academies, meaning that local authorities will no longer maintain schools. Instead, the preferred model is for communities, including parents and pupils, to be empowered in raising standards in education. Promoting an intensification of a market logic, Hatcher (2011) observes that the free school initiative is 'the most overtly market oriented' policy of the Coalition government.

The education marketplace is positioned to address a number of educational challenges. The Coalition government's vision for a reformed education system is outlined in the schools White Paper (Department for Education, 2010) and reinforced in *Educational excellence everywhere* (Department for Education, 2016a). In the light of England's faltering position on the Organisation for Economic Co-operation and Development PISA (Programme for International Student Assessment) rankings, the imperative to reform education in order to ensure that standards are among the best in the world is expressed in these Department for Education documents. As well as needing to keep up with international competitors, concern is also expressed regarding educational inequalities on a domestic level. An achievement gap, between pupils from poorer backgrounds and their more wealthy peers, is a theme referred to throughout the schools White Paper (Department for Education, 2010) and *Educational excellence everywhere* (Department for Education, 2016a). In particular, it is highlighted that such attainment gaps are less stark in other countries.

Free schools are positioned as one vehicle by which education can combat social injustice. Not only is their existence predicted to raise attainment, the schools White Paper envisages that free schools will be located in the most deprived neighbourhoods, addressing the 'significant dissatisfaction with the choices available' (Department for Education, 2010, p52) in these locations. Evidence from Sweden has been drawn upon to make predictions for similar success in England. For example, Bohlmark and Lindahl (2007) conclude that the parental choice associated with the publicly funded private schools in Sweden resulted in increased levels of attainment. Similarly, Sahlgren (2011) claims that voucher reforms have led to increased levels of attainment as well as increased levels of parental satisfaction. The apparent success of the Swedish system is used to support claims that increased competition will lead to an improvement in educational outcomes (Bunar, 2010). Further, in the English context it is predicted that the attainment gap between pupils in receipt of free school meals and their peers will be narrowed (Hatcher, 2011; Miller, 2011). With parental choice being a central feature of contemporary schooling landscapes, it is recognised that 'school choice is a widely endorsed school improvement policy' (Burgess et al, 2015, p1262).

However, free schools extend this principle of parental choice (Avis, 2011), by being demand-led, this being their 'defining characteristic and rationale' (Goodwin, 2011, p412). As will be discussed in subsequent sections, this demand is expressed in Newtown's application for a free school to the Department for Education.

Responsive to local need and demand, the free school initiative relies on a form of 'active citizenship', as evidenced by discourses of empowerment (Wright, 2012) in places such as the schools White Paper. According to these discourses, citizens are empowered to take 'charge of their own communities' (Morris, 2011, p215). This can also be seen as a form of social justice, enabling the mobilisation of 'the resources of concerned parents to support teachers in creating schools with a strong ethos, that work to the benefit of the great majority of those who attend them' (Leeder and Mabbett, 2011, p143). As Leeder and Mabbett (2011, p133) also observe, by empowering parents, free schools have the potential to enhance 'roles of neighbourhoods'. For Newtown, this active citizenship is emphasised. Describing 'its grass roots beginnings', the free school initiative is seized upon as offering a means of highlighting the needs of the neighbourhood, through references to an imagined community, in terms of an additional school for local young people.

The community of Newtown

Anderson's (2006) concept of the imagined community is applied in describing the community of Newtown, in which this free school came to be situated. Drawing on this concept, it is claimed that Newtown as a community is imagined because it has finite boundaries (Anderson, 2006), defined by two neighbouring wards (Newtown North and Newtown South). While these two wards sit within a local authority area of over 25 wards, Newtown nevertheless emerges as a distinct community in its own right. In the free school application document, Newtown is simultaneously referred to as a community as well as a town. This suggests that it is imagined as a physical, as well as a symbolic place. Spatially, there are geographic reference points (ward boundaries) to define the community. The spatial imaginings of Newtown as a community are further reinforced in references to wards beyond Newtown's borders. For example, the application document makes numerous references to the young people who are educated in 'schools within the boundaries of the Borough', while the consultation document emphasises that many of these young people are not educated 'within their community'. Although forming part of the same local authority area, often neighbouring wards, these places are positioned as separate communities to which the residents of Newtown do not belong. It is this separateness that underpins the justification for a free school.

To borrow another characteristic of imagined communities, within the discourses examined 'lives the image of ... communion' (Anderson, 2006, p6) between the residents, revealing Newtown to be, symbolically, an imagined community. This can be seen in the application document, which refers to Newtown as 'a popular area, particularly for people with young families'. Furthermore, the lack of social problems is highlighted, as 'it has good primary schools' as well as 'a low crime rate'. Diversity within Newtown is recognised, as the occupations of residents range from 'tradesmen ... to professionals and premiership footballers', but this is used to emphasise the broad appeal of Newtown as a 'popular place to live', rather than to highlight any social inequalities. Nevertheless, the application document does acknowledge that a 'sense of community' is lacking in Newtown, however this is expressed, with a desire to engender such communion via the creation of a new school. Drawing on Anderson's (2006) discussion on imagined communities, it is evident that any notion that Newtown may be characterised by inequality is ignored; instead, the common interests of the community in benefiting from a new free school are emphasised.

Newtown is relatively affluent, both locally and nationally. However, the free school application describes the young people living in the community as marginalised. According to the 2015 Index of Multiple Deprivation, Newtown North and Newtown South are the least deprived wards in the local authority area, as well as being among the 25% least deprived wards in England. One of the wards is among the 10% least deprived wards in England (Department for Communities and Local Government, 2015). This position is based on the Index of Multiple Deprivation (IMD) rank, meaning that the two wards may experience greater levels of deprivation on some domains than some other wards in the local authority area. However, overall, these two wards are the least deprived wards in the local authority.

Not only is the *community* ranked as experiencing less multiple deprivation than other wards in the local authority, but the two wards also occupy starkly opposite positions in that ranking to many of the other wards in the local authority. Briefly, the deprivation experienced by residents in half the wards in the local authority is among the worst in the country, as those wards fall within the 25% most deprived wards in England. Further, half of these wards experience levels of multiple deprivation that result in them being ranked among the 10% most deprived wards in England. For example,

Newtown North and Newtown South are poles apart from other wards in the local authority. Newtown is not, however, a 'pocket of affluence' in an otherwise deprived local authority. For example, the wards immediately neighbouring Newtown also have low levels of deprivation, and contain two schools that the Newtown young people might otherwise attend.

Marginality, certainly in terms of multiple deprivation, would not be immediately associated with this community. It is, after all, a community made up of residents who, on average and in comparison with residents in other parts of the local authority, have higher levels of income and less overall deprivation, and it is ranked alongside the least deprived wards in England. Despite these key features, the discourse of marginality was a central feature of the free school application document. Specifically, the lack of sufficient secondary school places for the young people of Newtown was posited as providing material and symbolic evidence of this marginalisation.

A free school for our community

The neighbourhood is recognised as being centrally important in the landscape of schooling (Reay et al, 2013). Burgess et al (2015, p1263) observe a 'strong preference for proximity' when it comes to parents' preferred choice of school. But this preference for proximity is also part of class-based strategies in relation to school choice. As Bacqué et al comment, 'neighbourhood is a key ingredient in the schooling strategies of the middle classes for their children' (Bacqué et al, 2015, p135).

For Newtown, the geographic boundaries that frame the community are a key ingredient underpinning the demand for a free school. In the approved free school application document, Newtown is referred to as a 'town' as defined by the wards of Newtown North and Newtown South. The identified admission zone is bounded by these wards. That Newtown is also referred to in the application document as a community is an example of how it is imagined and, simultaneously, reflects a perceived lack of community. For example, in outlining the educational vision for the Newtown free school, it is recognised that the town 'lacks a cohesive community'. The idea of community is, however, a recurring theme in the approved free school application document. An imaginary of a community is being pursued through the establishment of this free school. Importantly, it is the lack of sufficient secondary school places that contributes to this lack of community and, as such, the Newtown free school is positioned to address this and to 'engender community cohesion'. The Newtown free school will address the marginalisation that the application document claims the young people in the town experience.

According to the approved free school application form, in Newtown there is 'an unprecedented parental demand for additional secondary school places within the community'. This is a claim that the existing schooling provision is insufficient, and can only be addressed by creating more places, via a free school within the community, as defined by the geographic boundaries of Newtown. In the approved free school application document, it is observed that there are approximately 1,500 secondary-age pupils living in Newtown (this figure rose to 1,600, when consultation opened the year following the submission of the application). These pupils can be considered to be in the admission zone of three nearby secondary schools. One of these schools is located in Newtown, while the other two are located in neighbouring wards, outside Newtown but within the local authority area.

The first of these schools is a secondary school located in Newtown. According to school performance tables it can be considered one of the top-performing schools in the local authority area. However, its capacity at around 600 pupils limits the number of Newtown children who 'can be educated within their community'. The number of school places available at this school is presented as evidence of the underresourcing of the community. Expanding the number of places at this school is not considered to be a viable solution to the lack of school places in Newtown, because it is a faith school. This designation is drawn on to emphasise how this results in 'marginalising some children and limiting parental choice ... due to their religious beliefs', as highlighted in the free school application document. Therefore, the current secondary school provision marginalises the young people of Newtown, not only because of insufficient places, but also because of the existing school's faith designation.

As a consequence, the majority of Newtown's secondary school-age pupils attend schools outside the community, although no exact figures are quoted in the application or consultation documents. These documents do suggest, however, that Newtown's remaining secondary-age pupils attend one of two secondary schools in neighbouring wards. However, as has been discussed, the wards are considered to be outside the community. The free school application document draws on this situation, in claiming that 'the majority of our young people continue their statutory education outside of the town', to emphasise the marginalisation of the young people of Newtown.

The two schools situated outside the community, but forming the catchment area for the secondary pupils within Newtown, are located in wards that (according to their 2015 IMD ranking) experience higher levels of multiple deprivation than the Newtown wards. Nevertheless, these wards are also among the least deprived wards in the local authority and are among the 25% of least deprived wards in England (Department for Communities and Local Government, 2015). The two schools are also among the top-performing schools in the local authority area, with higher than average proportions of pupils achieving five or more A★-C grades, including English and Maths, at GCSE. By objective measures of school performance, the admission zone in which Newtown is located is served by 'good' schools. It cannot be claimed that these schools are associated with 'middle-class imaginaries of demonisation' (Reay, 2007, p1192). Yet, the marginalisation of the young people of Newtown is a recurring theme in the approved free school application document. For example, in claiming that the existing schooling arrangement 'instils a sense of division in our young people', a concern with a geography of schooling is revealed. This can only be addressed by the provision of another school within the boundaries of Newtown. The community identity of Newtown is posited as being dependent on this.

For example, one recurring theme of the ways in which the young people of Newtown are claimed to experience marginalisation is that, as a consequence of having to travel outside the community to attend school, extracurricular opportunities are limited. Moreover, it is claimed that the young people of Newtown are 'deprived of extracurricular' activities as a result of the location of their secondary school. This deprivation is exacerbated by 'a lack of suitable transport' after the end of the school day. Transport is also highlighted as problematic to facilitating the standard school day. While it is acknowledged that the two schools outside the community may be proximate to Newtown, the consultation document highlights the lack of 'safe walking route from either school back to [Newtown]'. As such, the proximity of Newtown to the two schools in neighbouring wards is not reflected in bus journey times. To emphasise the marginalisation that results from bussing, the consultation document highlights how pupils attending schools outside Newtown may experience an additional hour in travel time at both the start and the end of the school day. It is claimed that a free school in Newtown would remove the need for pupils to be bussed out of the community. In contrast, the application document claims that the free school will be located on a 'carefully chosen site that is accessible to all residents'. In further support of the claim that travelling out of the community is damaging to Newtown, the application document emphasises that a free school is the 'environmentally friendly option' as a result of the reduced need for bussing.

The geography of the new free school is further emphasised in discussions regarding an 'inner admission zone' in relation to transport. The inner admission zone is that area of Newtown that is closest to the free school. Pupils living in this zone will be allocated a place at the school, having priority over pupils living in the 'outer admission zone' in the rest of Newtown, who will be subject to random allocation of places. This move will give 'all schoolchildren greater opportunity to walk and cycle to school', supported by Newtown's 'excellent network of footpaths and cycle paths' – further emphasising that the Newtown free school is a school *in* the community and *for* the community.

Further isolation of young people occurs, according to the approved free school application document, because of a lack of existing resources in Newtown, again directly associated with the lack of school places. This discourse supports a strong imaginary in the approved free school application document that a new school will have the ability to 'foster a further sense of community' within Newtown. That there is no strong sense of community in Newtown is directly attributed to the lack of school places. The free school, it is claimed, would further contribute to the development of a community, by 'becoming a hub for community activity'.

An additional feature in Newtown could be what Wilkins (2010) describes as a 'seduction of community', a belief that a new school will help to bring about a cohesive community in Newtown. Reay et al argue:

> In the twenty-first century we still have powerful imagined communities, but there is scant empirical evidence that communities, rooted in the local and with the power to reach across class and ethnic boundaries actually exist. People may share neighbourhoods as a living space but this not does mean they will interact together as a community. (Reay et al, 2013, p57)

A free school in our community

Newtown Free School opened in September 2014. Located in temporary premises, the school is still in development, with imaginations of what the school will look like and how it will serve the community.

The school currently consists of three year group; Years 7, 8 and 9 with a sixth form intake anticipated in September 2019.

As it is a new school, limited data are available; certainly there are no data in terms of performance. For 2014/15, the year in which the school opened, the school reported that just over 35% of its pupils (Year 7 only) were eligible for pupil premium funding. This was approximately four times the rate of that for the existing secondary school in Newtown, and approximately three times higher than the rate for the two secondary schools in the neighbouring wards. By 2015-16 the proportion of pupils (Years 7 and 8) eligible for Pupil Premium funding in Newtown Free School had fallen to just over 21%; again, a higher rate than the other schools that Newtown pupils are likely to attend. On this evidence alone it could be claimed that Newtown Free School, rather than admitting fewer pupils from deprived backgrounds, is admitting higher proportions of pupils from deprived backgrounds and is therefore addressing educational inequalities. However, given that there are currently only two year groups in the school, caution needs to be exercised here, before making any conclusions in this regard.

While the new school adds 'choice' in the educational marketplace, it remains that there are still an insufficient number of school places to accommodate all the secondary-age pupils in Newtown, who potentially continue to be marginalised through the lack of available school places. Further, it is not possible to map the residency of the pupils attending Newtown Free School, meaning that it cannot be ascertained with any certainty that the pupils attending this school are resident in the community it is intended to serve.

However, for the first year in which Newtown Free School was in operation (2014-15) an analysis of preference allocations revealed that of the 70-plus pupils admitted in this first year, over 20 places were allocated to pupils resident outside Newtown (WhatdotheyKnow, 2014). This means that, approximately, one quarter of the pupils came from outside the community, as defined in the discourses examined here. Given that geographic marginalisation and separateness from the rest of the local authority area were cited as justifications for a new school, this figure raises interesting questions about which community – or communities – this school serves. As Newtown Free School approaches full capacity, further, more detailed, examination of school preference allocation data may prove useful in addressing the extent to which free schools may be associated with continued marginalisation and segregated intakes (Green et al, 2015).

Conclusion

This chapter has sought to examine discourses of marginality in the establishment of a free school in the North East of England. An analysis of the discourses, specifically, the approved free school application document and the consultation booklet, is drawn upon, as a means of highlighting current marginalisation and thus a need for a free school. These documents highlight that the young people of Newtown are marginalised as a result of a limited number of secondary school places within what is deemed to be the local community. The fact that most young people have to travel to neighbouring wards to attend secondary school is further drawn on, in highlighting the marginalisation of these young people. Of particular note in this regard is the lack of opportunities to take part in school–based extracurricular activities.

As a result, these documents highlight the potential role of a new free school in helping to create a sense of community. Having received approval, Newtown Free School is operational within the boundaries of the community. However, what remains unclear is the extent to which Newtown Free School is a school serving the young people who reside in the community of Newtown. Early data reveal that pupils from outside this area made up one quarter of the first year's Year 7 intake. As Newtown Free School approaches full capacity, further examination of data is needed, to explore the extent to which the marginalisation of young people in Newtown is addressed via this free school.

References

Academies Act (c.32) (2010) London: The Stationery Office.

Anderson, B. (2006) *Imagined communities: Reflections on the origin and spread of nationalism*. London: Verso Books.

Avis, J. (2011) 'More of the same? New Labour, the Coalition and education: Markets, localism and social justice', *Educational Review*, Routledge, 63, 4: 421–38.

Bacqué, M.-H., Bridge, G., Benson, M., Butler, T., Charmes, E., Fijalkow, Y., Jackson, E., Launay, L. and Vermeersch, S. (2015) *The middle classes and the city: A Study of Paris and London*, London: Palgrave Macmillan.

Ball, S. J. (2012) 'The reluctant state and the beginning of the end of state education', *Journal of Educational Administration and History*, 44, 2: 89–103.

Bohlmark, A. and Lindahl, M. (2007) *The impact of school choice on pupil achievement, segregation and costs: Swedish evidence.* IZA Discussion Papers. http://papers.ssrn.com/abstract=987491

Bunar, N. (2010) 'Choosing for quality or inequality: Current perspectives on the implementation of school choice policy in Sweden', *Journal of Education Policy*, 25, 1: 1-18.

Burgess, S., Greaves, E., Vignoles, A. and Wilson, D. (2015) 'What parents want: school preferences and school choice', *The Economic Journal*, 125, 587: 1262-89.

Department for Communities and Local Government (2015) English indices of deprivation 2015. https://www.gov.uk/government/statistics/english-indices-of-deprivation-2015

Department for Education (2010) *The importance of teaching,* Cm 7980. London: The Stationery Office.

Department for Education (2013) *Increasing the number of academies and free schools to create a better and more diverse school system.* https://www.gov.uk/government/policies/increasing-the-number-of-academies-and-free-schools-to-create-a-better-and-more-diverse-school-system

Department for Education (2016a) *Educational excellence everywhere*, Cm 9230. London: The Stationery Office.

Department for Education (2016b) 'Free school applications'. https://www.gov.uk/government/collections/free-school-applications

Gerrard, J. (2013) 'Counter-narratives of educational excellence: free schools, success, and community-based schooling', *British Journal of Sociology of Education*, 35, 6: 876-94.

Goodwin, M. (2011) 'English education policy after New Labour: Big Society or back to basics?', *The Political Quarterly*, 82, 3: 407-24.

Green, F., Allen, R. and Jenkins, A. (2015) 'Are English free schools socially selective? A quantitative analysis', *British Educational Research Journal*, 41, 6: 907-24.

Hatcher, R. (2011) 'The Conservative–Liberal Democrat Coalition government's 'free schools' in England', *Educational Review*, 63, 4: 485-503.

Leeder, A. and Mabbett, D. (2011) 'Free schools: Big Society or small interests?', *The Political Quarterly*, 82, 133-44.

Lupton, R. (2011) '"No change there then!" (?): the onward march of school markets and competition', *Journal of Educational Administration and History*, 43, 3: 309–23.

Miller, P. (2011) 'Free choice, free schools and the academisation of education in England', *Research in Comparative and International Education*, 6, 2: 170.

Morris, D. (2011) 'Building a big society: will charity's creeping reach generate a new paradigm for state schools?', *Journal of Social Welfare and Family Law*, 33, 3: 209-26.

Morris, R. (2014) 'The admissions criteria of secondary Free Schools', *Oxford Review of Education*, 40, 3: 389-409.

Morris, R. (2015) 'Free Schools and disadvantaged intakes', *British Educational Research Journal*, 41, 4: 535-52.

Reay, D. (2007) '"Unruly places": Inner-city comprehensives, middle-class imaginaries and working-class children', *Urban Studies*, 44, 7: 1191-1201.

Reay, D., Crozier, G. and James, D. (2013) *White middle-class indentities and urban schooling*. Basingstoke: Palgrave Macmillan.

Sahlgren, G. H. (2011) 'Schooling for money: Swedish education reform and the role of the profit motive', *Economic Affairs*, 31, 3: 28-35.

Walford, G. (2014) 'Academies, free schools and social justice', *Research Papers in Education*, 29, 3: 263-7.

West, A. (2014) 'Academies in England and independent schools (fristående skolor) in Sweden: policy, privatisation, access and segregation', *Research Papers in Education*, 29, 3: 330-50.

WhatdotheyKnow (2014) '[School Name withheld] a Freedom of Information request [Name witheld] Council'. https://www.whatdotheyknow.com/request/[School Name Withheld]

Wiborg, S. (2010) 'Learning lessons from the Swedish model', *FORUM*, 52, 3: 279-84.

Wilkins, A. (2010) 'Community and school choice: geographies of care and responsibility', *Journal of Community & Applied Social Psychology*, 21, 1: 1-13.

Wright, A. (2012) 'Fantasies of empowerment: mapping neoliberal discourse in the coalition government's schools policy', *Journal of Education Policy*, 27, 3: 279-94.

TWELVE

The marginalisation of care: young care leavers' experiences of professional relationships

Emma Davidson and Lisa Whittaker

Introduction

In 2003/04, in the UK, there were more people in poverty aged over 65 than aged 16–25. The opposite is now true (MacInnes et al, 2015). Young people, as the other chapters in this collection reveal, are becoming the 'new poor' as they struggle to cope with increasingly precarious transitions into in(ter)dependent living. This chapter focuses on marginality within a specific group of young people: care leavers. This is a group internationally recognised as being among the most disadvantaged and excluded in society (Stein and Munro, 2008; Fernandez, 2010; Mendes, 2012; Van Breda, 2015) and therefore the most vulnerable to service cuts associated with austerity in the UK.

Through retrospective biographical interviews with 15 care-experienced young adults and discussions with current practitioners, the authors explored the ways in which professional relationships in care can shape someone's identity and imagined futures. This chapter focuses specifically on the authors' interview data with young adults, giving prominence to their voices and experiences. The narratives collated emphasise the importance of long-term, personal relationships while in care – and their absence. Structural, organisational and attitudinal barriers contributed to a relational 'golden thread' (The Care Inquiry, 2013) being marginalised in corporate parenting, and challenging to maintain. Legislation is changing in recognition of the incompatibility of institutional relationships with young people's own need for support. These are positive changes, but ones which, in the economic context of austerity, may be limited in their capacity to shift the powerfully embedded inequalities faced by care leavers.

Marginalised relationships in care

There is a wealth of research and practitioner-based evidence on the importance of developing and maintaining positive relationships for, and with, young people in care (Ruch, 2005; Happer et al, 2006; Stein and Munro, 2008; Winter, 2009; Munro, 2011; Ryan, 2012). This body of work has repeatedly emphasised that positive, sustained relationships *in* care are vital if care leavers are to experience trusting relationships in adulthood. These relationships are often central to enabling young people to manage and overcome earlier traumatic experiences, while at the same time contributing to a sense of belonging and connectedness (Ward, 2011; Wilson and Milne, 2013). The absence of nurturing professional relationships has also been discussed as a contributing factor in care leaver outcomes (Stein, 2006; Rogers, 2011; National Audit Office, 2015; Scottish Government, 2016).

The comprehensive body of evidence on outcomes demonstrates that, in spite of recent improvements, care leavers are far more likely to have poorer outcomes when compared to peers who have not grown up in care: in education, employment, physical and mental health, housing and social relationships. At the same time, public sector budget cuts are continuing to place pressure on both care providers and vulnerable families, prompting concerns over local authorities' ability to safeguard young people in care (The Care Inquiry, 2013; Community Care, 2014; National Bureau for Children, 2015; Hastings et al, 2015).

Both legislation and policy are responding under the weight of this evidence. *Staying Put Scotland* (Scottish Government, 2013) emphasised the need for consistent positive relationships, which transcend both settings and roles. The Children and Young People Act (Scotland) 2014 has begun to take forward these commitments, by extending the right to continuing care to the age of 21 and the provision of advice, guidance and assistance to care leavers up to the age of 26. In England and Wales, local authorities have a statutory duty to 'monitor and support' staying put arrangements, enabling a young person to stay in their foster placement until they are 21, although the same options are not available to those in residential placements.

While legislating extensions to care is critical, it has been suggested that nurturing relationships in corporate care remain marginalised by an approach focused on outcomes, standards and regulation (Coady, 2014). This includes a creeping culture of managerialism that has required social workers to adopt more instrumental, bureaucratic and procedural approaches to their work (Gilligan, 2004; Meagher and Parton, 2004; Broadhurst et al, 2010a; Broadhurst et al, 2010b). Social work services are becoming increasingly risk averse, with the workforce's own vulnerability to allegations being cited as a reason for relational practices not being prioritised (Horwath, 2000; Cree and Wallace, 2009). Challenges remain, including: time constraints on staff; the movement of young people between multiple placements; a cultural focus on independence; and the inflexibility of professional relationships to move across organisational boundaries. These challenges discourage nurturing relationships from developing.

Defining a nurturing relationship

Relationship matter in care – but how are such relationships formed, and what qualities do they comprise? Research on relationships has looked at the family as the normative environment for nurturing young people. Family relations can provide the biographical origins of self (Mead, 1934; Erikson, 1951; Berger and Luckmann, 1967; Widmer and Jallinoja, 2008; McCarthy, 2012), and despite being renegotiated as young people grow up, for most they continue to be a condition of a secure sense of self and a scaffold for understandings of loyalty, fairness and responsibility.

The home itself performs an ontological function, providing not only a place in which relationships and daily routines can be performed, but also a space in which a rooted sense of identity, belonging and stability can be developed (Cooper Marcus, 1995; Silva, 2007; Samuels, 2009). The nurtured young person moves from complete parental dependence, to being part of a network of interdependent relationships encompassing siblings, peers and other significant adults, with emotional bonds, love, warmth, stability and protection from harm all judged as key to facilitating positive outcomes (Lemay and Ghazal, 2007).

Relationships that matter do not necessarily map onto 'the family', with other significant relationships also capable of enabling a sense of belonging (Jamieson et al, 2006; Widmer and Jallinoja, 2008; Gabb, 2011). Close and special relationships are sustained by practices of intimacy (Jamieson, 2011), which can include giving and sharing, spending time with, knowing, practically caring for, feeling attachment and expressing affection. Intimate relationships also, like parent and youth relations, 'embody a temporal perspective, including a history and an imagined future' (Reis and Shaver, 1988, p383). They are built around an accumulation of past experiences – good and bad – and the anticipation of future events, where time together provokes qualities such as security, trust, mutual respect and dependability.

Brownlie's (2011, 2014) research on 'being there' also highlights the significance of time and temporality in relational practices. 'Being there' can literally mean having a physical presence and can represent a more symbolic 'reachability' or the potential for an emotional connection. 'Being there' is thus about the mundane, everyday practice of relationships; built and sustained over time. Research with young people who are in care or who have experienced care shows that they desire intimacy, emotion and, critically, continuity from their corporate parents. Young people value workers who are honest, respectful and committed to supporting them 'through the best and worst of times' (Winter, 2011, p5). They value having an authentic caring relationship (McLeod, 2010), which is sustained and consistent over time (Schofield and Stevenson, 2009). In Bickel's (2015) research, young people voiced the desire for an adult figure whom they could trust to care for them 'genuinely' and who could help them to prepare emotionally for the transition out of care.

Research methods

The interview sample for this study consists of 15 young adults with experience of the Scottish care system. These experiences were diverse in terms of the duration of time spent in care, and the type of care received (residential care settings, foster care or a combination of both). The authors were interested in understanding the ways in which corporate care can affect a young person's transition into adulthood and, in turn, how it might shape an individual's prospective sense of who they are. The interviews were biographical, and provided participants with the opportunity to tell their story. The point of enquiry focused on how support – both informal and formal – featured in these storied accounts of state care and the ways it mediated their 'future selves'. Temporality was thus a central component, both conceptually and methodologically. The approach was aware of time, and its passing, as being a subjective experience, where pace changes for different events and experiences, and memories are shaped by hindsight and a retrospective (re)evaluation of future prospects (Conrad, 2011).

The research setting was Scotland, with all participants being recruited through a charity that works with young people in, and leaving, care. Using a combination of residential and community-based support, the aim of the organisation is to enable young people to overcome social challenges, to make positive choices and to 'realise their potential'.

All participants had taken part in one of the organisation's residential programmes (not together) in 2006, 2007 or 2008 as teenagers. This purposive sampling approach meant that participants were in their early 20s when they were interviewed in 2013 and, officially at least, had already completed their transition into adulthood. Moreover, participants would come from the same historical cohort and have a similar social and economic context underpinning their narratives. A further benefit of selecting participants involved with the same third sector intervention was that it provided a point of comparison across the cohort between statutory and third sector approaches to support.

The authors initially approached their data through multiple readings of the transcripts, followed by a process of open coding. What was most striking across all the narratives was the distinction that participants drew between caring for, and caring about. Thus, while practical acts of care were important, it was their relational and emotional content that was most valued. To explore this, additional focused coding centred on exploring the implicit content and form of the care practices described by participants.

Care in an institutional setting

Previous research has shown that the significant relationships of young people in care are shaped by the organisational structures that create them, and are therefore framed differently from familial relationships (Winter, 2009). The data from this study confirmed this. The most revealing expression of this finding was in young adults' use of institutional language to describe their experiences of care. Participants frequently used vocabulary not typically present in narratives of everyday life (Miller et al, 1990), referring for instance to 'life skills', 'identity work', 'risk assessments' and techniques of restraint. Meanwhile, examples of care often related to the bureaucratic and organisational aspects of corporate parenting, such as supervision meetings, behavioural contracts, structured routines and the function of professional roles (the social worker, 'the unit chef').

These narratives revealed an 'institutional othering' of corporate parents. Alison's account illustrates this phenomenon, although to some extent it was present in all our transcripts. Alison was 25 at the point of interview and had been in and out of foster care, secure care and children's homes. As a child she had experienced abuse, which she was still trying to come to terms with as an adult. In Alison's account of her journey through care, she rarely gave names to the adults who were designated with her care. Rather, the institution of care was positioned as an 'other', responsible for doing things to, not for, her:

'They put me in secure [accommodation] for my own safety. That's what they say but I don't know.

[I remember being restrained] and that just makes you worse. Somebody restraining you and then they take all your stuff out of your room and lock you in your, room, cell thing.

[at 16] they put me in a hostel. They just dumped me.' (Alison)

Part of the relational distancing articulated by Alison was a consequence of the absence of continuity in her care, causing her to note: "it was different staff every day". This issue was familiar across the sample, but more pressing for those accommodated in residential units, where continuity related to both the stability of staff within units, and the number of placements that young people were allocated to. Stephen considered his move to foster care "lucky", describing his own experience of a children's home as the unhappiest he had ever been:

'I was put in a home and that was just a mental place. I can see the point why it exists, but it's just like a horrible place [...] I was living with 6, 7, 8 children at the same time. It was a battle. I can understand because I've been there, you just don't care. At that point, life is nothing, as a child. You've got nothing, you've got no parents or lack of them. You don't have that loving affection that most children do.' (Stephen)

Stephen's account implied that foster care is better placed to deliver care more akin to familial relations. This was articulated not as a need for practical help, but for love and affection from those caring about him. Yet the distinction between foster placements and residential units was not always clear. Foster care placements can be large. Stephen's foster placement, for example, included six other young people. The difference, he suggested, was that his foster parents "made him happy". Now, as an adult, they could be relied on to help him: he had recently returned home after a failed attempt to move to a large city. This supportive relationship was as much symbolic as it was material; simply knowing that he could 'fall back' on his foster parents was enough to provide him with order, continuity and ontological security (Giddens, 1991).

Another participant, Michael, lived in one foster placement from the age of 10. Like Stephen, it was a large household, but it differed in that multiple children "came and went" around him. At the age of 17 he moved out. He returned to visit his foster parents shortly after leaving, to find that they had moved house. He never saw them again:

> Michael: 'When I turned 15 or 16, I had to basically do my own stuff, like washing and cooking sometimes. Things like that. They made me, got me ready for the big bad world, basically.

> Interviewer: 'Were you living with ... were there other young people in the family?'

> Michael: 'There were, but they came and went. I was like 10 when I went there and they'd just moved to [area] too. I was there until I was basically 17. I think I was the longest kid they had there [...] They moved somewhere there or something after I left. That was the last time I saw them. I've not seen them since.'

The value of Michael's foster parents was that they provided practical skills for independence. Yet like Alison, Michael had no emotional or intimate connection to his corporate parents. Nor was there any continued relationship in adulthood. Michael left care and returned to the city where he was born: he stated that this was his return "home". He had found little stability, having moving almost 20 times, and had been unemployed for several years. However, he had developed, in his words, a "wee support network" of close friends. This friendship network was sustained not only by the practical help they gave each other (for example, borrowing money or providing a sofa to sleep on) and from their shared time socialising, but also by their knowledge that they had shared life experiences:

> 'The last couple of years, it's been more emotional between us, especially with his family background and that. He talks to me about all his problems and that, I'm happy to do that. We get drunk, get a case of beer and then he just talks about his problems. Sometimes I talk about mine, sometimes I don't. That's it.' (Michael)

A consistent theme was that the most important component of a relationship was an emotional or intimate connection. While receiving practical support was necessary, such acts carried far greater weight when they were associated with forms of care that were less explicit and were connected to trust, empathy and respect.

The importance of being there

There is a strong connectivity to how care-experienced young people define significant professional relationships as 'being there' (Brownlie, 2014). Three examples are discussed here: Billy, Summer and Kyubbi.

Billy talked about 'Jan', the manager of the residential unit who he said just 'got' what it meant for young people to be in care. Jan had worked with Billy over a long period, and had given him responsibility, respected his views and, crucially, had listened and acted on them.

> 'She came in and said, "Look, there's a new guy [staff member] coming. You've been here one of the longest, is it alright if we [make] him your key worker and you can show him the ropes?" She used to sit in the living room with us and we'd have meetings and that. She would openly turn around and say, "Is there any staff members you've got a problem with? Have any of them said anything?" It would be an open discussion.' (Billy)

Similarly, Summer described a significant relationship that, over time, she developed with keyworker 'Debbie'. Debbie was one of the few professionals whose advice and support Summer was willing (at this point in her life) to take. A large part of this related to the investment that Debbie gave to forming and sustaining a trusting relationship:

> 'She'd built up a working relationship with me. I trusted her, you know what I mean? She'd been there for me, consistently so it wasn't like, some of the workers that have come and gone or they were locums, so they were between different units. Or you'd see them once and then you wouldn't see them for another six months. She was there all the time.' (Summer)

Kyubbi had 18 different placements during her time in care, excluding the temporary ones. The majority of her time is care was, in her words, "hellish". However, in one of her many placements she developed a strong connection to her keyworker, and the unit overall. Her keyworker successfully managed to reignite Kyubbi's love of animals, and was the first to address her anger towards the care system:

'The care's different [in this unit]. They care. That was it. It was simple. They actually cared about ... like when they said to you, how are you feeling? They were actually genuinely concerned about how you were feeling.' (Kyubbi)

The research found that positive professional relationships had core characteristics:

- that young people in care felt they were being listened to;
- that they were trusted;
- that the relationships were formed not through a pre-existing script, but rather through a genuine desire to care for the young people.

Underpinning all this was that these relationships were the product of time, evolving organically through the accumulation of experiences; through sharing everyday activities like shopping or cooking; chatting and laughing together; and mutual experiences (for example, weekend trips or shared activities such as caring for an animal).

Where these relationships failed was in ensuring that their significance was recognised and invested in. As a result, positive relationships ended abruptly when young people moved into new placements or into supported accommodation, or when staff moved to a new position. The formation of more emotional or intimate bonds were also restricted by perceived bureaucratic procedures and risk assessment protocols, with relationships in two cases being forced to end as a result of them being judged 'inappropriate' by senior workers. In Summer's case, the difficulty came with trying to define, and control, what type of relationship a corporate parent should have. For her, the relationship ending made little sense, since it was as meaningful as any she had yet to experience:

'They tried to discourage it [maintaining contact after Debbie moved post] because I was a young person and she was a professional. It wasn't an "appropriate relationship" they said. I was like, "Well, hold on a minute, it's not like ... it's somebody that's been a significant part of my life. That's done quite a lot of intensive work with me. How can you say that's not a proper relationship?' (Summer)

In such endings, young people rarely had any involvement in decision making, which led to feelings of confusion and resentment towards the care system and professionals providing ongoing care. Emotional trauma was a commonly mentioned consequence of a relationship ending. For some, this continued into their adult life and future relationships.

Marginalised identities

The beginning of this chapter discussed the focus given to the outcomes of care leavers. Such indicators are critical, since they demonstrate the structural marginalisation that young people can face after leaving care, and are a means for measuring the extent to which this is changing over time. This research revealed that outcome measures were closely associated with participants' own care identities and their relationships in adulthood. Care-experienced adults were aware of their unequal life chances, with two specifically highlighting national care leaver statistics to illustrate their own employment situations. However, it was not simply that young adults were aware of care leavers' (and therefore their own) economic and social marginalisation, but also that these outcomes formed part of a deeper rhetoric about how being care experienced was perceived. This, in turn, shaped how care-experienced adults saw themselves, and how they related to others:

> 'I think you know. You feel it your whole life. You are always separated from your peers [...]. Regardless of your background or how much you try and put in, you're always going to be stigmatised.' (Vanessa)

This notion of the care identity being 'felt' was expressed by several other participants, with it being a recognisable source of stigma and embodied source of self-recognition. Some participants went as far as to actively conceal their care experience in their adult relationships, due to embarrassment about their past or fear of being labelled a troublemaker:

> 'I've always felt ashamed of my past growing up. Like, I always felt ashamed to say that I was in care.' (Susan)

Others translated care leaver marginalisation as something they needed to challenge as an adult. Participants spoke, for example, about the need to "prove them wrong" or the need to "do it for myself". For Grant, he needed to "work hard":

> 'When I left care I was very clear that there was two roads that I could have went down. I could have went down the road that people expect you to go down or I can work hard not to go down that road.' (Grant)

What is notable in these data is the notion of individualism, where the care leaver is depicted as someone who needs to fight against the system in order to succeed. Comments such as "it is down to me" or "I can only rely on myself" were commonly used by young adults to describe expectations for their 'future self'. Many were, at the point of interview, dealing with loneliness, social isolation, mental health issues and limited supportive social networks. This finding directly links to The Care Inquiry (2013, pp8-9), which found that past relationships affected care leavers' confidence in forming and sustaining relationships in adulthood. While it is not possible to assume a causal link, it is reasonable to suggest that these narratives are associated with the focus given to preparing care leavers for *independent* living. While practical skills are clearly important, a gap remains in enabling interdependence, which emphasises relationships, emotions, intimacy, making positive connections and fitting in with one's social context.

Prioritising relationships in austerity

Young people in, and leaving, care are the most vulnerable in society, marginalised within many domains of society. Data for England show that the number of looked-after children is now higher than at any point since 1985 (Stevenson, 2015), a trend worryingly linked to austerity.

This chapter has focused broadly on the marginalisation of relational practices in corporate parenting. The young care leavers interviewed consistently reported the absence of someone who was there for them. 'Being there' was not just a physical presence, but rather a relationship formed through common activities, events, practices and, importantly, over time. Consistency in support was critical, yet concerns about professional boundaries were described as preventing ongoing nurturing relationships. Emotional distance was a consequence of supportive relationships not being appropriate to the caring role, or unable to continue across transition points. This resulted in valued and trusting relationships ending in a way that was unnatural to young people. Many spoke about leaving care with a lack of trust and feelings of anger, rage or frustration, while others struggled to maintain positive relationships outside the care system.

Several leading charities are campaigning for increased support for young people leaving care in the UK. The NSPCC found that the emotional health of looked-after young people was often regarded as the responsibility of specialist mental health services; it calls for a relational approach which gives young people voice and supports their social and emotional needs (Bazalgette et al, 2015). Barnardo's research sets out the financial cost of supported and unsupported journeys through care, emphasising the substantial consequences that continued support has on a young person's emotional wellbeing, and resultant savings to the public purse (Brady, 2014).

The inequalities faced by young people, both in and leaving care, are complex and varied. Austerity measures add to this complexity by placing further pressure on budgets and the capacity of practitioners. The consequence is that relational practices are marginalised when young people with experiences of the care system need them most.

Conclusion

This research demonstrates that there is a place for emotion, love and permanence in corporate parenting. Young people know the difference in significant others who care 'for' them versus caring 'about' them. Past experiences in care leave a mark on present and imagined futures. There is a need to support relational practices within the care system: to raise expectations, change cultures and prioritise resources (Duncalf, 2013, p 6). It is important not to define young people based on their experience of care. However, growing up in care has a major influence on young people's lives, including the relationships they form and the support they access.

Policy makers and those working in the care system have a huge responsibility to young people. The challenge now moves to putting the new commitments to care leavers into practice. That is not always easy, especially during times of austerity and funding cuts. Relationships – loving ones – are key to a successful care experience, which poses challenges for services and the workers. Young people want positive relationships with the workers and carers in their lives that are genuine and not time limited. There is no quick fix. The care system requires long-term investment – social, emotional and financial – if it is to fulfil its policy commitments.

References

Bazalgette, L., Rahilly, T. and Trevelyan, G. (2015) *Achieving emotional wellbeing for looked after children*. London: NSPCC.

Berger, P. L. and Luckmann, T. (1967) *The social construction of reality: A treatise in the sociology of knowledge*. London: Allen Lane, The Penguin Press.

Bickel, A. (2015) *Kicked out kids!: A literature review considering the experiences of young people transitioning from residential care to independent adulthood*. Portsmouth: University of Portsmouth.

Brady, R. (2014) *The costs of not caring: Supporting English care leavers into independence*. Essex: Barnardo's.

Broadhurst, K., Hall, C., Wastell, D., White, S. and Pithouse, A. (2010a) 'Risk, Instrumentalism and the humane project in social work: identifying the informal logics of risk management in children's statutory services', *British Journal of Social Work*, 40, 1046-64.

Broadhurst, K., Wastell, D., White, S., Hall, C., Peckover, S., Thompson, K., Pithouse, A. and Davey, D. (2010b) 'Performing "initial assessment": identifying the latent conditions for error at the front-door of local authority children's services', *British Journal of Social Work*, 40, 352-70.

Brownlie, J. (2011) '"Being there": Multidimensionality, reflexivity and the study of emotional lives', *The British Journal of Sociology*, 62, 462-81.

Brownlie, J. (2014) *Ordinary relationships: A sociological study of emotions, reflexivity and culture*. Basingstoke: Palgrave Macmillan.

Coady, P. (2014) *Relationship boundaries in residential child care: intimacy and safety in group care relationships*. Edinburgh: University of Edinburgh.

Community Care (2014) 'Cuts to safeguarding teams and looked-after children services as council spending drops', 16 April.

Conrad, R. (2011) '"My future doesn't know ME": Time and subjectivity in poetry by young people', *Childhood*, 19, 204–18.

Cooper Marcus, C. (1995) *House as a mirror of self: Exploring the deeper meaning of home*. Berwick, ME: Nicolas-Hays.

Cree, V.E. and Wallace, S. J. (2009) 'Risk and protection', in R. Adams, M. Payne and L. Dominelli (eds) *Practising Social work in a complex world*. Basingstoke: Palgrave Macmillan.

Duncalf, Z., Hill, L. and McGhee, K. (2013) *Still caring? Supporting care leavers in Scotland*. Glasgow: Centre for Excellence for Looked After Children

Erikson, E. H. (1951) *Childhood and society*. London: Imago Publishing Company.

Fernandez, E. (2010) 'Growing up in care: an Australian longitudinal study', in E. Fernandez and R. P. Barth (eds) *How does foster care work? International evidence on outcomes*. London: Jessica Kingsley.

Gabb, J. (2011) 'Family lives and relational living: taking account of otherness', *Sociological Research Online*, 16, 10.

Giddens, A. (1991) *Modernity and self-identity: Self and society in the late modern age*. Cambridge: Polity Press in association with Blackwell.

Gilligan, R. (2004) 'Promoting resilience in child and family social work: Iissues for social work practice, education and policy', *Social Work Education*, 23, 93-104.

Happer, H., Mccreadie, J. and Aldgate, J. (2006) *Celebrating success: What helps looked after children succeed*. Edinburgh: Social Work Inspection Agency.

Hastings, A., Bailey, N., Bramley, G., Gannon, M. and Watkins, D. (2015) *The cost of the cuts: The impact on local government and poorer communities*. York: Joseph Rowntree Foundation.

Horwath, J. (2000) 'Childcare with gloves on: protecting children and young people in residential care', *British Journal of Social Work*, 30, 179-91.

Jamieson, L. (2011) 'Intimacy as a concept: explaining social change in the context of globalisation or another form of ethnocentricism?', *Sociological Research Online*, 16, 15.

Jamieson, L., Morgan, D.H.G., Crow, G. and Allan, G. (2006) 'Friends, neighbours and distant partners: extending or decentring family relationships?', *Sociological Research Online*, 11.

Lemay, R. and Ghazal, H. (2007) *Looking after children: A practitioner's guide*. Ottawa: University of Ottawa Press.

MacInnes, T., Tinson, A., Hughes, C., Born, T. B. and Aldridge, H. (2015) *Monitoring poverty and social exclusion*. York: Joseph Rowntree Foundation.

McCarthy, J.R. (2012) 'The powerful relational language of "family": togetherness, belonging and personhood', *Sociological Review*, 60, 68-90.

Mcleod, A. (2010) '"A friend and an equal": Do young people in care seek the impossible from their social workers?', *British Journal of Social Work*, 40, 772-88.

Mead, G.H. (1934) *Mind, self and society, From The standpoint of a social behaviorist*. Chicago: University of Chicago Press.

Meagher, G. and Parton, N. (2004) 'Modernising social work and the ethics of Care', *Social Work and Society Interantional Online Journal*, 2.

Mendes, P. (2012) 'Examining the experiences of young people transitioning from out-of-home care in rural Victoria', *Rural Society*, 21, 198–209.

Miller, P. J., Potts, R., Fung, H., Hoogstra, L. and Mintz, J. (1990) 'Narrative practices and the social construction of self in childhood', *American Ethnologist*, 17, 292–311.

Munro (2011) *The Munro Review of Child Protection: Final report: a child centred system*. London: Department for Education.

National Audit Office (2015) *Care leavers' transition to adulthood*. London: Department for Education.

National Bureau for Children (2015) *Cuts that cost: Trends in funding for early intervention services*. London: National Bureau for Children.

Reis, H. and Shaver, P. (1988) 'Intimacy as an interpersonal process', in S.W. Duck (ed) *Handbook of personal relationships*. London: John Wiley and Sons Ltd.

Rogers, R. (2011) '"I remember thinking, why isn't there someone to help me? Why isn't there someone who can help me make sense of what I'm going through?": "instant adulthood" and the transition of young people out of state care', *Journal of Sociology*, 47, 411–26.

Ruch, G. (2005) 'Relationship-based practice and reflective practice: holistic approaches to contemporary child care social work', *Child & Family Social Work*, 10, 111–23.

Ryan, M. (2012) *How to make relationships matter for looked after young people: A handbook*. London: National Children's Bureau.

Samuels, G. M. (2009) 'Ambiguous loss of home: the experience of familial (im)permanence among young adults with foster care backgrounds', *Children and Youth Services Review*, 31, 1229–39.

Schofield, G. and Stevenson, O. (2009) 'Contact and relationships between fostered children and their birth families', in G. Schofield and J. Simmonds (eds) *The child placement handbook: Research, policy and practice*. London: Baaf.

Scottish Government (2013) *Staying put Scotland: Providing care leavers with connectedness and belonging*. Edinburgh: The Scottish Government.

Scottish Government (2016) *Children's Social Work Statistics Scotland 2014/15*. Edinburgh: The Scottish Government.

Silva, E. (2007) 'Security, self and the home', in S. Carter, T. Jordan and S. Watson (eds) *Security: Sociology and social worlds*. Manchester: Manchester University Press.

Stein, M. (2006) 'Research review: young people leaving care', *Child and Family Social Work*, 11, 273–79.

Stein, M. and Munro, E.R. (eds) (2008) *Young people's transitions from care to adulthood: International research and practice*. London: Jessica Kingsley.

Stevenson, L. (2015) *Number of looked-after children at 30-year high, government data reveals.* 1 October 2015. http://www.communitycare.co.uk/2015/10/01/number-looked-children-30-year-high-government-data-reveals/ Accessed on 02.03.17

The Care Inquiry (2013) *Making not breaking: Building relationships for our most vulnerable children: Findings and recommendations of the Care Inquiry.* England: The Care Inquiry. www.Nuffieldfoundation.Org/News/Care-Inquiry-Calls-Decisions-Based-Need-Not-Legal-Status

Van Breda, A. D. (2015) 'Journey Towards independent living: a grounded theory investigation of leaving the care of girls & boys town, South Africa', *Journal of Youth Studies*, 18, 322-37.

Ward, H. (2011) 'Continuities and discontinuities: issues concerning the establishment of a persistent sense of self amongst care leavers', *Children and Youth Services Review*, 33, 2512-18.

Widmer, E. and Jallinoja, R. (2008) *Beyond the nuclear family: Families in a configurational perspective.* Basingstoke: Peter Lang Ag.

Wilson, S. and Milne, E. J. (2013) *Young people creating belonging: Spaces, sounds and sights.* Stirling: University of Stirling.

Winter, K. (2009) 'Relationships matter: the problems and prospects for social workers' relationships with young children in care', *Child & Family Social Work*, 14, 450-60.

Winter, K. (2011) *Building relationships and communicating with young children: A practical guide for social workers.* London: Routledge.

Part three:
Resistance and ethnography

THIRTEEN

[B]othered Youth: marginalisation, stop and search and the policing of belonging

Seán F. Murphy

Introduction

This chapter examines the contemporary issues surrounding the nature and impact of policing within disadvantaged communities in England and Wales. It seeks to critically explore how young people's encounters with the police can have a stigmatising and marginalising effect. The main focus for discussion is an exploration of the controversies surrounding the current policy and practice issues of 'stop and search' police powers (for example the Police and Criminal Evidence Act 1984 and section 60 of the Criminal Justice and Public Order Act 1994). It introduces the notion of *[B]othering* to explain how policing can be identified as the embodiment of respectability and acceptability, and offers some new insights into young people's lived experiences and their responses to encounters with the police.

The author offers some theoretical thoughts into the role of policing as a 'spatial practice' (Lefebvre, 1991), within what can be defined as 'marginal spaces' (Thompson et al, 2013) to illustrate how it is that certain young people, through stigmatisation and the process of 'othering', are marginalised and their use of space is regulated and controlled. Importantly, the concept of *[B]othered Youth* sees the dualistic notions of structure and agency as problematic, and draws upon Evans' (2002) concept of 'bounded agency' to examine young people's attempts to make sense of, and to take control of, their lives.

The chapter offers a critical look at policing strategies, and questions the effectiveness of methods that are based on instrumental goals and legal interpretations of 'stop and search'. It concludes by advocating for a policing role that incorporates a more nuanced understanding of youth and recognition of its pastoral and inclusive capabilities.

The meaning of *[B]othered Youth*

The author's initial concern is to look at the use of 'stop and search' powers to explore how such a policing practice can be considered as *[B]othering* – meaning a form of social practice which stigmatises disadvantaged young people and informs their sense of belonging, thereby contributing towards their marginalisation and wider social exclusion in Britain today. The term *[B]othered Youth* is coined here to encapsulate a range of key concepts and findings from contemporary research literature, which collectively describe the specific set of policing strategies and social conditions that, when applied to marginalised young people, help to explain their lived experiences.

The term draws upon the sentiments expressed by TV sketch show character Lauren Cooper, who popularised the saying 'Am I bovvered?' as part of *The Catherine Tate Show* (BBC TV, 2004-06). It came to symbolise the DIY generation, in the sense of an emergent new reflexivity in youth, as a form of habitus or what Bourdieu calls 'embodied cultural capital' (Threadgold and Nilan, 2009) that remains inequitably distributed along class lines. The term uses the concept of 'othering' to explain why the historical, cultural and social process of stereotyping and stigmatisation results in young people from disadvantaged groups becoming represented as 'the Other' and subject to a range of policing approaches and disciplining practices.

The concept of *[B]othered Youth* encapsulates the important factors of place, class and race, and articulates how the impact of poverty and location structure the opportunities for young people growing up in poor neighbourhoods (MacDonald and Marsh, 2005). Such lack of opportunity can best be described as structured marginalisation, which leads to the fractured and 'ragged transitions' (Loader, 1996; Furlong and Cartmel, 2007). Moreover, it is within a contemporary discourse on youth which can be defined as the 'institutionalised mistrust of youth' (Kelly, 2003) that prescribes youth as a binary of 'at risk' and 'dangerous'. Therefore, *[B]othered Youth* is a representation of youth who are the object of surveillance as they attract the gaze of public policy and become subjected to a raft of state interventions which are symptomatic of 'problem-orientated' policing approaches and methods.

Jensen (2011, p65) states: 'such discursive processes affirm the legitimacy and superiority of the powerful and condition identity formation among the subordinate'. For him, the concept of 'othering' is: 'well suited for understanding the power structures as well as the historic symbolic meanings conditioning such identity formation, but problematic in terms of agency' (Jensen, 2011, p63). However, the discussion on structured marginalisation is also symptomatic of such subordinating discourses. As such, it can be criticised as a form of structural thinking that denies young people's capacity to resist such identity formations and conditioning. Here the author suggests that Lauren Cooper's character in *The Catherine Tate Show* is representative of today's *[B]othered Youth*, which includes degrees of agency within specific contexts and is seeking to contest representations and to challenge orthodox notions about being young and experiencing marginalisation.

The role of policing

Policing has always played a pivotal role in the life of communities. It has helped to ensure the community's safety and contributed to its sense of belonging and wellbeing. Storch (1976) suggested that since the inception of 'new policing' in the early 19th century, policing could be described as a form of 'domestic missionary', whose role stretched beyond crime and public disorder. He argued that they operated as moral guardians, acting as an 'all-purpose lever of urban discipline' and 'brought the arm of municipal and state authority directly to bear upon key institutions of daily life in working class neighbourhoods' (Storch, 1976, p481). Moreover, it is important to recognise that the routine police practice of monitoring and control of the streets often ran counter to local customs and leisure pursuits of the working class, and led to rioting, protest and resistance.

Loader (2006) argues that there have been continuities and shifts in relation to the role of the police – from the maintenance of social order, community safety and crime detection, through to zero-tolerance and the more pervasive form of policing. It can be argued that this missionary zeal is in operation again within a contemporary 'neighbourhood policing' strategy that incorporates the notion of intelligence-led and targeted approaches. It symbolises a form of *[B]othering*, as there is substantial evidence to suggest that the role and purpose of policing is becoming less associated with crime prevention, crime detection and public order, instead operating as a more pervasive and intrusive force in people's everyday lives in a manner that maintains social order and enforces 'self-regulation' (Rose, 1999).

Reiner (2010) refers to this process as the criminalisation of youth through the use of stereotypes, stigmatisation and the amplification of deviance, a form of 'police fetishism', suggesting that policing is as much about visibility and reassurance than crime detection, acting more as a social problem-solver rather than a crime-solving unit. Similarly, Loader (1996) described it as 'ambient policing', in which central to the role of policing is the targeting of crime hot-spots, focused on prolific offenders, and fulfilling the instrumental role of the removal of risks, order maintenance and quick responses. Here the notion of *[B]othering* is manifested through the increased use of surveillance and control methods targeted at young people, such as curfews, dispersal orders, anti-social behaviour orders, parenting orders and most recently pre-court sentencing within youth justice policy.

The controversial nature of 'stop and search'

The policing practice of 'stop and search' has had a long and controversial history in England and Wales. It is one of the earliest police powers known as the 'sus law' (Section 4 of the Vagrancy Act 1824), which provided police constables with the power to search a 'suspected person', that is someone considered likely to commit an arrestable offence. The contested nature of such powers has featured prominently in public debates regarding policing of communities. As Storch's (1976) historical analysis prophetically described, 'the basic technique of daily surveillance of the streets and recreational centres of working-class districts proved a lasting one, and would ultimately be applied not only to nineteenth-century Leeds or Manchester but – in highly sophisticated variants – to twentieth-century police work as well' (Storch, 1976, p496).

The Scarman Inquiry Report into the 1981 Brixton 'disorders' identified that the relationship between the police and minority ethnic communities was problematic (Souhami, 2014), and it cited the excessive use of the 'sus laws' as a key contributory factor. Later, the MacPherson Inquiry into the death of Stephen Lawrence concluded that institutional racism was endemic in the police services and had significantly contributed to the failure of the police investigation. In particular, it noted that the disproportionate use of 'stop and search' within disadvantaged and minority ethnic communities played a salient role in undermining the 'legitimacy of the police, they are likely to weaken the public's willingness to comply with the law' (Quinton, 2011, p257). Since the Scarman Report, revisions have been made to the use and monitoring of 'stop and search' powers, such as the introduction of a Code of Practice as part of the Police and Criminal Evidence Act 1984 (PACE), which Reiner (2010, p212) described as the 'single most significant landmark in the modern development of police powers'. However, other key legislative changes, such as the introduction of Section 60 powers (Criminal Justice and Public Order Act 1994), introduced more draconian measures, which provided the power to 'stop and search' with 'no grounds of suspicion'.

However, despite such reforms, the practice of 'stop and search' remains highly controversial. It featured prominently in the causes of the English 'riots' of August 2011. *The Guardian* report *Reading the Riots* stated that: 'a key factor in the August riots was discontent with the police – with stop and search one of the most hated aspects' (Prasad, 2011, online). The then Home Secretary, Theresa May (2014), speaking following a review of 'stop and search' in England and Wales, indicated that only 38% of young people (aged 18-24) thought 'stop and search' powers are effective, and she highlighted her concerns about the misuse of 'stop and search', which can be counterproductive. She stated that: 'when innocent people are stopped and searched for no good reason, it is hugely damaging to the relationship between the police and the public' (May, 2014).

The decline in the use of 'stop and search'

Recent Home Office data (Home Office, 2015) indicate that there were 540,870 searches carried out in 2014/15 in England and Wales (see Table 13.1). This represents a fall of 64% compared to the peak rate (1,519,516 searches in 2008/09). This year-on-year fall in searches indicates a policy shift away from the widespread use of 'stop and search' as a policing practice for crime detection and prevention. Most significant has been the reduction in searches conducted under Section 60 (Criminal Justice and Public Order Act 1994), which has seen a dramatic fall of 93% in the searches conducted from its peak of 150,174 searches in 2008/09.

Table 13.1: Stop and search, by legislation, England and Wales

Year	Type of search			Total
	Section 1	Section 60	Section 44/47A	
2008/09	1,159,374	150,174	210,013	1,519,561
2009/10	1,177,327	119,973	108,685	1,405,985
2010/11	1,229,324	62,429	11,787	1,303,540
2011/12	1,142,909	46,973	—	1,189,882
2012/13	1,012,196	5,346	—	1,017,542
2013/14	900,129	3,960	—	904,089
2014/15	539,788	1,082	—	540,870

Source: Home Office (2015) Stop and Search statistics

Murphy (2014) highlighted concerns around discriminatory effects and ineffectiveness of Section 60 powers, citing its extremely low arrest rates, and questions whether any other 'public service would be allowed to continue a practice with such poor outcomes' (Murphy, 2014, online). The recent Home Office data (Home Office, 2015) show that the arrest rate remains low at just 3% (32 arrests), which indicates no change over the period. Thus Section 60 represents a policing measure that creates great anxiety and mistrust, while yielding poor results.

The number of searches conducted under Section 1 of the Police and Criminal Evidence Act 1984 (PACE) was 539,788 in 2014/15, which represents a reduction of 40% on the previous year 2013/14 (895,975 searches), and moreover demonstrates a 53% reduction compared to the peak year of 2008/09 (1,159,374 searches). Significantly, the arrest rate for the 539,788 searches in 2014/15 was 14% (74,680 arrests), which represents an improvement from 10% (113,680 arrests) in 2008/09 (the peak 'stop and search' year) and illustrates that fewer searches do not lead to fewer arrests.

However, the data reveal that concerns surrounding ethnic profiling and the disproportionate use of 'stop and search' remain. Overall, the 'stop and search' rate in England and Wales for 2014/15 was 15 searches per 1,000 population (see Table 13.2). But an examination of the data in relation to the ethnicity (self-defined) of the persons stopped and searched reveals a different picture. For instance, the stop and search rate for White people is 8 searches per 1,000 population, but for Black/Black British the rate is 34 significantly higher, and for Asian/ Asian British the rate is 11. Overall, there was a significant reduction in the number of searches of Black and Minority Ethnic (BME) groups between 2010/11 and 20014/15, falling from 51 searches per 1,000 population, down to 16. Despite the overall reduction in searches

Table 13.2: Stop and search rates (per 1,000 population), by ethnicity, England and Wales (2010/11 to 2014/15)

	White	Black (or Black British)	Asian (or Asian British)	Chinese or Other	Mixed	All BME groups
			Self-defined ethnicity			
2010/11	112	36	19	30	51	
2011/12	16	95	32	16	29	45
2012/13	15	65	24	13	23	32
2013/14	13	55	19	12	20	27
2014/15	8	34	11	8	13	16

Source: Home Office (2015) Stop and Search statistics

conducted, the data indicate that you are still twice as likely to be stopped and searched if you are from a BME background, and 4.25 times more likely to be stopped if you are Black.

Policing and youth

Muncie (2014) argues that youth justice policy across England and Wales over the last two decades can be characterised as the demonisation and criminalisation of young people. This pervasive and targeted approach to policing has had a dramatic impact on young people and their use of social spaces. Loader (2006) categorises such practices as the 'policing of belonging' and links it to the formation of beliefs within police culture where young people on the streets are categorised as a 'police property' and subjected to social constructs of respectability and order. Therefore, it is through the notion of becoming 'police property' that young people become *[B]othered*, i.e. subject to frequent police encounters under the guise of suspicions. As Waddington (1999) suggests, the recurrent police-initiated contacts result in the construction 'the usual suspects' as marginalised young people find their behaviour and use of public spaces continuously questioned and contested.

Ariza (2014) suggests that police practice tends to focus on 'individuals with prior police contact and whose friends have had prior police contact' (Ariza, 2014, p219) and this form of *[B]othering* can be termed 'policing by association', meaning that young people are overpoliced and their interests underrepresented in policing. Similarly, Ralphs et al identified that being labelled as a gang member or associate creates a greater vulnerability to police attention and surveillance, and thus to becoming a 'permanent suspect', which is 'based on socio-economic status as much as on serious and persistent offending' (Ralphs et al, 2009, p487).

Bradford's (2014) research into police and youth argues the need for greater acknowledgement and recognition of the stigmatising effect of negative police encounters on young people's sense of wellbeing. The study investigated experiences of BME young men from London and concluded that '[e]ncountering negative policing styles may serve to encourage a pre-existing or nascent sense of difference and alienation from the wider social and political community' (Bradford, 2014, p23). He identified that there is a strong link between being treated fairly and people's willingness to cooperate with the police, noting that policing has a strong symbolic role, which affects people's sense of wellbeing, including social identity, collective belonging, as well as feelings of inclusion or exclusion. Bradford (2014) states that the police 'are a highly visible representation of the state, a concrete instantiation of its (often failed) claim to protect and represent all its citizens' (p23), and concludes that those excluded or included will draw important lesson regarding their social status from such encounters with the police.

Loader's (2006) study of youth encounters with the police clearly articulates the impact on young people and communities of such 'spatial practices' and representations, stating that:

> Every stop, every search, every arrest, every group of youths moved on, every abuse of due process, every failure to respond to a call or complaint, every racist snub, every sexist remark, every homophobic joke, every diagnosis of the crime problem, every depiction of criminals – all these send small, routine, authoritative signals about society's conflicts, cleavages, and hierarchies, about whose claims are considered legitimate within it, about whose status identity is to be affirmed or denied as part of it. (Loader, 2006, p211)

This evidence upholds the resentment experienced by *[B]othered Youth*. As Quinton's (2011) research into police officers' interpretation of suspicion indicates, 'the categories that dominated police thinking were highly symbolic and would have resulted in suspicions falling disproportionately on the socially marginal young men, black people, and the "regulars"' (Quinton, 2011, p366). Similarly, Delsol (2011) suggests that the experience of repeat and frequent encounters with the police 'can be frightening and humiliating' and that the '[d]isproportionate stops and searches of ethnic minorities serve to stigmatise whole groups and continue to drive mistrust between communities and the police' (Delsol, 2011, p20). Also, Jacobs (2011, p22) has equated stop and search with criminalising the innocent, and raises question as to whether the 'criminalisation of the next generation of youth is being achieved by accident, or is it design?'.

These findings suggest that *[B]othering* comes to symbolise the policing in disadvantaged communities through regular surveillance, police raids and 'stops and searches', and stigmatises individuals and families. In this sense, it embodies a set of policing tactics and practices that shape and mould desirable characteristics and behaviours. Its focus is on desirability and appropriateness – who can go where, who is allowed to be somewhere, and when and how they use public spaces. Essentially it is not focused on crime prevention or detection, but instead on what is considered acceptable behaviour and addressing wider social fears about youth presence.

Policing as a 'spatial practice'

The concept of *[B]othering* is centred on understanding how young people's use of space becomes problematic. Lefebvre (1991) uses the idea of space as 'lived experiences' – as part of the production and reproduction of everyday life. He uses the concept 'representations of space' to explain how the use of space is mediated by official discourse and government policy to become socially constructed and to shape the way spaces are used.

However, postmodernist theorists have suggested that an individual's choice and autonomy are less restricted by structural forces and social background, arguing that globalisation has led to a process of 'individualization' and 'de-traditionlization' within a late modern society (Beck, 1992). Also, theorists such as Giddens (1991) have downplayed the importance of place, noting that growing geographical mobility has resulted in everyday experiences becoming increasingly disembodied from physical location. However, this decoupling of class and place has been widely criticised by youth studies academics, who articulate the enduring significance of class and place in youth experiences. Shildrick et al (2009) are critical of a postmodern, postsubcultural theory, which places a greater emphasis on agency and the individual at the expense of more nuanced and critical discussion of the social structures and institutions that continue to marginalise some sections of young people.

Ralphs et al (2009) re-examine the importance of place and space as a key function for young people's identity and belonging. They refer to the 'spatialisation' of young people's experiences and state that '[g]rowing up in poor neighbourhoods, leaving the parental home and the navigation of everyday life all have physical and metaphorical spatial dimensions' (Ralphs et al, 2009, p65). They suggest that those young people categorised as 'the Others' are identified as problematic and 'high risk', leading to them having to 'continually negotiate a range of risks bound up with the territory that they inhabit and subsequent spatial boundaries that are formed' (Ralphs et al, 2009, p483), and resulting in exclusion, marginalisation and victimisation.

Moreover, Lefebvre (1991) refers to 'spatial practices' to define social acts and interventions, such as policing methods and the types of strategies deployed that inform their work. So accordingly, *[B]othering* is a 'spatial practice' – a form of social interaction and encounters that become governed by dominant discourse or 'representations of space', which in turn inform public policy. Thompson et al (2013) go further, suggesting that social places become categorised as 'marginal spaces', for example sink schools, depressed areas or crime blackspots. This categorisation of a place as marginal or 'special' will have a significant impact on 'spatial practice': it can attract regeneration grants and new resources but, equally importantly, it can generate increased levels of stigmatisation and marginalisation. Thus, the policy formation and responses for disengaged young people are spatially conceived as 'marginal places' (Thompson et al, 2013, p67) – as the places where youth are formally *[B]othered*, for example special units in school, exclusion units or pupil referral units and work-based learning provision.

Young people's agency: resistance and reaction to regulation

Thus far, the discussion on *[B]othered Youth* can be criticised as a form of structural thinking that denies young people's capacity to resist such identity formations and conditioning. Therefore, in terms of identity formation and youth culture, this orthodox way of defining 'othering' can be problematic. Young people are perceived within a recurring binary – troubled or trouble – and it forms a frame of reference that negates the possibility for young people to be creators or agents in co-constructing identities.

Lauren Cooper in *The Catherine Tate Show* is pivotal to understanding the notion of *[B]othered Youth* because the TV sketch show character embodies a young person seeking to contest taken-for-granted representations and seeks to challenge orthodox notions about being young. A useful concept here is what Evans (2002) terms 'bounded agency' as a socially situated process, meaning that individuals are influenced – but not determined – by structures. The research illustrates how 'the experiences and orientations of young people [are] differently positioned within the social and institutional landscapes' (Evans, 2002, p255). Therefore, *[B]othered Youth* sees the dualistic notions of structure and agency as problematic. In reality, young people's lives are complex and full of contradictions, as they navigate the 'interplay of structural forces and individual's attempts to control their lives' (Evans, 2002, p265).

Gray and Manning's (2014) research illustrates how young people react to police regulation and seek to reconfigure spatial practices and dominant representations of social spaces. Their work highlights how young people perceive such discourse and identities as problematic, as they seek to 'position themselves as both knowing about the need for regulation, while also resisting such regulation as applying to them directly' (Gray and Manning, 2014, p650). Therefore, *[B]othered Youth* are seen as 'knowing agents', often subverting the intended purpose of police surveillance and the regulatory controls of 'moving them on' or 'talking them home'. Young people deployed a variety of actions or spatial practices: hiding themselves and/or their drink in bushes, or returning to places immediately after being moved on. Very often, they viewed the attempts at spatial regulation as 'laughable' and unenforceable, thereby 'transforming a potentially serious attempt at regulation of their presence (and behaviour) in public into a comical and ultimately harmless game' (Gray and Manning, 2014, p650). The research showed how young people reconstructed the meaning of being taken home by the police into getting a 'free ride' home, or as a convenient way of getting home, especially in winter. In this way, 'they reworked regulation as something that could ultimately be of straightforward benefit to them (as a service) – subverting its intended purpose and neutralising it as a form of sanction or control' (p650). Therefore, young people demonstrated the capacity to determine what was considered appropriate or inappropriate behaviour within 'marginal places' as a form of resistance or 'bounded agency'. They would reposition their own behaviour as appropriately 'in place', in order to construct police action as being inappropriate and/or 'out-of-place'. Generally, *[B]othering* encapsulates the scope for agency within the social constraints and regulation of spatial practices, with participants showing the ability to work out which behaviours are appropriate and when certain behaviour can be controlled.

Shifts in policy discourse on 'stop and search'

There appears to be some evidence that policy discourse and rhetoric are shifting towards consideration of the illegal and discriminatory nature of excessive use of 'stop and search', and recognise the need to develop confidence in police use of these powers through promoting more accountability and community involvement. The Equalities and Human Rights Commission (EHRC, 2010, p5) suggested that current police use of 'stop and search' powers 'may be unlawful, disproportionate, discriminatory and damaging' to community relations.

Similarly, the then Home Secretary Theresa May announced in 2014 a review of police 'stop and search' practice, stating that 'when innocent people are stopped and searched for no good reason, it is hugely damaging to the relationship between the police and the public' (May, 2014). In 2015, HMIC Chief Inspector Stephen Otter stated that: '[t]oo many police leaders and officers still don't seem to understand the impact that the use of powers to stop and search people can have on the lives of many, especially young people, and those who are from black and minority ethnic backgrounds' (Otter, 2015).

In response, a number of recent initiatives have been proposed. These include a *Best Use of Stop and Search Scheme*, introduced in 2014 and intended to encourage local police service improvements to 'achieve greater transparency, community involvement in the use of stop and search powers and to support a more intelligence-led approach, leading to better outcomes' (Home Office/College of Policing, 2014, p2) and encouraging lay observations of patrols using 'stop and search'. Since the establishment of Police and Crime Commissioners across England and Wales in 2012, there has been greater scrutiny and transparency through Community Scrutiny Panels thematic groups, such as Stop and Search Panels. Other initiatives include: the College of Policing devising a national curriculum for 'stop and search' training and accreditation; and new protocols and recording requirements for searches involving the removal of young people's outer clothing and strip-searching in public places.

However, while revisions and the recent reduction in the number of 'stop and searches' are welcomed, there remains a need for policing to embrace an inclusive approach to its practices, to foster cooperation between police and the public, and to encourage fairness and proportionality. Bradford (2014) suggests 'communities that have historically been "over-policed" in a style that has damaged trust and legitimacy have also often been "under-protected" (Kushnick 1999), and the failure of the police to protect citizens may have been as keenly felt as any experience of unfairness' (2014, p27). Such policing intensifies young people's experience of being *[B]othered* at a personal level, and has a detrimental effect, by conferring a negative status and a stigmatising effect.

Deuchar et al (2015) identify the need for a pastoral role within the police, suggesting that they can act as enablers of community engagement and can reduce social fears surrounding young people on the streets. They propose a positive approach that fosters participation and dialogue between young people and older generations within communities (McAra and McVie, 2010), developing a more nuanced understanding of young people, in particular in recognition of critical life moments, for example loss or bereavement, or becoming a parent. McAra and McVie's research suggests that policy makers and youth justice service approaches need to be more holistic in their understanding of young people, and tailored to specific needs rather than the generalised and stigmatising approach.

Research by Nolas (2014) focused on socially excluded young people and identified that youth clubs can offer a 'shelter from the storm' (p35), thus acting as a buffer against the stigmatising and negative impact of *[B]othering*, by creating safe havens within 'marginal spaces'. She suggests that youth inclusion programmes can offer opportunities that enable young people to participate in the community and make sense of their lives through 'unstructured' activities. These leave them: 'free to sail in and out and like a family they were unconditionally accepted at the Centre ... and in contrast to other institutional and public spaces (school, streets) that featured in these young people's narratives, neither age nor statutory obligation determined membership' (Nolas, 2014, p35).

Conclusion

The idea of *[B]othered Youth* is drawn from the concept of 'othering', defined as the discursive processes by which powerful groups in society define minority or subordinate groups in a manner that imbues them with inferior characteristics and prescribes their behaviour as problematic. The term *[B]othered Youth* encapsulates the important factors of place, class and race in describing how the impact of poverty and location can structure the opportunities for poor youth, resulting in further marginalisation.

But, importantly, the concept recognises that just like the TV character Lauren Cooper stating 'Am I bovvered?', young people are able to contest dominant representations and to challenge orthodox notions about being young. Recent police–youth studies have demonstrated degrees of 'bounded agency' (Evans, 2002), by acting as 'knowing agents' (Gray and Manning, 2014), often subverting the intended purpose of police surveillance and the regulatory controls within such police encounters.

However, as the chapter has articulated, the notion of *[B]othering* within the spatial practice of policing and the use of 'stop and search' is a pervasive and dominant factor that shapes young people's sense of wellbeing and status – acting as a powerful signifier of acceptance and belonging. The youth studies research illustrates that being *[B]othered*, i.e. subject to frequent police contact, is a common a feature of young people's daily experience and symptomatic of the formation of 'the usual suspects' (Waddington, 1999), and beliefs within police culture where young people on the streets are categorised as 'police property'.

The impact of 'stop and searches' on young people's sense of belonging and wellbeing and their place in the community has failed to be adequately addressed by changes to policy and procedure. For while the police reforms may address the tone of the 'ambient policing' and seek to navigate around a police culture and institutionalised racism which labels and targets the 'usual suspects', the practice still results in youth experiencing being *[B]othered*. What is required is a more holistic understanding of young people's lives and approach from policy makers and practitioners, based on young people's needs. Nolas (2014) recognises the importance of youth clubs and safe havens for young people growing up in 'marginal places', and Deuchar et al (2015) recognise the generational gap in attitudes towards young people and call for a greater role for 'pastoral policing' to facilitate dialogue and understanding.

To achieve a shift towards a more inclusive form of policing requires further guidance and training for police officers in ways which take them beyond achieving an accreditation in the legal basis for 'stop and searches'. Inclusivity requires the policing to develop a greater appreciation of their role as a signifier of status and exclusion. The notion of *[B]othering* offers a more nuanced understanding of the complex set of social practices which frame young people's sense of belonging and wellbeing. It suggests that revisiting the way in which places and people are constructed provides the potential to reappraise the importance of proportionality, fairness and justice when working within marginalised spaces.

References

Ariza, J. (2014) 'Police-initiated contacts: young people, ethnicity, and the "usual suspects"', *Policing and Society: An International Journal of Research and Policy*, 24, 2: 208-23.

Beck, U. (1992) *Risk society: Towards a new modernity*. London: Sage.

Bradford, B. (2014) 'Policing and social identity: procedural justice, inclusion and cooperation between police and public', *Policing and Society: An International Journal of Research and Policy*, 24, 1: 22-43.

Delsol, R. (2011) 'Stop and search – renewed powers, less accountability?', *Criminal Justice Matters*, 86, 1: 20-1.

Deuchar, R., Miller, J. and Barrow, M. (2015) 'Breaking down barriers with the usual suspects: findings from a research-informed intervention with police, young people and residents in the West of Scotland', *Youth Justice*, 15, 1: 57–75.

Equality and Human Rights Commission (EHRC) (2010) *Stop and think again: Towards race equality in police PACE stop and search*. https://www.equalityhumanrights.com/en/publication-download/stop-and-think-again-towards-equality-police-pace-stop-and-search

Evans, K. (2002) 'Taking control of their lives? Agency in young adult transitions in England and the New Germany', *Journal of Youth Studies*, 5, 3: 245–69.

Furlong, A. and Cartmel, F. (2007) *Young people and social change*. Maidenhead: McGraw Hill.

Giddens, A. (1991) *Modernity and self-identity: Self and society in the late modern age*. Cambridge: Polity.

Gray, D. and Manning, R. (2014) '"Oh my god, we're not doing nothing": young people's experiences of spatial regulation', *British Journal of Social Psychology*, 53, 4: 640–55.

Home Office (2015) *Stop and search statistics – Police powers and procedures, year ending 31 March 2015*. https://www.gov.uk/government/statistics/police-powers-and-procedures-england-and-wales-year-ending-31-march-2015-data-tables

Home Office/College of Policing (2014) *Best use of stop and search scheme*. Home Office.

Jacobs, P. (2011) 'The use of section 60 powers in Brent', *Criminal Justice Matters*, 86, 1: 22–3.

Jensen, S. Q. (2011) 'Othering, identity formation and agency', *Qualitative Studies*, 2, 2: 63–78.

Kelly, P. (2003) 'Growing up as risky business? Risks, surveillance and the institutionalized mistrust of youth', *Journal of Youth Studies*, 6, 2: 165–80.

Lefebvre, H. (1991) *The production of space*. Oxford: Wiley-Blackwell.

Loader, I. (1996) *Youth, policing and democracy*. Basingstoke: Macmillan.

Loader, I. (2006) 'Policing, recognition and belonging', *The ANNALS of the American Academy of Political and Social Science*, 605: 201.

MacDonald, R. and Marsh, J. (2005) *Disconnected youth? Growing up in Britain's Poor Neighbourhoods*. Basingstoke: Palgrave.

May, T. (2014) 'Stop and search: comprehensive package of reform for police stop and search powers', an oral statement to Parliament, 30 April. https://www.gov.uk/government/speeches/stop-and-search-comprehensive-package-of-reform-for-police-stop-and-search-powers

McAra, L. and McVie, S. (2010) 'Youth crime and justice: Key messages from the Edinburgh Study of Youth', *Criminology and Criminal Justice*, 10: 179-209.

Muncie, J. (2014) *Youth and crime* (4th edn). London: Sage.

Murphy, S. (2014) *Rethinking stop and search:Changing 'ways of thinking' about marginalised youth*. Runnymede Trust/Race Card. www.racecard.org.uk/blog/rethinking-stop-and-search-ways-of-thinking-about-marginalised-youth

Nolas, S.-M. (2014) 'Exploring young people's and youth workers' experiences of spaces for "youth development": creating cultures of participation', *Journal of Youth Studies*, 17, 1: 26-41.

Otter, S. (2015) *Police forces failing to understand the impact of stop and search*. https://www.justiceinspectorates.gov.uk/hmic/news/news-feed/police-forces-failing-to-understand-the-impact-of-stop-and-search/

Prasad, R. (2011) 'Reading the riots: "Humiliating" stop and search a key factor in anger towards police', *The Guardian*, 6 December. https://www.theguardian.com/uk/2011/dec/06/stop-and-search

Quinton, P. (2011) 'The formation of suspicions: police stop and search practices in England and Wales', *Policing and Society*, 21, 4: 357-68.

Ralphs, R., Medina, J. and Aldridge, J. (2009) 'Who needs enemies with friends like these? The importance of place for young people living in known gang areas', *Journal of Youth Studies*, 12, 5: 483-500.

Reiner, R. (2010) *The politics of the police* (4th edn). Oxford: Oxford University Press.

Rose, N. (1999) *Governing the soul: The shaping of the private self* (2nd edn). London: Free Association.

Shildrick, T., Blackman, S. and MacDonald, R. (2009) 'Young people, class and place', *Journal of Youth Studies*, 12, 5: 457-65.

Souhami, A. (2014) 'Institutional racism and police reform: an empirical critique', *Policing & Society*, 24, 1: 1-21.

Storch, R. (1976) 'The policeman as domestic missionary: urban discipline and popular culture in Northern England, 1850–1880', *Journal of Social History*, 9, 4: 481-509.

Thompson, R., Russell, L. and Simmons, R. (2013) 'Space, place and social exclusion: an ethnographic study of young people outside education and employment', *Journal of Youth Studies*, 17, 1: 63-78.

Waddington, P. (1999) 'Police (canteen) sub-culture: An appreciation', *The British Journal of Criminology*, 39, 2: 287-309.

FOURTEEN

On the margins: the last place to rebel? Understanding young people's resistance to social conformity

Jane McKay and Frances Atherton

Introduction

Young people have for decades been the subject of repeated 'moral panics' (Cohen, 2002) in Western society. From the troubles of the 'teenager' in the early post-war period, the mods and rockers of the sixties, the anarchic punk subculture of the seventies, through to the most recent moral panic of the 'NEET' (not in employment, education or training) generation, there has been an apparent tension between the empowerment and subjugation of young people. This has manifested itself through discourses of children's rights, voice and participation, and the competing discourses of failure, risk and problematisation.

The media portrayal that fuels the moral panic of unruly and out-of-control young people portrays them as frightening not only to other members of society, but also to one another (*The Independent*, 2009). This sense of moral panic around young people relates closely to the ownership of public spaces and what has been perceived as young people's 'disruptive use of public space', whereby young people are accused of disrupting spaces in parks, on estates, on playing fields and on street corners (Robinson, 2009, p510).

In contrast, this chapter considers how young people themselves understand and view their position in relation to their social environment. It also offers an illustration of the complex and unintended ways in which young people are marginalised in everyday life. Marginalisation is not considered as an end-product of social dysfunction; rather, it emerges as a *process*, by which the young people themselves may negotiate their position in different social situations in order to effect autonomy and self-determination, even within the smallest and most mundane activities.

Drawing on Erikson (1972), we consider what Erikson refers to as the 'leeway of mastery in a set of developments or circumstances', which suggests 'free movement within prescribed limits' (p691) – a literal translation being space of, or space for, play; what the rules of the game allow. The concept of social play is an important feature of Erikson's work and relates to the fifth stage of psychosocial development: adolescence.

The importance of play in the early years is a well-rehearsed discussion. However, the concept of play in the transition stage from childhood to adulthood – adolescence – provokes a reconsideration of the ways in which young people explore and learn about themselves and their world. We consider freedom and autonomy for the young person to follow their own particular motivations, yet within 'prescribed limits'. We explore how space is negotiated and, at particular points of intersection, how potential conflict is tempered to maintain the freedom that boundary spaces may offer. We consider the role of resistance at places of intersection, where the desire to define a new liberty, a free space (Robinson, 2009) is bargained. For, as Robinson suggests, 'leisure practices can ... involve opposition, resistance and transgression' (p508), and these are the key emerging elements of the young people's social play that we examine in this chapter.

A case study of resistance

The social competence paradigm of Prout and James (1990) provides a way to frame our understanding of the spaces in which young people express themselves. Thus, young people are described as 'active in the construction and determination of their own social lives' (Prout and James, 1990, pp8–9), while their status as 'children' (in developmental and legal terms) is defined largely within the interactional setting in which they find themselves.

Young people, then, are considered here as *being*; whole and distinct persons with complete personalities, thoughts and beliefs about themselves and the world around them. Too often, young people are regarded as *becoming*; not yet adult, somehow 'other'; in deficit by virtue of their age and life stage. According to Cannella (1999), young people have been identified as distinctly different from those who are older, a difference that has come about since the emergence of an enlightenment/modernist focus on science. This 'otherness' has been constructed within the context of modernist beliefs that assume a predetermined truth, in which science 'has revealed what we can expect from [children] at various ages, how we should differentiate our treatment of them in [educational] settings' (Cannella, 1999, p37). This identifies a temporal nature in the way that young people are considered in relation to many social 'problems' and moral panics in recent years. For Brannen (1999), a preoccupation with age and generational contexts has been responsible for failing to account for the cultural and contextual nuances that occur within the broad categorisation of 'childhood'. Thus, young people move from the limits prescribed for them by significant adults in their earlier years, to the self-imposed limits of discovery during the adolescent phase. At these points of intersection between childhood and autonomous adulthood, the dangerous and the mundane meet.

The way in which these 'prescribed limits' (Erikson, 1962, p 691) are explored and contested by young people are considered here, through ongoing research that seeks to explore the lived experienced of the mundane, the daily and the everyday aspects of young people's lives. Our participants were a group of around 15 young people, varying in age from 16 to their mid-20s. Some were still in school or college (seven); some were employed (two); and some were unemployed/ NEET (six). Broadly, there were equal numbers of males and females in the group and there did not appear to be any evident hierarchy. Our approach was shaped by the young people we encountered, in that it was collaborative, participatory, co-constructed and organic.

Access to the group was elicited in the first instance through an existing relationship with one of the young people, with negotiated access for data collection with the other group members taking place at each meeting. It was apparent that the young people themselves were keen to express their views, and the ensuing discussions that we conducted were open, relaxed and took place over a number of separate gatherings. We did not audio-record conversations; rather, notes were taken of the observations of activities that the group engaged in, together with supplementary photographs (some of which are included in this chapter). Consent for use of notes, verbatim comments and photographs was obtained at the time of data collection.

Youth observed on the Meadows

A number of encounters were recorded as part of the research, but here we focus on one particular encounter that took place on a summer afternoon in 2013. The Meadows is an ancient patch of wetland and grassland adjacent to the River Dee in the centre of Chester, a small city in the north of England. 'A peaceful place to enjoy, surrounded by nature,' so the 'Friends of the Meadows' boast, procured with the intent to be forever 'maintained and preserved as a recreation ground for the use of citizens' (www.friendsofthemeadows.org.uk).

Dog walkers, joggers, anglers, birdwatchers and other assorted enthusiasts take full advantage of this civic gift. A careful distance is maintained by the more energetic few. Solitary in their endeavour, distinguishing uniforms for striving fitness describe a homogeneous group. Taut elastic fabric binds the flaunting few, with billowing tracksuits disguising the bashful. They shuffle past, respectfully hushed, so as not to disturb the wildlife enthusiasts in their silent, still pursuits.

Seeking a freedom

They are accompanied by another group; equally deliberate in their intent to find a place, similarly eager to protect and preserve their place, in this place, where existence and being can, momentarily, become more (un)real. We draw on the experiences of a group of young people we got to know at the Meadows. They find their way there and find themselves. They share in the salvation that this place offers with other disciples whose practices similarly, and necessarily, seek seclusion not available in the heart of the city but for this redemptive grassland. The story that unfolds here is one of the active construction of a social domain through self-imposed marginalisation from 'normal' spaces. The young people seek out a space, apart from others, noted for its isolation. Here there is the opportunity for expression, and being, a place where there is a sense of progression from boundaries imposed from the adult world, to the self-imposed boundaries of the 'becoming' adults. In the times spent here with the young people, strident exchanges unfold, unexpected relationships evolve and insights into often turbulent lives are glimpsed, as details enact around us.

The journey that the young people make to the Meadows begins in the city centre. Usually they would gather outside shops, where any dreamy imaginings of what could be, any lure towards convention, is rejected, as browsing and purchasing are forsaken. Gazing longingly through shop windows, however furtively executed, would not be tolerated, nor any secret succumbings to the seductive temptation of hypnotic consumerism. Manikins flaunt wares, yet this exhibitionism has no impact on this group, when gathered as a group. Becoming shoppers would interrupt their preferred sense of being. As their rowdy banter forces local proprietors to issue invitations to leave, these innocuous revolutionaries attempt to forge a new identity as they journey to the Meadows:

'If we hang out in town, it's like don't stop there, don't stand outside our shop …'

'I don't care what they say.'

'Yeah but it's not worth it, right.'

More rebellious group members are tempered by those less willing to be oppositional at this point of intersection, where antagonism could have fuelled an unseemly altercation. They choose to submit themselves to the regulatory insistence of the traders, but paradoxically, in so doing, continue to the Meadows empowered.

As Adams (1996, p5) acknowledges, empowerment is 'the means by which individuals, groups and/or communities become able to take control of their circumstances and achieve their goals'. Cooper (1994, p441), however, rejects the idea of power as emancipatory, preferring to concede its potential to debilitate. She states that power has 'the capacity to create subject identities who accept or internalize their position'. Powerfulness is a dynamic concept here, as the group members seem to play with the ideas of restraint and release. They are attuned to the acceptable and inhibit their own behaviour accordingly in a Freudian (1920) attempt (Freud and Strachey, 1984) to postpone satisfaction to achieve later reward. The reality of transitory forbearance is the debt to pay for deferred satisfaction.

The power of resistance

In recent years, the notion of resistance has featured strongly in subcultural studies, notably those focusing on working-class youth, such as the studies by the Centre for Contemporary Cultural Studies at the University of Birmingham. Resistance is a seemingly inevitable by-product of the effects of power; and is therefore seen an integral element of class-based studies of social interactions. Raby (2005) discusses the differing considerations of resistance, identifying two key categories – resistance as appropriation; and resistance as deviance – based on the work of Leong (1992). This provides a useful framework for understanding how the young people in this study make sense of their unfolding interactions.

The Meadows is symbolic of resistance, defiance, empowerment and freedom and is the peripheral edge of society, where the group prefers to locate. At this margin, a kind of egalitarian sovereignty unfolds, which identifies a new and different group – a group which presumes a certain kind of power and captures Foucault's (1978) notion of power as a productive force. Here we observe the resistance of the young people as localised and specific to the circumstances of their gathering; it is a means by which they can disrupt the normal, the institutional, the social order that they choose to extricate themselves from in order to be 'free' here:

> *'Why do you come to the Meadows?'*
> 'We just chill, somewhere to go that's out of the way.' (young person 1)

> *'Out the way of what?'*
> 'Everyone!' (young person 1)

> 'Yeah like hassle … trouble an' shit.' (young person 2)

> 'It's ours … Fuckin' free man … We get left alone.' (young person 1)

The young people do not attempt to conceal themselves in the more shadowy corners of the Meadows (see Figure 14.1). There are no cautious whisperings; there is no evasion or vigilant attention to anything beyond themselves. The group appears liberated by its desire to discard the mundanities, restrictions and regulations of the routine. There is amiable posturing as they lounge and banter with each other, and innocuous passers-by are discounted as irrelevant and ignored. Appropriation, then, of the free space, serves as the first element of their resistance.

Inevitably, the social domain of the young people is subject to interruption by others. It seemed that there were varying degrees of concern and attention given to these interruptions. In some instances, adults may well pass by the group, or even interact with the group, but their comments and behaviours would be largely ignored. The vague disapprovals that were evident in furtive gazes and muttered remarks were laughed away, or flouted by these young people. They did not want to interact. Significantly, they were not seeking approval or inclusion in the temporary social; they were forming their own social world without the need for external input.

Figure 14.1: The young people at the Meadows

Source: Photo taken by researcher/author Jane McKay

Self-marginalisation and soliciting partition

Giroux (1991) recognises the distancing process of 'othering', which Lahman (2008, p286), in the context of marginalisation, would undoubtedly describe as 'othered'. The group of young people we came to know at the Meadows embraced segregation; they deliberately sought to sever contact with ordinariness and to be 'other' people, to be 'others', paradoxically not in an 'other' place, but in a place which others used.

If the values of the other were not the values of one's own, Vidich and Lyman (2000) question whether there can ever be mutual understanding. The young people purposefully solicited partition and established an 'otherness', an ostracised position of self-imposed detachment, a self-marginalisation, which supposed this lack of understanding between the 'others' and themselves across an impossible divide. Those interfering old 'biddies' won't leave us alone. That intimidating mob of unruly louts threatens the sedate tranquility of our lush haven. An uneasy truce maintains as the incompatible factions fake acceptance with begrudging tolerance.

Uneasy interactions in negotiated space

Others are less easily overlooked, and it is the presence of the police that forces a particular method of interaction. This particular part of the Meadows becomes a point of intersection, a point of potential conflict. The young people who have intentionally marginalised themselves are drawn back from their preferred state of exile, as the public nature of their private sanctuary exacts a kind of recompense.

Interruptions by the police were taken seriously. The police themselves openly acknowledged that they were acting preventatively. While the police framed their interruption as being 'informal' in the way that they sought to engage and interact with the young people, it was the very fact that their action was viewed more formally by the young people showed that it was recognised and given credence by them.

The young people were keen to engage on a level with the police – physically and intellectually. Recognising the authority of the police and the potential impact of their presence, the young people played with methods of interaction, in order to secure recognition of their concerns, and the right to remain in situ, despite the noted disapproval of onlookers or passers-by.

So, for example, as the police approached, the young people would stand up to talk with them, removing any potential barrier of domination; they were keen to demonstrate their understanding of by-laws with regard to issues such as littering, drinking and social gatherings. These activities were integral to the overall establishment of their 'free space', so the young people were keen to negotiate their position and to retain their perceived territory of social action.

Unwelcome disturbance may easily be a catalyst for altercation, yet the encounters between the young people and the police are remarkably affable. At this point of intersection, inequalities are realised, understood and bargained. Various arbitrations unfold, as cautious connections, easily fractured, are covertly and necessarily maintained; no intimidating bluster here, as both police and young people carefully manoeuvre around each other. The willingness to mediate is clear from both parties. This trading of options and concession reciprocates, as an accepted position is sought.

Negotiation, then, features as an important element of the way that young people could justify their position on the margins. They were able to demonstrate an ability to negotiate their position, and did so. The police acknowledged this, and so what ensued was a kind of bargaining – a trading of options and concessions until an agreed position could be found. It was evident that the young people would be prepared to follow some rules in order to be able to transgress others at a later date (Freud and Strachey, 1984).

The image in Figure 14.2 shows the young people talking with the police. In the foreground is a collection of litter in plastic bags that

Figure 14.2: The young people with the police

Source: Photo taken by researcher/author Jane McKay

the young people had collected to demonstrate their responsibility and willingness to adhere to some imposed rules. After the police had left, the young people were then able to continue to drink and smoke – part of the routine of their social gathering.

The extent to which transgressive behaviour is tolerated by the police and tempered by the young people is evident at these points of contact, where cultural diversity plays out. When the boundary existence which the young people find at the Meadows is breached by the police, understandings around rights, power, inequality, peripheral being, resistance and conformity are haggled:

'… you get left alone on the meadows …'

'Except when the police come to talk to you!'

'The police fuckin' love us [mutual laughter].'

Valentine (2007) suggests that individuals experience different social structures concurrently. Mayo (2007, p68) confirms this, stating that 'identities work in strategies and counterstrategies, that categories are insufficient, crucial, and unstable, and that [at the point of intersection] no category of identity works alone'. Rodó-de-Zárate (2013, p925), in her work developing 'relief maps' as a way of representing intersectional data, also argues for flexibility in asserting that without using categories rigidly, both 'privilege and oppression' can be taken into account.

Therefore, to reconceptualise the place of convergence as divergent, as that which is undoubtedly fluctuating, even erratic, requires a mosaic understanding of intersectionality. Rose (1993) and Garry (2011) reject any binary understandings of space characterised by insider–outsider, powerful–weak, free–restricted, compliant–rebellious descriptions in a recognition of the inconsistent and precarious nature of space. More appropriate is an acceptance of the tangled nature of intersecting space, where complex threads are tied and untied, become knotted, are unpicked, cut and weaved together, continually.

The group at the Meadows rehearses a range of social practices, including status, position, relationship and employment both with each other and with additions to this exclusive group who seek to occupy this place with them. Figure 14.3 shows the Meadows as a point of intersection.

Crenshaw's (1991) structural intersectionality, concerned with the intersection of unequal social groups, is picked up in McCall's (2005) later distinction of approaches in using the concept of intersectionality, including the intra-categorical. McCall states that the focus of this approach is on 'particular social groups at neglected points of intersection', which allows for intricate aspects of lives to be revealed. McCall does, however, acknowledge the drawback of such a fine-tuned focus in deflecting from the more overarching societal and political influences that may cause inequalities. Walby et al (2012, p236) also warn that it is important not to 'conflate a set of social relations and related projects but to recognise the distinction between them'.

Figure 14.3: The Meadows – a point of intersection

Source: Photo taken by researcher/author Jane McKay

Resistance as rebellion

Our discussion offers a reminder that the everyday actions and interactions of young people are framed by a wider social and political context that sets the boundaries, rules and possibilities of their lives. These wider prescribed limits offer points of transgression, often chosen or negotiated by the young people themselves, through which they seek to forge themselves as competent in their social action. So, for example, the negotiation to remain on the Meadows using knowledge of rules and by-laws demonstrates how the mundane becomes dangerous; the ordinary provides extraordinary ways of being. It also recognises the uniqueness of each individual's experiences, while also identifying emerging patterns of marginalisation. Resistance as deviance and rebellion are captured and portrayed through our data.

To an extent, it could be argued that aspects of the empowerment discourse are appropriated and used as regulatory tools to support the subjugation discourse. For example, by offering 'safe' places for young people and 'safe' activities, we are more able to problematise young people who choose not to conform to these safe options. By providing the means to listen to young people's voices, we can problematise those young people who choose not to speak out (McKay, 2014). Once problematised, it is then easier to increase the regulatory and punitive actions against young people.

The young people whose experiences we share here choose not to engage in the safe places and activities that the adult world suggests to them; instead, they seek out their own safety away from the negative judgements and stereotypes that blight their everyday lives. This chapter argues that the cruelty of neo-liberalism has created a world where many young people seek the margins for solace from the lack of opportunity, lack of care and lack of tolerance for being themselves.

Recent cuts in public spending under the auspices of 'austerity' have targeted youth services particularly hard (Unison, 2014). As Portfilio and Carr (2010) suggest, neo-liberalism and the growth of market forces in public service delivery has generated increasingly negative attitudes towards young people, especially those who lie at the periphery of social desirability. Sanctions for transgressions become increasingly punitive and less forgiving in a society that blames young people for much of the world's social problems (Giroux, 1997). The young people here recognise all too well that the world around them affords less room for error, less space for play, less time to grow and learn. The social play that Erikson (1972) suggested as being integral to young people's successful transition to adulthood has taken the form in recent years of a damage limitation exercise, especially for those young people forced to enact their social play in public, open spaces, by virtue of circumstances of class or disadvantage.

Conclusion

We conclude by questioning what this means for our understanding of the ways that children and young people are marginalised. This can either be by others or by themselves; a means of removal from social situations to those of their own making in order to be 'free'. We demonstrate how marginalisation occurs in the micro-interactions of the mundane (which is often overlooked by protagonists), relating our findings to the wider, competing discourses of risk, problematisation, rights and voice.

The spaces where young people are afforded a voice – and the mechanisms for hearing their views and including them in the mainstream, conservative, acceptable social order – are structured in such ways that many young people feel disenfranchised not just by virtue of their social class, but also because of an inevitable difference. This difference of being young in a world designed by those seen as 'other' – by the young people themselves, by those older, by those better off, by those in uniform, and by those they do not recognise as their own potential future selves – is a lived reality for many of the young people we got to know in this study. In seeking out a separation, in order to 'be', these young people have found themselves constructed as a potential problem in the social order, occupying a shared social space where their own social play is viewed as a deviant act.

Being resistant – and continuing resistance – is a complex and volatile facet in a subculture of the young. Resistance, however, appears reciprocal here. An adult who may wish to recognise and accommodate perceived 'subordinates', but will do so only if the young person is prepared to be assimilated into a 'culture of the older,' presents an impossible dichotomy. This, to the younger, can be an intolerable submission and a point, therefore, of turbulent (mutual) opposition.

References

Adams, R. (1996) *Social work and empowerment*. London: Macmillan.

Brannen, J. (1999) 'Reconsidering children and childhood: Sociological and policy perspectives', in E.B. Silva and C. Smart (eds) *The New Family?* Sage: London: 143-58.

Cannella, G. (1999) 'The scientific discourse of education: Predetermining the lives of others – Foucault, education and children', *Contemporary Issues in Early Childhood*, 1, 1: 36-44.

Cohen, S. (2002) *Folk devils and moral panics 30th anniversary edition*. London: Routledge.

Cooper, D. (1994) 'Productive, relational and everywhere?: Conceptualising power and resistance within Foucauldian feminism', *Sociology*, 28, 2: 435-54.

Crenshaw, K.W. (1991) 'Mapping the margins: Intersectionality, identity politics, and violence against women of colour', *Stanford Law Review*, 43, 6: 1241-99.

Erikson, E. (1972) 'Play and actuality', in J. Bruner, A. Jolly and K. Sylva (eds) (1976) *Play – Its role in development and evolution*. Basic Books: 688-704.

Foucault, M. (1978) *The history of sexuality: Volume 1: An introduction*. New York: Vintage Books.

Freud, S. and Strachey, J. (1984) *On metapsychology: The theory of psychoanalysis* (new edn). Middlesex: Penguin Books.

Friends of the Meadows (2016) www.friendsofthemeadows.org.uk

Garry, A. (2011) 'Intersectionality, metaphors and the multiplicity of gender', *Hypatia*, 26, 4: 826-50.

Giroux, H. (1991) *Postmodernism, feminism and cultural politics*. New York: State University of New York Press.

Giroux, H. (1997) *Youth in a suspect society: Democracy or disposability?*, New York: Palgrave Macmillan.

Lahman, M. (2008) 'Always Othered: ethical research with children', *Journal of Early Childhood Research*, 6: 281.

Leong, L. W. (1992) 'Cultural resistance: the cultural terrorism of British male working-class youth', *Social Theory*, 12: 29-58.

Mayo, C. (2007) 'Intersectionality and Queer Youth', *Journal of Curriculum and Pedagogy*, 4, 2: 67-71.

McCall, L. (2005) 'The complexity of intersectionality', *Signs*, 30, 3: 1771-1800.

McKay, J. (2014) 'Young people's voices: disciplining young people's participation in decision-making in special educational needs', *Journal of Education Policy*, 29, 6, 760-73.

Portfilio, B.J. and Carr, P.R. (2010) (eds) *Youth culture, education and resistance*. Rotterdam: Sense Publishers.

Prout, A. and James, A. (1990) 'A new paradigm for the sociology of childhood? Provenance, promise and problems', in A. James and A. Prout (eds) *Constructing and Reconstructing Childhood*. London: Falmer Press.

Raby, R. (2005) 'What is resistance?', *Journal of Youth Studies*, 8, 2: 151-71.

Robinson, C. (2009) '"Nightscapes and leisure spaces": An ethnographic study of young people's use of free space', *Journal of Youth Studies*, 12, 5: 501-14.

Rodó-de-Zárate, M. (2013) 'Developing geographies of intersectionality with relief maps: reflections from youth research in Manresa, Catalonia', *Gender, Place and Culture*. doi: 10. 1080/0966369X.2013.817974.

Rose, G. (1993) *Feminism and geography*. Cambridge: Polity Press.

The Independent (2009) '"Hoodies, louts, scum": How media demonises teenagers', 13 March. www.independent.co.uk/news/uk/home-news/hoodies-louts-scum-how-media-demonises-teenagers-1643964.html

Unison (2014) 'Government cuts plunge youth work into crisis, warns UNISON report', 11 August. https://www.unison.org.uk/news/article/2014/08/government-cuts-plunge-youth-work-into-crisis-warns-unison-report/

Valentine, G. (2007) 'Theorizing and researching intersectionality: a challenge for feminist geography', *The Professional Geographer*, 59, 1: 10-21.

Vidich, A.J. and Lyman, S.M. (2000) 'Qualitative methods: the history in sociology and anthropology', in N.K. Denzin and Y.S. Lincoln (eds) *Handbook of qualitative research* (2nd edn). Thousand Oaks, CA: Sage, 37-84.

Walby, S., Armstrong, J. and Strid, S. (2012) 'Intersectionality: multiple inequalities in social theory', *Sociology*, 46, 2: 224-40.

FIFTEEN

'Binge' drinking devils and moral marginality: young people's calculated hedonism in the Canterbury night-time economy

Robert McPherson

Introduction

Young people have long been associated with being 'folk devils' (Cohen, 2002), who are morally marginalised by the moral indignation and controversy related to media portrayals of recreational substance use (Young, 1971). This chapter examines the media framing of the contemporary alcohol consumption practice known as 'binge' drinking, and how negative media representations of young people and this practice have produced moral indignation and marginality in the UK (Cohen, 2002). It argues that media terms such as 'binge' drinking create negative connotations, which act to marginalise young people in the UK today, and that prioritising the experiences of young people and alcohol consumption can lead to a reframing of the term to: 'calculated hedonism' (Griffin et al, 2008). The argument is associated with young people being granted more agency and control within their alcohol consumption 'management' than suggested in mainstream media representations and government policy documents. This features a prioritisation on expressing the life experiences of participants involved in the night-time economy by featuring examples of young people drinking.

The chapter builds upon the reframing of the term 'binge', by reflecting this as a problematic term as outlined by the definitions associated with the practice. It also reflects on the argument that 'empirical research suggests that young people intentionally manage their levels of desired and actual intoxication by using strategies that incorporate aspects of perceived risk' (Measham, 2006, p261). This is a central feature of contemporary academic discourses around young people's alcohol consumption.

'Folk devils' and discourses of youth: media misrepresentations of young people and moral panics

Media discourse regarding substance use among young people in particular has long been highlighted as being both a marginalising and a myopic view. Stanley Cohen describes the negative impact of misleading media representations on public perceptions in *Folk devils and moral panics*:

> the media have long operated as agents of moral indignation in their own right: even if they are not self-consciously engaged in muck-raking, their very reporting of certain 'facts' can be sufficient to generate concern, anxiety, indignation or panic. (Cohen, 2002, p7)

While Cohen's view of a strategic media amplification of certain 'facts' was originally associated with his study into the youth subculture of mods and rockers in the 1960s, this view is also explicitly linked to the contemporary media representations of UK 'binge' drinking. These are exemplified by headlines such as: 'UK among worst "binge drinkers"' (*BBC News Online*, 1 June 2006); 'Britain is the "binge-drinking capital of Europe"' (*The Telegraph*, 22 April 2010); and 'UK's teenage girls are biggest binge drinkers in Europe' (*Mail Online*, 1 July 2012). Kelly (2006, p30) argues that these representations became a source of: 'Stories perpetuating negative images of youth [which] apparently appeal to many adults and sell newspapers'. These negative images evoke tensions in public perceptions, which are the result of the translation and portrayal by media outlets, ranging from tabloid newspapers to local press and television documentaries, which create a 'discourse of moral panic around young people's "binge drinking" [which] has pervaded popular media, public policy and academic research' (Griffin et al, 2008, p3).

Tellingly, 'binge' drinking features as the first two words of the then Prime Minister David Cameron's foreword to *The Government's Alcohol Strategy* (Home Office, 2012, p2), which highlights the negative social and cultural connotations associated with alcohol consumption:

> Binge drinking isn't some fringe issue, it accounts for half of all alcohol consumed in this country. The crime and

violence it causes drains resources in our hospitals, generates mayhem on our streets and spreads fear in our communities. My message is simple. We can't go on like this. We have to tackle the scourge of violence caused by binge drinking. And we have to do it now. (Home Office, 2012, p2)

This account from the British Prime Minister reinforced the moral marginalisation of alcohol use, by using the term 'binge' drinking alongside emotionally resonant language such as 'crime', 'violence', 'mayhem', 'fear' and 'scourge'. The Prime Minister further declared that: 'Binge drinking is a serious problem. And I make no excuses for clamping down on it' (Home Office, 2012, p2). Consequently, this chapter argues that the constructed media representation of 'binge' drinking has defined a moral marginalisation of young people and alcohol use within public perceptions.

Becker (1963, p149) relates this definition of young people to the notion of the 'Moral Entrepreneur'. He explains that: 'moral crusades are typically dominated by those in the upper level of social structure – [this] means that they add to the power they derive from the legitimacy of their moral position, the power they derive from their superior position in society'. This has been related to previous youth subcultures that were associated in the media with the use of specific substances. For example, the mods were aligned with amphetamine use and the hippies with LSD during the 1960s; and also the media furore surrounding the subsequent youth subculture of the acid house movement of the late 1980s provoked widespread interest in, and condemnation of, the drug ecstasy and its users.

Young (1971) expands on the idea of moral condemnation of young people in *The Drugtakers: The social meaning of drug use*. For Young's subject 'drug taker', it is easy to reframe as 'binge' drinker within a contemporary context:

> the mass media portrayal of the drug taker [or 'binge' drinker] is not a function of random ignorance, but a coherent part of consensual mythology ... by fanning up moral panics over drug use ['binge' drinking], it contributes enormously to public hostility toward the drug taker ['binge' drinker] and precludes any rational approach to the problem. (Young, 1971, p415)

These views of Cohen, Young and Becker broaden the scope of a coherent moral marginalisation towards young people and intoxication across decades. This is strategically managed through media portrayals and is a result of power relations exerted upon young people by the upper echelons of the social structure. This chapter seeks to examine this controversy by a focus on voicing the life experiences of young people participating in the night-time economy with which the term 'binge' drinking is associated.

'Binge drinking': defining and redefining a problematic term

Measham (2006, p265) highlights the common media usage of the term 'binge' drinking and its negative connotations for young people, arguing that: 'the current media, political, and public perception of unbridled British "binge" drinking youths rampaging the city streets after dark needs tempering'. The controversy associated with the term 'binge' and its mainstream usage in both media products and government policy helps to consolidate this view, which confirms the negative public perception of young people and 'binge' drinking.

The controversy associated with the term 'binge' drinking is further evidenced by the difficulty in locating a precise definition of the term. Close inspection of multiple sources demonstrates that 'binge' drinking is a complex term to define with any great accuracy, due to the multiple connotations that its definitions are shown to carry. Plant and Plant (2006) contextualise this complexity to the point of a distinct complacency in its construction and meaning, stating that 'binge' drinking is a terminology that 'has been used in two distinct ways' (p viii). Initially, they contend, 'binge' was a term used by health professionals to describe the activity of going out on a 'bender', which was 'a prolonged drinking spree during which an individual drinks in a sustained manner and gives up other activities for at least two or three days' (p viii). Subsequently, Plant and Plant state that 'binge' has been redefined into a further and more popularly considered meaning, which 'relates to a single drinking session intended to or actually leading to intoxication. This session need not be prolonged but is assumed to be at least potentially risky' (p ix). Where these perspectives meet in agreement is within the suggested context of possible participation in risky behaviour by consumers of alcohol, or the suggestion that the individual involved will be unable to participate in regular everyday activities within the duration of this period of intoxication. The general impression created is of how an individual connected with the term 'binge' is the subject of a moral marginalisation with regard to their substance use and level of intoxication.

Adding to the confusion regarding a clear and succinct interpretation of the term 'binge drinking', bodies such as the National Institute on Alcohol Abuse and Alcoholism (NIAAA) in the US and the UK Home Office respectively define 'binge' as: 'a pattern of drinking alcohol that corresponds to consuming five or more drinks for a male or four or more drinks for a female in about 2 hours' (NIAAA, 2003); or 'people who reported having felt "very drunk" once or more in the past 12 months' (Mathews and Richardson, 2005). The ideas emerging here concern less the length of duration of alcohol consumption, as suggested by the earlier examples, but a proposition of the idea as framed within the NIAAA perspective that consumption *versus* time = binge. Consequently, speed and volume of consumption become the focus of the definition. Recent evidence also supports this confusion, as White and Hingson (2014, p201) argue that there is no clear or specific definition: '[E]xcessive or "binge" drinking is defined ... as consuming five or more drinks in an evening, although the instruments vary in the specified time frames given'.

Conversely, Griffin et al (2008, p4) oppose the open use of the term 'binge' drinking, stating that it is an 'emotive term', due to its common use in media circles. Alternatively, they advocate the potential reframing of the term 'binge' drinking towards the more inclusive term 'calculated hedonism', whereby young people are attributed with more agency towards their decisions regarding alcohol consumption within the context of the night-time economy. Previously, Measham and Brain (2005) argued towards the term a 'new culture of intoxication', where young people were subject to multiple attractions in the night-time economy, which contributed to a style and approach to alcohol consumption that became identified with the hard-to-define and controversial terminology of 'binge' drinking.

Measham and Brain (2005) cite several key developments over the previous few decades that contributed to this 'new culture of intoxication'. The emergence of dance music culture in the late 1980s saw a shift among young people from the use of alcohol towards dance drugs such as ecstasy, and the alcohol industry responded by recommodifying alcohol as a psychoactive product targeted at a more diverse group of young users. Blackman (2004, p80) expands upon this idea: 'It is possible to suggest that the alcohol industry responded with a calculated strategy which utilized aspects of dance culture at a general level through marketing'. Smith (2014, p8) describes this as producing 'specific cultures of alcohol consumption – the determined drunkenness commonly referred to as "binge drinking" against the commodified experience offered by the night-time high street'.

These specific cultures of alcohol consumption resulted in a wider range of alcoholic products appearing, which were designed to appeal to young adults as 'psycho-active consumers' (Brain, 2000). These included: FABs (flavoured alcoholic beverages); RMDs (spirits-based, ready-to-drink mixers); 'buzz' drinks based on legally available substances such as caffeine; and, more recently, cheap shots of spirits and liqueurs usually downed in one for an instant 'hit' (Measham, 2006). These developments have led to the conclusion that: 'the reality is that many young people are deliberately engaging in hedonistic drinking where the "buzz" effect of alcohol has become an important commodity within the contemporary leisure culture' (Fry, 2011, p65). This is related to origins within the alcohol industry and outside of the moral marginalisation of 'binge' drinking perpetuated by media images of young people consuming alcohol.

By highlighting these changes in alcohol consumption elicited by the changes made by the alcohol industry across the previous two decades, the research described in this chapter supports the redefinition of 'binge' drinking towards the alternative term 'calculated hedonism'. The latter term refers to 'a way of "managing" alcohol consumption which might be viewed as excessive' (Griffin et al, 2008, p3), rather than the moral marginalisation that has been propagated through media portrayals of young people and alcohol. Young people's ways of 'managing' alcohol are highlighted in the ethnographic case studies in the following section.

Alcohol management by young people in the night-time economy: distinct styles of drinking, pre-defined drinking parameters and a sense of community

In this section, alcohol consumption sessions (which may be defined as 'binge' drinking in terms of their consumption *versus* time) are referred to as heavy episodic drinking, with the emphasis on highlighting a sense of 'calculatedness' in young people's drinking. This relates to distinct styles of drinking among young people in the night-time economy, the pre-defined drinking parameters such as pre-planning of the evening and exit strategy, and the sense of community which young people gain from drinking inclusively within a group setting.

The research was an ethnographic study into young adults' (aged 18-34) alcohol consumption in the cathedral city of Canterbury, south-east England. Chatterton and Hollands (2002) describe cities as:

sites of entertainment and pleasure seeking [where] a central focus of recent rebranding has been the promotion of the night-time economy, much of which is characterised by the ritual descent of young adults into city-centre bars, pubs and clubs especially during the weekend. (Chatterton and Hollands, 2002, p95)

Two case studies have been selected, which focus on understanding alcohol use in young people through their own life experiences not as 'binge' drinking, but as 'drinking [which] is constituted and managed as a potential source of pleasure' (Griffin et al, 2008, p4). This is supported by an emphasis on the accounts of the experiences of young people within the Canterbury night-time economy. The research correlates with Measham and Moore (2009, p438), who argue: 'The expansion of the British night-time economy has led to a growing body of research focused on drinking, alcohol-related crime and broader cultural and criminological aspects of the alcohol-focused licensed leisure industry'.

By arguing that drinking can be both excessive and fun, the term 'calculated hedonism' will empower young people with the responsibility to understand and tailor their alcohol consumption in the context of their own leisure time. This will reduce the moral marginalisation aroused by media perceptions or the influence of the term 'binge' drinking; also fulfilling the 'need to consider the cultural entrenchment of young adults' alcohol consumption and the way they manage their alcohol experiences' (Fry, 2011, p 65).

Throughout the fieldwork in the Canterbury night-time economy, it was apparent that young adults made a distinction between styles of alcohol consumption. This managed and strategic consumption supported a reframing of the term 'binge' drinking towards 'calculated hedonism'. As an example of this distinction between styles of alcohol consumption, in case study one, James (aged 21, student) offered an insight into the variety of social occasions among young adults where alcohol was consumed and how. He stated:

'Well, there's going out for a couple of pints and a quick chat or a game of pool, which might just take place in the afternoon or the evening. That's what I like to do. Heavy drinking – shots or spirits – is also common. This isn't really for me, I see people hammering back the shots, but I've never really liked the idea of it myself. I just prefer a few beers, and so do quite a few of my friends. My housemates are always up for getting smashed on the shots and good luck to them, but they plan their evening around where they are going and when they are going to get back. It's fun to watch them and see how they react to being so drunk, but they always know what they are doing.'

This statement by James from the field diary was gained after a series of fieldwork trips out in the night-time economy. This data extract supports the argument by Griffin et al (2008) that young people have devised ways in which to manage their alcohol consumption in order to become heavily intoxicated within a level of consumption that would correspond with any of the earlier stated definitions of 'binge' drinking. James states that he is aware that the practice of heavy episodic drinking occurs among his peers. Although not participating fully in the practice himself, he is happy to engage with his friends while they participate in this activity. James demonstrates an awareness of heavy episodic alcohol consumption, while also making it clear that he has made a conscious decision not to participate, based around this awareness drawn from personal experience of being around the activity. He also expands on how his friends manage their own alcohol consumption, when he gives an insight into how they plan their alcohol consumption in advance by deciding on their destinations and also by being aware of when they are returning home.

Rather than creating an impression of reckless, thoughtless drinking – which the media and government policy refer to as a social burden that must be tackled or clamped down on – this example of the experience of young people in relation to alcohol consumption constructs an unfamiliar narrative of young people drinking in a calculated fashion that is strategically planned and practised by its protagonists. These fieldwork data develop the impression that James accepted heavy episodic drinking as a part of the freedom of choice made within his friends' social lives and even enjoyed watching them partake in these practices, further stating: 'it doesn't really affect me what they choose to do'. In defending the rights of his friends to undertake extreme drinking practices, and the potential entertainment it provided to onlookers and participants, James demonstrated acquired knowledge of the culture of extreme drinking practices informed by close proximity to this activity. This is outside of the mediated views that Cohen and Young argue develop into a moral marginalisation for young people involved in intoxication. James was able to view both the practice and the aftermath of it through his personal experience of the practice of alcohol consumption management – by both himself and his friends. By virtue of this, he was able to make informed decisions as to his own participation in – and perception of – extreme drinking, while acknowledging that what other young adults do had little impact on his own life.

In case study two, Tara (24, office worker) offered an account from the fieldwork diary that provided an insight into the practice of heavy episodic drinking occurring in the Canterbury night-time economy:

> 'I was out the other week with work colleagues on a Friday night in Canterbury, and was being pestered to do this shot, or a shot of that. It's not that I have a problem with people drinking like that, I have done shots before, but I really don't enjoy feeling that drunk or how it makes you feel afterwards. If I was really up for a heavy night out, I might have one or two, but definitely no more. I had to keep saying: "But I'm OK drinking my wine" or "Not this time" as different colleagues kept asking me to join them. They weren't pushy, just drunk really, and wanting everyone to join in. I stayed firm, and just enjoyed my evening at my own pace. I enjoyed watching them getting really drunk, they were having a great time and just relaxing after a long week at work. They have their evening mapped out – we had three pubs planned out before a club – and the taxis were ordered for a specific time. Some of my colleagues were really drunk by the end of the evening, but we each got in our cabs, and made our way home safely.'

Tara's account correlates with that of James and also reinforces the argument of Griffin et al (2008) towards the notion of 'calculated hedonism', by revealing a distinction between styles of drinking related to speed and volume of consumption and the type of alcoholic product being consumed. This distinction of styles is specific to the conscious decisions of individuals within the night-time economy. Tara also demonstrates acceptance towards heavy episodic drinking, which is based on her previously acquired knowledge of this practice through personal experience.

Tara admitted that she had experienced shots for herself before, but did not enjoy the feeling of intoxication that it entailed and preferred to drink at her own pace; whereas James was familiar with the activities of his housemates, but was not attracted to participating in this practice. Both participants accepted that heavy episodic drinking featuring the consumption of multiple shots of liqueur is a familiar aspect of participation within the night-time economy, which fulfils the criteria of the various definitions of 'binge' drinking relating to speed and volume of consumption, and also the type of alcoholic product consumed.

Importantly, Tara and James also demonstrated an acceptance of these styles of drinking, which referred to the fun or entertainment that could be gained from the role of onlooker towards heavy episodic drinking. This highlights 'the importance of collective forms of alcohol consumption in the establishment and reinforcement of key aspects of both subjective and group identities' (Smith, 2013, p1069), which are often overlooked in media portrayals of young people drinking.

Both James and Tara relate that their friends were involved in pre-planned heavy episodic drinking sessions. These had clearly defined parameters that pre-defined the outcome of the evening in terms of a safe conclusion, by providing a finite end destination and return transport home; also a sense of community and group identity among young people, which can be experienced by participants both inside and outside the specific style of alcohol consumption. This is demonstrated by James's friends being clear on their destinations and their mode of transport for their return home. Tara's account, which also establishes that young people in the Canterbury night-time economy demonstrated a calculated strategy towards drinking that features hedonistic pleasure in the shape of drinking high-ABV alcohol quickly but also having pre-planned destinations and a pre-planned exit strategy from the Canterbury night-time economy correlates with the account of James. Fun and laughter, which were not gained at the expense of other people's good times and enjoyment, characterised the presence of heavy episodic drinking in the Canterbury night-time economy. Both Tara and James's accounts alluded to strategic approaches to alcohol consumption that reject the negative media representation of 'binge' drinking, which formulates a morally marginalising view of young people acting neglectfully within the night-time economy while in the pursuit of pleasure.

James also offered this further account, recorded in the field diary, which developed more context of 'calculatedness' in his friends' drinking and there being a sense of community outside the often reckless image portrayed by the media of young people 'binge' drinking:

> 'There are occasions where you hear negative stuff about young people drinking – fighting, or breaking stuff in the street, stuff like that – and you do see the occasional idiot

around in Canterbury, but I've never seen anyone I know cause any trouble to anyone. They're generally too busy having a good time with our group; and that's what it's about really, joining together and having a few drinks – or a lot of drinks if that's what you fancy, but not allowing anything to get out of hand. If anyone starts to annoy anyone or looks like doing anything silly, there's people around to make sure that it doesn't happen. You know, people do know when to stop, or when they've had enough, and if they don't then someone else will tell them.'

This reference to a lack of engagement in violence or vandalism among James and his friends also challenges the moral marginalisation of young people made through media representations, by offering the unfamiliar perspective of young people participating in heavy episodic drinking while making active decisions about how to behave within the night-time economy. This was guided by calculated individual understandings of the limits of alcohol consumption, which were also reinforced by having other people around within a group who were prepared to intervene, were there to be any potential misbehaviour by group members. While James is aware of infrequent acts of violence or vandalism occurring within the Canterbury night-time economy, he is also clear from the members of his group – and across the general population – that such instances related to heavy episodic drinking are isolated. According to the accounts of both James and Tara, drinking in groups provides a calculated structure within which young people manage their alcohol consumption and also their behaviour within the night-time economy. This represents a level of agency towards young people that is absent from mainstream media representations of young people 'binge' drinking.

The term 'binge' drinking has provided an outline of moral marginalisation relating to young people and alcohol consumption through mainstream media representations, but the broad scope of definitions related to this activity have failed to provide a sense of focus or purpose to how young people manage their alcohol consumption and behaviour in the night-time economy. The term 'calculated hedonism' (Griffin et al, 2008) provides a less-emotive structure of definition, within which young people can be recognised to manage their alcohol consumption and behaviour, especially within drinking groups of various styles of consumption and levels of intoxication. This demonstrates that the 'the night-time economy now functions as the field upon which many people attempt to develop a sense of communitas and belonging' (Smith, 2013, p1069).

Conclusion

This chapter has argued that 'binge' drinking is a problematic term, which has led to moral marginalisation of young people. However, it is also a commonly recognised drinking style in the Canterbury night-time economy, which features strong elements of calculation and planning among participants. By voicing the life experiences of two young people within the Canterbury night-time economy, morally marginalising media representations of young people drinking have been countered with accounts of planned and managed alcohol consumption that resulted in young people sharing good times with one another in group settings and communities.

This chapter has referred to previous work on youth cultures by Young (1971), Cohen (2002) and Becker (1963), which argued that representations of intoxicated young people are constructed through a media lens. This construction led to young people's portrayal as 'folk devils' and towards their moral marginalisation in society, which is a result of power structures in society as recognised through government policy towards 'binge' drinking and how this defines young people's image within the night-time economy.

The introduction and discussion of the hard-to-define term 'binge' drinking demonstrated that the contemporary debate around young people drinking was characterised by an association with carelessness and even violence, but outside of clearly identifiable parameters. This was countered by the introduction of the oppositional term 'calculated hedonism' (Griffin et al, 2008), which developed a reframing of the idea of young people 'binge' drinking carelessly towards more responsible and pleasurable outcomes through ethnographic data examples from the field. This highlighted a 'calculatedness' among young people in group settings in the night-time economy, characterised by management of alcohol consumption and behaviour, alongside the development of a sense of community founded upon groups of drinkers of various levels of consumption and intoxication.

References

Becker, H. (1963) *Outsiders: Studies in the sociology of deviance*. The Free Press.

Blackman, S. (2004) *Chilling out: The cultural politics of substance consumption, youth and drug policy*. Open University Press.

Brain, K. (2000) *Youth, alcohol, and the emergence of the post-modern alcohol order*. Institute of Alcohol Studies.

Chatterton, P. and Hollands, R. (2002) 'Theorising urban playscapes: producing, regulating and consuming youthful nightlife city spaces', *Urban Studies*, 39, 1, 95-116.

Cohen S. (2002) *Folk devils and moral panics* (3rd edn). Routledge: London.

Fry, M.-L. (2011) 'Seeking the pleasure zone: Understanding young adult's intoxication culture', *Australasian Marketing Journal* (AMJ), 19, 1, 65-70.

Griffin, C., Szmigin, I., Mistral, M., Bengry-Howell, A., Weale, L. and Hackley, C. (2008) 'Re-framing "binge drinking" as calculated hedonism: Empirical evidence from the UK', *International Journal of Drug Policy*, 19, 5, 359-66.

Home Office (2012) *The Government's Alcohol Strategy*. London: Home Office.

Kelly, D. (2006) 'Frame work: helping youth counter their misrepresentations in media', *Canadian Journal of Education*, 29, 1, 27-48.

Mathews, S. and Richardson, A. (2005) *Findings from the 2004 Offending, Crime and Justice Survey: Alcohol-Related Crime and Disorder*. Research Findings 261. London: Home Office

Measham, F. (2006) 'The new policy mix: alcohol, harm minimisation, and determined drunkenness in contemporary society', *International Journal of Drug Policy*, 17, 4, 258-68.

Measham, F. and Brain, K. (2005) '"Binge" drinking, British alcohol policy and the new culture of intoxication', *Crime, Media, Culture*, 1, 3, 262-83.

Measham, F. and Moore, K. (2009) 'Repertoires of distinction: Exploring patterns of weekend polydrug use within local leisure scenes across the English night time economy', *Criminology & Criminal Justice*, 9, 4, 437-64.

National Institute of Alcohol Abuse and Alcoholism (NIAAA) (2003) https://www.niaaa.nih.gov/research/guidelines-and-resources/recommended-alcohol-questions

Plant, M. and Plant, M. (2006) *Binge Britain: Alcohol and the national response*. Oxford: Oxford University Press.

Smith, O. (2013) 'Holding back the beers: Maintaining "youth" identity within the British night-time leisure economy', *Journal of Youth Studies*, 16, 8, 1069-83.

Smith, O. (2014) *Contemporary adulthood and the night-time economy*. London: Palgrave.

White, A. and Hingson, R. (2014) 'The burden of alcohol use: excessive alcohol consumption and related consequences among college students', *Alcohol Research*, 35, 2, 201–18.

Young, J. (1971) *The drugtakers: The social meaning of drug use.* Harper Collins.

SIXTEEN

The new 'spectral army': biography and youth poverty on Teesside's deprived estates

Anthony Ruddy

'I need a job but no one will help me. I'd do anything, I swear to God, anything. I just want a job man. I just want to be able to get a job. I've tried and tried.' (Carl, 26, unemployed)

Introduction

In spite of the significant interventions over successive decades, including the implementation of national government legislation (since repealed) to mitigate the effects of poverty and even to try to eradicate it, there are millions of people spanning all age groups who continue to live in poverty in the UK today. The Office for National Statistics (2016) shows that around one third of all people in the UK were living in income poverty at least once between 2011 and 2014, while the Child Poverty Action Group (2015) shows approximately 3.5 million young people alone who are currently living in poverty – equivalent to more than one quarter of the UK's entire youth population. Echoing Walter Greenwood (1933), they are the new 'spectral army'.[1]

Contrary to popular belief, most of these young people will be living in households where at least one parent is working. Poverty and Social Exclusion (PSE, 2015) and the Joseph Rowntree Foundation (MacInnes et al, 2015) also estimate that up to half of all young people in the UK are living in poverty – a rate that is increasing over time. Currently there are around one million unemployed young people in the UK and many millions more who are underemployed in jobs that bring little in way of income, security or satisfaction (Shildrick et al, 2012). The social and economic impact of the global financial crisis – and the resulting austerity programme that followed in the UK – has affected young people significantly, but little is known about the real consequences of poverty for the young and poor in the UK today. By and large, the underlying basis for undertaking the research upon which this chapter is based was mostly founded on a lack of qualitative research in the field of contemporary youth poverty (Blackman, 1997; Craine, 1997).

In Britain, there is already an impressive body of research evidence, which has built up over many years, studying the nature, extent and consequences of poverty. The University of Bristol (PSE, 2015) published what it considers to be the most comprehensive study of poverty undertaken to date in the UK. Yet, although research about poverty in the UK is extensive, it is also typically centred on younger children (Bradshaw, 1990; Ridge, 2009) or older age groups such as the elderly, rather than young people. Instead, research about youth poverty is scarce and tends to be largely quantitative in nature. Very few UK studies focus closely or exclusively on youth poverty. Apart from some notable exceptions (for example Fahmy, 2006, 2014), most youth poverty research tends to be founded on long-standing international studies (Canto-Sanchez and Mercader-Prats, 1999) or grounded in research that has been largely constructed around the secondary analysis of large-scale international datasets (Iacovou and Arnstein, 2007).

This chapter is based on research focusing on the experiences of young people growing up in contexts of multiple deprivation and material hardship in a small, deindustrialised town in north-east England. The main aim of the research was to interrogate the interplay between youth poverty and material inequality, youth cultural practice and the day-to-day lives of young people from marginalised communities. The research explores the complex interface between socioeconomics, everyday life and the identities and values of young people during the course of their transition to adulthood.

The structure of this chapter

A key feature of the research was to study the structural context of youth poverty, such as local youth labour-market conditions and the effects of recent government welfare reforms. The aim was to try to get a sense of the struggle to gain meaningful employment at a time of nationally imposed austerity and the various pressures associated with the recent changes to the UK welfare system. In particular, participants talked openly and honestly about their strong commitment to work, against a backdrop of intermittent (under)employment and seemingly permanent recession within a severely depressed youth labour market in the local area.

This chapter explores the multiple hardships described by 25 young people who were living in contexts of poverty, inequality and marginality. The chapter describes *the concertina effect* of interconnected hardships and also explores the corrosive effects of poverty, demonstrating how the consequences cut across many aspects of social, economic and family life. For many research participants, the effects culminated in complex and challenging lifestyles, characterised by a combination of deep financial hardship, social and economic discrimination, new forms of labour-market exploitation, difficult home lives, a deep sense of regret and remorse, low self-worth and resulting poor mental health. The final section attempts to show the range of diversity that existed within the same socioeconomic group and how this variety manifested itself in the differing daily lives, values and aspirations of young people – the kind of diversity that we might ordinarily expect to see across or between social groups but not within the same group.

Methodology and fieldwork

The research used to inform this chapter was grounded in the ethnographic tradition of Becker (1963), Polsky (1967) and Whyte (1943) as well as some landmark studies in the UK (Willis, 1977), in Europe (Bourdieu et al, 1999) and in the US (MacLeod, 1987). The study was constructed from biographical methods, observations and field notes, but was principally informed by lengthy in-depth interviews with participants, in order to draw out the rich subjective narratives and life stories of some of the UK's poorest young people (Hart, 2010).

The research setting or fieldwork site was selected using objective national datasets for measuring deprivation levels down to small areas. Based on data published by the Department for Communities and Local Government (2011), the research locale (which we shall call 'Boomtown' to maintain its anonymity), was classified as the 12th most deprived ward in England. The fieldwork site was a post-industrial urban town, suffering from chronic, long-term socioeconomic decline, disinvestment and uninterrupted structural degeneration since the 1980s. Apart from one brief mention in earlier research by Townsend et al (1988), the fieldwork site has not featured in any previous research study until now. Fieldwork for the research was undertaken in 2013 and 2014, which included 25 completed interviews with young people aged between 16 and 26 years old.

Research findings

Using descriptive quotations from participants, the following sections try to give an idea of the multiple difficulties experienced by young people in poverty. Almost immediately, what materialised from conversations was the thick volume of adversities that young people had to endure every day, largely due to a lack of money. The following sections use illustrative examples to show the multifaceted nature and compounding effects of youth poverty, looking at young people's accounts of unemployment and welfare. For the majority of participants, being out of work was the trigger that initiated and brought about the resulting hardships. For many of the participants, it was the combined effects of unemployment and a punitive welfare regime that were the root cause of many of their consequent troubles.

Unemployment and the cold shoulder of welfare capitalism

Young people's accounts of growing up on Teesside's poor estates repeatedly referred to their current economic status and their search for work within a deeply depressed labour market in the local area. The following responses, which were characteristic of the vast majority of those who took part in the research, reflect the frustration and disappointment of participants when work was hard to find. The feedback from young people showed evidence of a strong work ethic and a willingness to look for work, rather than the predictable narrative of young people as feckless:

> 'I'd like to get a job but I'm finding it hard. There's not many jobs going. The jobs are like dead-end jobs.' (John, 19, unemployed teenager)

> 'I've been looking but I can't seem to get nothing / I mean, I've been applying for jobs and stuff but I never hear anything back / I've always worked until I had my first son and I've never, ever signed on the dole or anything like that; so, to go from that to relying on other people for your money, it's not really what you want is it? I'd rather be out there earning my own money and paying for my own things / I just want to get back out to work and start earning my

own money / I want to be out there again, I don't want to be sat around and relying on the dole / It's just the fact that people think that anybody who is on benefits is lazy and they don't want to work and they can't be bothered and they just tar you all with the same brush really … we are not all just lazy gits who sponge money off people to live. There's people out there who do want to work and make a life for themselves, it's just that the jobs aren't there for people / That's all I want to do, just get back out to work.' (Lilly, 26, unemployed single mum)

'There's nowhere to go, nothing to do, there's no work. I used to work in Corus and then when it got mothballed I lost my job and then after that I can't get no work / It's hard living down here, really, especially on Jobseekers Allowance and all because it's hard to live on what you're getting.' (Dean, 24, unemployed steelworker)

With few opportunities in the labour market, many participants talked about how they had taken their chances with alternative openings for work. Some young people discussed doing voluntary work, while others talked about how they had taken on caring roles. Others talked about doing 'fiddly jobs' for 'cash in hand', such as short-term labouring work, or becoming involved in criminal networks, which were widespread in the local area. Many participants had been engaged in some form of *precarious* employment and talked about their experiences of low-paid, transitory employment, often with large, well-known multinational companies based in the surrounding area (for example Asda). Consistent with the type of evidence and arguments set out by Standing (2011) in his descriptions of the new global youth labour market and its new forms of exploitation, employment experiences were characterised by: poor pay and poor working conditions; a lack of permanency and security; or hazardous and dangerous work (for example asbestos stripping).

Many young people also recalled their experiences of poor training courses that they had participated in, either at the local colleges or with a number of national training providers (for example Carillion), which, they believed, did not adequately prepare them for employment. Added to this, other young people described themselves as being discriminated against, explaining how they felt economically marginalised because of where they lived (Tunstall et al, 2014). Research participants believed they had been deliberately locked out of the local labour market due to postcode discrimination, which privileged people from more affluent neighbourhoods. The blend of poor employment opportunities, inadequate training provision and the perceived discrimination of participants had steered many young people to engage with *the informal working economy* (Katungi et al, 2006). Some young people even viewed crime as a reasonable alternative career:

> 'There's always crime going on around here, yes, there's a lot, daily. It's a way of life for some people I know, but I don't want to say any more about that, like I've said, it's a living.' (John, 19, unemployed teenager)

The combination of unemployment and a broken labour market left many young people with no option but to claim their legal entitlement to a variety of low-value, rudimentary welfare benefit payments, typically consistent with *welfare capitalism* (Esping-Anderson, 1990). The low worth of state benefits was made worse for some young people, who were also affected by the initial impact of the government's new social austerity measures. For example, the introduction of benefit sanctions and the 'bedroom tax' both had a particularly negative affect on young people. Often, this resulted in a significant reduction in the participants' benefit payments, placing even greater financial and personal strain on young people:

> 'Well I've been sanctioned at the moment because I never went to a course through the job centre. I've been living on £52 a fortnight from the 2nd August. I'm struggling at the moment, I can't do nowt, I'm borrowing more than I'm actually getting.' (Dean, 24, unemployed steelworker)

> 'It's just because I'm in a three-bedroom house and I've got the bedroom tax, so obviously I need to down size ... it's like because I have two bedrooms that I aren't using I have to pay £11 a week towards them, which all in all is about £44 or something and it's impossible on the dole, absolutely impossible.' (Claire, 23, unemployed female)

These responses highlight the harmful effects of social austerity for some of the poorest people in the UK and the forms of social suffering that pervade their lives because of the introduction of radical welfare reforms. These reforms particularly affected young people already struggling to survive on rudimentary benefit payments, who would now be penalised further, either through the bedroom levies or by having their basic benefits reduced even more. Similar to the experiences described by O'Hara (2015), these findings are also consistent with research published by Watts et al (2014), which is now starting to reveal the negative impact of benefit sanctions. Unable to participate in their communities or to maintain any degree of independence as part of their natural transition to adulthood, some young people had no option but to consider returning home to their parents.

The weight of the world

The participants who took part in the Teesside research experienced suffering that closely relates to Bourdieu et al's (1999) *The Weight of the World*, based on growing concerns about the harmful effects of globalisation, especially on those most vulnerable, and on Bourdieu's ideological opposition towards neo-liberalism and the consequent policy reforms in France at that time. Bourdieu wanted to understand more about the lived reality of these reforms, and designed a comprehensive ethnographic study to interrogate the consequences of globalisation on ordinary people. The study revealed new forms of social suffering directly resulting from government policies, and recorded the daily struggles of ordinary people unable to participate in their communities and poorly adapted to the rapidly changing world around them. The study still represents one of sociology's most determined attempts to understand the types of social exclusion, despair and hopelessness experienced by those forced to exist on the margins of society. (See also Chapter One.)

What makes the research by Bourdieu et al (1999) particularly impactful is the wide variety of people who participated in the study, and the amount and scope of the hardships that participants experienced daily:

> To understand what happens in places like 'projects' or 'housing developments' as well as in certain kinds of schools, places which bring together people who have nothing in common and force them to live together, either in mutual ignorance and incomprehension or else in latent or open conflict – with all the suffering this entails – it is not enough to explain each point of view separately. (Bourdieu et al, 1999, p1)

The Weight of the World mainly comprises conversations covering the disparate social worlds of many people. At first sight, these stories, certainly when viewed individually, could appear trivial and unimportant. However, when the conversations are analysed together as part of an amassed study, they reveal a clear, well-defined picture of the multiple pressures experienced by ordinary citizens exposed to the harsh reality on the margins of society (which can also be attributed, quite directly, to the forces of structural change, rather than individual preference). By the same token (albeit, without the same gravitas as Bourdieu's research), for the participants who took part in the research described in this chapter, it was the multitude of hardships that weighed down on them, rather than their perceived indifference to work, or the result of a single problem or hardship. Whether one lives on the outskirts of Paris or in north-east England, if the forces of globalisation and government institutions and policy are against you, then you will more likely suffer from their consequences than not.

The author undertook a closer examination of the experiences of young people living in poverty, without employment, with little money and at the mercy of the welfare benefits system. It highlighted how the cumulative material disadvantages were both encumbering and damaging to their lives. For example, many participants were unable to travel around or outside the area where they lived, because they could not afford to pay for public transport or find the resources to secure their own means of transport, such as learning to drive or owning a car (see also Chapter Seven). Celebratory events tended to be few, and most people tended to keep things simple. Many participants failed to recall how, or even if, they had celebrated their 16th, 18th or 21st birthdays, and most young people had never experienced a family holiday or short break.

Participants' narratives also showed that many young people had never experienced taking a day trip out of the local area, and the vast majority of participants were unable to afford to go to a restaurant. Even some of the more basic necessities, such as food and clothing, were often inaccessible to participants. In harmony with Bourdieu et al (1999), what these stories seem to exhibit is the tremendous sense of social suffering that permeates the daily lives of young people in poverty and the variety of hardships that infuse them:

> 'You have to budget. I'm always writing lists, making lists to make sure that I don't go over my money / People say do you want to come out for your dinner or do you want to come out with the kids somewhere and I have to say no

because I need my money, and I won't go out and borrow money to do something when I couldn't eat the week after / It just comes down to money, the financial situation.' (Lilly, 26, unemployed single mum)

'Money, that's it, it's money … 'till I can get a job, then, I don't know, it is just hard to live with / I can never get anything for me.' (Kelly, 18, unemployed teenage parent)

'There's a lot of stress for my Mam, it's just a stressful environment, all the bills and stuff, but you just have to get on with it / I wake up every morning in a good mood but then getting back to having no money and that, stuff like that can affect your mood / Arguing with my Mam, lack of money, no job, boredom, when I'm bored sat at home over thinking things / Not having enough money to do things like pay for driving lessons or go on to University maybe.' (John, 19, unemployed teenager)

Without the routine and organisation usually associated with employment, boredom and isolation became key features in the lives of many of the young people who took part in the research. Time passed slowly for most people, and days went by with nothing to do and nowhere to go. They talked about 'feeling stuck' or 'just staying still'; their lives appeared to give the impression that they were trapped in the place where they lived:

'It's no life is it, on the dole … I can't take them on holiday can I, on the dole? It worries me that it'll be like this all the time, like I feel stuck.' (Kelly, 18, unemployed teenage parent)

'I think that's why a lot of young people in particular nowadays are getting into trouble because there is just nothing for them to do / Mine is just looking after my kids, on a weekend I get my own time to do my own stuff like going out to see my friends or maybe the odd night out / My life is quite boring to be honest / Money is an issue for everyone isn't it but because I'm on benefits … I mean, I can drive but I can't get a car to get out anywhere because like I say I'm a single parent and I can't afford the expense.' (Lilly, 26, unemployed single mum)

'I get up about ten, have some breakfast first, then go to the gym ... chill with some friends who are about my own age, who don't work ... maybe check out what football matches are on the telly later ... nothing really, because there is nothing else to do really / I'm in the wrong place.' (John, 19, unemployed teenager)

'I don't do nothing / I get up, clean up, get ready, take the dog out, go to Nana's and see if she wants owt from the shops, probably go to the cemetery with her, come home, clean up again, and that's about it, sit and watch the telly / I don't really go out of the area / I don't really go anywhere / I just want a job, that's all, just a job, then I'll actually start going somewhere in life instead of just staying still.' (Claire, 23, unemployed female)

Reflecting on home life, young people repeatedly referred to their complicated and fragmented family structures and difficult home situations as being exceptionally challenging and 'messy'. Participants' narratives about home life tended to reflect relational problems with parents (often due to a lack of money), pressure to leave the family home and the consequent struggles to live independently due to the financial constraints from bills, bringing up young families, and the effects of various welfare reforms and austerity measures. Rent arrears and other related debts were common among young people who had decided to set up their own homes, and tended to be caused or compounded by other financial pressures from welfare reforms, as well as from other debts accrued due to payday loans, mobile phone contracts and some personal fines resulting from minor offences.

Inevitably, poverty appeared to have serious consequences for the mental health and emotional wellbeing of many young people who took part in the research. Apart from the material and social effects, the psychological resilience of participants was severely tested over time. Many participants seemed resigned and fatalistic about the future, particularly in terms of improving their current socioeconomic position, and some young people talked about experiencing symptoms of poor mental health, such as the stress and depression that resulted in some participants 'feeling really down'. A small number of participants also talked implicitly about having thoughts of self-harm or suicide, and almost all of the people who took part in the study either knew someone personally, or knew of someone young, who had committed suicide in the past two years:

'I went to the Doctor about my depression and he gave me some tablets. I kept going back and talking to the Doctor and then I got over a certain situation and it just went.' (Cathy, 18, part-time further education student on Income Support)

'It depresses me, not having a lot of money, because I can't just get up and go out whenever I want to … it is depressing.' (Kelly, 18, unemployed teenage parent)

'I've got a few friends who've passed away. They've just hung themselves and killed themselves. Not old at all, younger than me. Alan, he hung himself … Stu', he hung himself as well, over there, on the field. There's a couple, John as well, he was only a young lad, about twenty-four.' (Carl, 26, unemployed)

'There's been a lot of young people dying … God, there's been loads over the past two years / I knew them but not properly, I knew them, like who they were.' (Lilly, 26, unemployed single mum)

Another way out – better[2]

This section discusses another emerging theme from the research, which was more optimistic and hopeful than what has been presented so far. During the research, the author was taken aback by the different ways in which poverty was experienced and how it had different effects on young people who, objectively, were living in the same material situation. However, within the sample there were differences, which reflected participants' day–to–day lives, attitudes and values, and their aspirations for the future. In other words, there was diversity within the same material group, which exhibited the kind of diversity that we might expect to see across or between social groups, but not within the same, poor socioeconomic classification. These young people were poor, but they were also self-assured and positive about themselves and their futures.

Cathy's story typifies a small number of participants, whose overall narrative appeared more confident and dynamic than many of her young counterparts. Despite her current material conditions, which were still poor, Cathy's biography remained more encouraging and constructive on the whole. Cathy was 18 when she was interviewed and was living with her grandparents, after leaving her mother's home due to relational problems (Cathy does not know her father and has never met him). She finished her compulsory education without taking her GCSE examinations and said that she was bullied at school due to her quiet nature. She also had a poor school attendance record. However, Cathy was highly aspirational and stated that she was determined to make some positive changes in her life. She attended one of the local further education colleges, which she described as being the best thing that has ever happened to her. She had strong aspirations to go on to university and eventually to work and live in the United States. At the time of the interview, she was surviving on Income Support and, like everybody else who took part in the study, she had insufficient disposable income to do many of the things that she would have liked to do, such as take driving lessons, visit other places or go out with friends. Despite this (or maybe even because of it), Cathy's overall biography was positive, and she remained resolutely determined and purposeful about her future:

Interviewer: 'What did you do when you left school?'

Cathy: 'I was looking for a job and I was on Job Seekers Allowance but then every job that I tried to contact you needed GCSEs or other qualifications and so I thought that if every job is like this then I'll need to get the qualifications before I can go out and get a job, so, that's why I went to college and then after that it's off to University.'

Interviewer: 'What does it feel like to have no money?'

Cathy: 'It doesn't really bother me because I know that when I've finished University and got a good job I will have a lot of money to go out and do all those things.'

Interviewer: 'What are your main hopes for the future?'

Cathy: 'To finish college and get my dream job / To live and work in America / I'm going to go for it all the way / I want to see the world.'

Although Cathy was poor, she was lively and self-motivated. Cathy was disengaged from drugs and criminal networks and had a wider social network of college friends and people from outside the local area. She studied hard and viewed education as her main route out of poverty. Cathy was dynamic and she had a plan; she looked forward to the future with expectation.

Conclusion

This chapter has tried to provide an insight into the daily lives of young people growing up on one of the UK's poorest estates on Teesside, in north-east England. Using qualitative techniques to tell their stories, it highlights the daily hardships endured by young people as a result of poverty and the damaging, long-term consequences caused by a broken labour market, a welfare state in reprisal and a rolling programme of austerity measures.

One of the most common misconceptions associated with people who are poor is that they do not deserve to be helped because they are *lazy, feckless* and *don't want to work*. This idea is usually pointed at a particular social group, labelled by Murray (1990) among others, as the 'Underclass'. The deliberately disparagingly concept of the underclass and its related theories have a long history (see Welshman, 2013), but these unhelpful ideas have been largely exposed in recent years by more constructively measured, evidence-based research. This shows that poverty and worklessness are largely a national structural problem, rather than the result of an intended, chosen culture (MacDonald and Marsh, 2005; MacDonald, 2011).

In the same way, during the course of this research, the poverty and hardship experienced by the participants did not present as being a consequence of idleness or of being work-shy. Instead, all of the respondents who took part in this study held the notion of paid employment in extremely high regard, and demonstrated that they were dedicated to securing – and even desperate to secure – paid employment of their own:

> 'I need a job but no one will help me. I'd do anything, I swear to God, anything. I just want a job man. I just want to be able to get a job. I've tried and tried.' (Carl, 26, unemployed)

This chapter seeks to demonstrate that poverty is not a function of individual pathology or human agency. Instead, it is because *the very structure of opportunities has collapsed* in capitalist society that people *fall to the bottom*, not because they are weak, but because the social welfare, economic and political institutions of that society have failed (Mills, 1959). These system-wide failures, combined with the types of unhelpful victimisation that stigmatises and shames individuals, and squashes the self-esteem of an entire social group, can reduce a whole generation of good young people to nothing (Smith, 2011).

The chapter contests the insensitive discourse at the centre of contemporary developments in government policy and legislation concerning young people and *social justice* (Jones, 2012). It also calls for more qualitative research in the field of youth poverty, in order to highlight the lived reality and the hardships that young people experience in the UK, and to expose the popular – but unhelpful – myths about young people, which unfortunately exist in mainstream society today.

Acknowledgements

I would like to acknowledge the continuing support of my PhD supervisory team at Teesside University, Professor Robert MacDonald and Dr Donald Simpson, and at Leeds University, Professor Tracy Shildrick.

Dedication

For the 25 young people I talked to and for those young people that I couldn't talk to because it was too late.

Notes

[1] The title for the chapter and the concept of 'the spectral army' were taken from a section of Walter Greenwood's working-class novel, *Love on the Dole* (1933): 'Nothing to do with time; nothing to spend; nothing to do tomorrow nor the day after; nothing to wear; can't get married. A living corpse; a unit of the spectral army of three million lost men' (p170).

[2] This subheading was taken from the last sentence of a fictional book by Arthur Morrison, *Child of the Jago* (1896): *"Tell Mist' Beveridge there's 'nother way out – better"* (p165).

References

Becker, H. (1963) *Outsiders: Studies in the sociology of deviance.* New York: Free Press.

Blackman, S. (1997) '"Destructing a Giro": A critical and ethnographic study of the youth "underclass"', in R. MacDonald (ed.) *Youth, the 'Underclass' and Social Exclusion.* London: Routledge, 113-29.

Bourdieu, P. (1999) (ed) *The weight of the world: Social suffering in contemporary society*. Translated by P. P. Ferguson. Palo Alto, CA: Stanford University Press.

Bradshaw, J. (1990) *Child poverty and deprivation in the UK*. London: National Children's Bureau.

Canto-Sanchez, O. and Mercader-Prats, M. (1999) *Poverty among children and youth in Spain: The role of parents and youth employment status*. Document de Treball, 99, 07. Departament d'Economia Aplicada, Universitat Autonoma de Barcelona, Spain.

Child Poverty Action Group (2015) *Child Poverty in the UK: A few facts*. CPAG.

Craine, S. (1997) 'The "Black Magic Roundabout": Cyclical transitions, social exclusion and alternative careers', in R. MacDonald (ed) *Youth, the 'underclass' and social exclusion*. London: Routledge, 130-52.

Department for Communities and Local Government (2011) *The English indices of deprivation 2010*. DCLG.

Esping-Anderson, G. (1990) *The three worlds of welfare capitalism*. Princeton University Press.

Fahmy, E. (2006) 'Youth, poverty and social exclusion', in C. Pantzis, D. Gordon and R. Levitas (eds) *Poverty and social exclusion in Britain*. Bristol: Policy Press.

Fahmy, E. (2014) 'Poverty in Britain, 1999 and 2012: some emerging findings', *Journal of Poverty and Social Justice*, 22, 181-91.

Hart, C. (2010) (ed.) *The Legacy of the Chicago School of Sociology*. Kingswinsford: Midrash Publishing.

Iacovou, M. and Arnstein, A. (2007) *Youth poverty in Europe*. York: Joseph Rowntree Foundation.

Jones, O. (2012) *Chavs: The demonization of the working class*. London: Verso Books.

Katungi, D., Neale, E. and Barbour, A. (2006) *People in low-paid informal work: Need not greed*. York: Joseph Rowntree Foundation.

MacDonald, R. (2011) 'Youth transitions, unemployment and under-employment', *Journal of Sociology* (the Australian Sociological Association), 1-18.

MacDonald, R. and Marsh, J. (2005) *Disconnected youth: Growing up in Britain's poor neighbourhoods*. Basingstoke: Palgrave.

MacInnes, T., Aldridge, H., Bush, S., Tinson, A. and Born, T.B. (2015) *Monitoring poverty and social exclusion*. York: Joseph Rowntree Foundation.

MacLeod, J. (1987) *Ain't no makin' it: Aspirations and attainment in a low income neighbourhood*. Boulder: Westview Press.

Mills, C.W. (1959) *The sociological imagination*. New York: Oxford University Press.

Morrison, A. (1896) *A child of the Jago*. London: Oxford University Press (World's Classics, 2012).

Murray, C. (1990) *The emerging British underclass*. London: Institute of Economic Affairs.

Office for National Statistics (2016) *Persistent poverty in the UK and EU: 2014*. London: ONS.

O'Hara, M. (2015) *Austerity bites: A journey to the sharp end of cuts in the UK*. Bristol: Policy Press.

Polsky, N. (1967) *Hustlers, beats and others*. Chicago: Aldine Publishing Co.

Poverty and Social Exclusion (PSE) (2015) *The impoverishment of the UK: PSE UK first results: Living standards*. Bristol: Policy Press.

Ridge, T. (2009) *Living with poverty: A review of the literature on children's and families' experiences of poverty*. London: Department for Work and Pensions.

Shildrick, T., MacDonald, R., Webster, C. and Garthwaite, K. (2012) *Poverty and insecurity: Life in low-pay, no-pay Britain*. Bristol: Policy Press.

Smith, D. L. (2011) *Less than human: Why we demean, enslave and exterminate others*. London: Macmillan.

Standing, G. (2011) *The Precariat: The new dangerous class*. London: Bloomsbury Publishing.

Townsend, P., Philimore, P. and Beatie, A. (1988) *Inequalities in health in the north*. London: Croom Helm.

Tunstall, R., Green, A., Lupton, R., Watmough, S. and Bates, K. (2014) 'Does poor neighbourhood reputation create a neighbourhood effect on employment? The results of a field experiment in the UK', *Urban Studies*, 51, 4.

Watts, B., Fitzpatrick, S., Bramley, G. and Watkins, D. (2014) *Welfare sanctions and conditionality in the UK*. York: Joseph Rowntree Foundation.

Welshman, J. (2013) *Underclass: A history of the excluded since 1880*. London: Bloomsbury Publishing.

Whyte, W. (1943) *Street corner society*. Chicago: University of Chicago Press.

Willis, P. (1977) *Learning to labour: Why working class kids get working class jobs*. Hants: Saxon House.

SEVENTEEN

Conclusions: advanced youth marginality post-Brexit

Ruth Rogers and Shane Blackman

Contemporary issues affecting the UK

In this final chapter, we consider some of the contemporary issues affecting young adults in the UK as a result of economic insecurity post-Brexit. This is followed by three sections that address marginality in terms of:

- austerity measures targeting young people;
- the critical intersections of social class, gender and ethnic identities within political, cultural and popular discourses as they impinge upon the question of young people and social marginalisation;
- degrees of resistance and autonomy among young people, where agency appears highly vulnerable and young people struggle to maintain an independent voice.

Economic insecurity post-Brexit

The UK is entering a new period of economic instability since the referendum decision to leave the European Union in June 2016. While still in the early stages, we know that the referendum result had a significant impact on the fall in the value of the pound and an increase in the cost of imported products, including food. Given that the UK only produces 60% of the food it consumes, this is already having a direct impact on the supermarket shop (*The Guardian*, 2016a).

This economic instability, together with rising inflation and the increased cost of goods and foods needs to be considered within a context where the use of food banks was already at a record high and over a quarter of all young people living in the UK were already living in poverty (Garthwaite, 2016). These include families suffering from underemployment as well as unemployment. In 2013–14, the proportion of young people in poverty living in a working family rose from 54% in 2009-10 to 63% (Institute for Fiscal Studies, 2015). The numbers of young people living in poverty have been steadily rising since 2004, and young people are much more likely to live in low-income households than either pensioners or working-age adults (Poverty Site, 2016). The Institute for Fiscal Studies explains this divergence as a result of the various cuts to benefits, which it claims are projected to have a 'particularly large impact on child poverty rates in large families' (Institute for Fiscal Studies, 2015, p38).

Austerity measures targeting young people

Advanced marginality is with us due to extensive cuts to benefit entitlement over the last five years. These include the new sanctions scheme in 2012 (see Brooks, Chapter Four), the Spare Room Subsidy in 2013 (the so-called 'bedroom tax') and the abolition of the Return to Work Credit in 2013. Also, 2013 saw the introduction of the benefit cap, which put a maximum limit of £26,000 on the amount of benefit that a household could claim. This was reduced further to £20,000 in 2016. The cap was slightly higher for those living inside London, but lower for single people without children, where the maximum was reduced to £18,200 in 2013 and to £13,400 in 2016. Also in 2016, benefits for working-age people were frozen for four years, which was expected to save £3.9 billion a year. From April 2017, tax credits and family benefit are to be limited to the first two children only.

There have been a number of cuts that *specifically* target young people. For example, in 2015 it was announced that young people aged 18–21 would no longer be entitled to claim for Jobseeker's Allowance after they had been unemployed for six months. Instead, the government announced the Youth Obligation scheme for claimants aged 18–21 which, when rolled out in 2017, would require young people to attend a three-week intensive 'boot camp' (Buzzeo, 2016, p5).

Further, from April 2017, childless young people aged 18–21 have been barred from claiming Housing Benefit. This proposal was initially announced in the 2015 Conservative Party Manifesto, which stated: 'It is also not fair that taxpayers should have to pay for 18–21-year-olds on Jobseeker's Allowance to claim Housing Benefit in order to leave home. So we will ensure that they no longer have an automatic entitlement to Housing Benefit' (Conservative Party, 2015, p20). Crisis (national charity for homeless people) stated that the increased risks of homelessness significantly outweighed the limited financial savings that would be made from this policy change:

This is a scenario that implies where some young people decide to live off the state rather than live independently or remain within the parental home. It assumes that young people seek support from Housing Benefit in order to enable them to leave home; that they exercise considerable choice about where they wish to live; that receiving support towards their housing costs reduces their desire to find employment; and that the consequences of removing their entitlement to Housing Benefit will cause them to remain with their parents, get a job and break an otherwise seamless transition from state-supported education to state-supported indolence. (Crisis, 2015, p3)

For some young people, the opportunity to remain in the family home after turning 18 is not a safe option, owing to family disruption. This is a concern for vulnerable and disadvantaged young people, who are more likely to have already been blighted by insecurity. For example, research exploring the 'instant adulthood' of young people leaving care stated that many vulnerable young people 'neither have the luxury of a gradual transition into adulthood, nor do they have the safety net of family if they find themselves unprepared for the challenges of independent living' (Rogers, 2011, p414).

There has been a significant increase in the number of benefit sanctions, as discussed in Squires and Goldsmith (Chapter Two), Fahmy (Chapter Three) and Brooks (Chapter Four). What has not been reported on in the mainstream media is that young people under the age of 25 also have a substantially higher risk of being sanctioned than older people, with 8% of young people under 25 being affected per month, compared to around 5.5% of all claimants (Joseph Rowntree Foundation, 2014). Moreover, data on appeals against benefit sanctions show that there are also significant differences in the number of successful appeals by age group. For example, of all those who had made an appeal against a Jobseeker's Allowance sanction between October 2012 and March 2016, 39% had been aged 18–24. The number of appeals (and sanctions) also reduced according to the increased age of the claimant, and of all those who appealed: 11% were aged 30–34; 8% were aged 35–39; 7% were aged 40–44; and 6% were aged 45–55. Significantly, the older the person appealing against the sanction, the more likely they were to be successful. The 18-24 age group also had the highest proportion of unsuccessful appeals against a lower-level sanction than any other age group, with 67% being unsuccessful between 2012 and 2016. The same was also true for the intermediate and high-level claims, in that the younger the person appealing against the decision to receive a sanction, the less likely they were to be successful (Department for Work and Pensions, 2016, Table 1.6). In addition, the younger the claimant, the more likely they were to receive multiple sanctions. Of those who had received three or more low-level sanctions, 49% were aged 18–24, which is particularly striking when compared with just 0.5% being aged 60 or over receiving the same number (Department for Work and Pensions, 2016, Table 1.7).

The economic disadvantages facing young people, explored by Squires and Goldsmith (Chapter Two), Fahmy (Chapter Three), Brooks (Chapter Four) and Ruddy (Chapter Sixteen), are set to continue well into the 2020s and beyond. This affects young people on low incomes or claiming benefits, but also those more financially secure, who will no longer experience the advantages enjoyed by their older generation in terms of home ownership. Instead, home ownership rates have almost collapsed for younger generations over the past 20 years. For example, between the 1980s and early 2000s there were around 400,000 to 600,000 loans for first-time buyers each year. In 2008, there was a 47% decrease in this number, which has had a significant impact on the age of first-time buyers (Department for Communities and Local Government, 2016). In addition, whereas in 1991, 67% of people aged 25–34 were homeowners, by 2014, this had reduced to 36% (Office for National Statistics, 2016a). For the 16-24 age group, home ownership reduced from 36% to a mere 9% over the same period. This, coupled with the fact that in 2016 interest rates have reached a 322-year record low (*The Times*, 2016), it is now increasingly difficult for young people to save for a deposit for property.

Even further down the line, the occupational pensions previously enjoyed by baby boomers are now almost completely inaccessible to young people. Changes to introduce a new 'flat rate' pension will impact negatively on young people, with the Pensions Policy Institute reporting that the new system will result in three quarters of people in their 20s losing an average of £19,000 over the course of their retirement (BBC, 2016).

Intersections of youth marginality: ethnicity, gender and education

Under advanced marginality, young people encounter a complex experience between ethnicity, gender, poverty, family structure and educational access.

Ethnicity

The experiences of ethnic minorities, asylum seekers and immigrants are particularly concerning, given the political changes and uncertainty facing the UK following the referendum result to leave the EU in 2016 (see Chapter Eight by Robinson and Williams, and van Krieken Robson's Chapter Nine). In the month following the result, the number of racist or religious abuse incidents recorded by police in England and Wales rose by 41%; and in July 2016, there were 5,468 such crimes recorded compared to 3,886 in July the previous year. This increase in the number of recorded incidents began as early as April 2016, and while they began to decline in August, they remained at a higher level than prior to the EU referendum (Home Office, 2016, p18). The national press reported on a large number of these racial hate crimes in the weeks following the Brexit referendum. Examples included: letters being sent to residents in Tunbridge Wells saying: 'F★★★ off to Poland'; diners refusing to be served by Italian waiters in London; dog excrement being pushed through a letter box in Rugby; and a 25-year-old Asian man being stabbed in the back in Rochdale with such force that the knife blade came off, resulting in a nine-hour operation (Institute of Race Relations, 2016).

The tabloid media contributes to young people's feelings of anomie through stereotyping and scapegoating of immigrants and asylum seekers. It has also been responsible for inaccurate reporting (see Blackman and Rogers, Chapter Five). For example, in October 2016 it was revealed that previous estimates of the number of international students outstaying their visa in the UK had been grossly exaggerated. In January 2016, the *Daily Mail* had decided to run with the headline: 'nearly 100,000 foreign students a year from outside Europe are not returning home' (*Daily Mail*, 2016) and the *Daily Express* headline stated: 'Nearly 100,000 non-EU students STAYING in Britain after their studies' (*Daily Express*, 2016). However, in October 2016, exit check data found that the number of non-EU students breaching their visa by staying in the UK every year was not 100,000, but as few as 1,500 (*The Telegraph*, 2016a).

Gender

In relation to gender, there have been significant reductions in the number of teenage pregnancies in recent years. For example, teenage pregnancies fell by 6.8% for girls under the age of 18 and by 10% for girls under the age of 16 between 2013 and 2014 (Office for National Statistics, 2016b). However, there are some consistent themes, and 2013 data suggested that 70% of pregnant teenagers were not engaged in education, employment or training and were far more likely to live in deprived neighbourhoods than other parents.

Lower socioeconomic status was also a factor: one in three British teenagers from lower socioeconomic backgrounds were likely to become a teenage parent (Mental Health Foundation, 2013, p5). Young single mothers also suffer from stigmatisation (see Blackman and Rogers in Chapter Five, and Kehily in Chapter Six), and the charity Gingerbread said that many of the young mothers it works with feel isolated and alone after claiming to have been verbally abused by strangers. Gingerbread reported how one young mother explained to the charity: 'When I first started to show I was so proud, but all I would get is dirty looks ... It made me feel quite victimised so I stayed in quite a lot' (Gingerbread, cited in BBC, 2014).

Education

Finally, in relation to education, there are also significant potential changes occurring in the UK. The first of these relates to the development of free schools (see Tupling, Chapter Eleven). Free schools were introduced under the Academies Act 2010. They are either primary or secondary government-funded schools, and can be established by various independent groups, such as groups of parents, charitable organisations, community organisations, religious groups or businesses. The introduction of free schools has received a critical response, with the concern that they introduce more selection into mainstream education and take away much-needed resources from existing schools. For Tupling (Chapter Eleven), free schools, although officially non-selective, appear to attract more socially advantaged young people. Hatcher confirms this, stating that: 'Some free schools are private schools seeking state funding, and the siblings-first admissions rule, coupled with their image, would tend to perpetuate the disproportionately middle-class composition of their intake' (Hatcher, 2011, p494).

The move towards effectively segregating young people on the basis of academic attainment also has resonances with the move towards apprenticeships, which Ainley (Chapter Ten) argues is dividing 18-year-olds into two separate categories of either 'apprentices' or 'students' – and forcing the former to compete against the odds in an era of inflating academic qualifications.

Educational attainment also intersects with ethnicity and social class. It remains the case that black students do not benefit equally from attending academy schools as white students, and they are further disadvantaged by the emphasis placed on the introduction of the EBacc as an indicator of success. Gillborn argues that: 'the coalition's policies follow a path that increases disparities of achievement and, in the case of race inequity, amount to a war on Black children' (Gillborn, 2013, p483).

Degrees of resistance and autonomy

Throughout the book, different young people speak out with voices of resistance and risk. At times, this resistance appears to be focused at a micro level and whilst there is some resistance to young adults' local and personal experience of marginality, there is little that operates at the national level, or that is providing organised resistance to the wider political structures. Theoretically, resistance is most often associated with the Centre for Contemporary Cultural Studies theory of subculture and the work of Dick Hebdige (1979), where resistance by young people is seen as a sign of refusal.

One of the criticisms of this cultural studies approach was the lack of real political context to young people's actions (Blackman, 2014). However, in the 2016 referendum vote, young people did engage with the political system. Toby Helm reported in *The Guardian* on 10 July 2016: 'It is thought that young people who took part in the referendum voted 70%–30% in favour of Remain' (*Guardian*, 2016b). Despite this, the Conservative press stated: 'Young people have a right to be angry at Brexit – but not at their parents who voted Leave', alongside the patronising statement that: 'Brexit isn't about racism – students have a lot to learn' (*The Telegraph*, 2016b). This view was contradicted by Louise Ridley in the *Huffington Post*, who argued: '75% of people aged 18–24 claimed they voted for Remain in the YouGov survey after voting closed, a figure that falls as age increases' (*Huffington Post*, 2016). Jessica Elgot in *The Guardian* confirms that young people voted to remain but the older generation voted to leave, setting up a 'deep generational and social divide in the country' (*The*

Guardian, 2016c). Shortly after this, *The Guardian* printed a sample of emails it had received from young people immediately following the referendum result, which included quotations such as: 'I couldn't vote in what is probably the most important political decision the British people have ever made'; and 'I'm 17 but turn 18 in four days. This morning I've woken up to feel completely betrayed by my own country' (*The Guardian*, 2016d).

The qualitative work of Batchelor et al (Chapter Seven), Murphy (Chapter Thirteen), McKay and Atherton (Chapter Fourteen), McPherson (Chapter Fifteen) and Ruddy (Chapter Sixteen) has brought out the subjective nuances of resistance and risk, but also revealed how young people feel subject to forms of discrimination through their leisure activities. This concern is focused on by McPherson (Chapter Fifteen), who critically discusses how young adults are politically positioned through a constructed moral marginality that denies young people the legitimacy to voice feelings and thoughts because of the generalisation of a 'binge' drinking culture applied to all young adults through tabloid media.

For Ruddy and Murphy, in their studies on young people in poverty subject to hardship and police regulation, there are real feelings of anomie, which emerge from experiences of frustration and disappointment. It would appear that before some young people can become resistant, they are too fully engaged in cultures of survival, as shown by Brooks (Chapter Four), Kehily (Chapter Six) and Batchelor et al (Chapter Seven). Murphy's use of the term '[b]othered' as a feature of young adults' lives, speaks of offering young people a degree of agency in their contact with the police, as it enables young people to have a non–aggressive response to the police. In contrast, Ruddy's research participants are desperate for the normality of employment to move beyond work in the informal or illegitimate economy. For Ruddy, the 'weight of the world' brought young people closer to survival rather than resistance.

McKay and Atherton's case study (Chapter Fourteen) on young adults linked with a space known as the Meadows has parallels with Murphy's chapter (Chapter Thirteen), in terms of how young people encounter the police and to what extent forms of transgressive behaviour are tolerated by the police. For Murphy, in the North East it seems that the way in which the police use their 'stop and search' powers has a stigmatising and discriminatory effect on young adults, increasing their feelings of anomie within the community. By contrast, McKay and Atherton's green space of the Meadows is a point of intersection, where sets of young people engage in forms of resistance.

The social space of the Meadows as a location appears to have a key role in tempering their encounters with the police. The young people experience adult interruption and intervention, but they work through negotiation rather than confrontation. This may dampen resistance, but it reduces conflict with authority.

Conclusion

This chapter has explored how young people are disproportionately affected by the significant benefit cuts and restructuring of the benefits system in the name of austerity. Under advanced marginality, young people experience the antithesis of the baby boomer generation. They are not only disproportionately targeted in their youth, but they are also members of the generation who will continue to be affected into their old age by the cuts to the state pension, the gradual contraction of the NHS, and the increasing dominance of the market. These young people have experienced: a collapse in the youth labour market; a collapse in home ownership rates; the greatest levels of student debt; and fundamental changes to the education system in terms of the increase in academies, free schools and the likely return of segregation that is so central to the ideology behind the grammar school system of the current Conservative government.

Structurally and culturally, young adults are either politically disenfranchised by age or through their own disengagement with the system and struggle with anomie. Despite this, they are also among those who stand to lose the most from the political shifts and longer-term effects of Brexit. British young adults have seen the withdrawal of the Education Maintenance Allowance and the increase in the racist use of 'stop and search' powers by the police. Populist forms of state monitoring have seen the introduction of Challenge 21 and Challenge 25, which is a UK scheme whereby young people who look as though they *may* be under the age of 21 or 25 can expect to be asked for their ID before they can purchase products – even if they only have to be aged 16 or 18 to legally make the purchase. This scheme effectively forces young people to carry identification and to account for themselves on a daily basis. This makes young adults the only group of people where it is considered 'acceptable' to exclude on the basis of their membership of a particular group.

It is inconceivable to imagine an independent high street newsagent being allowed to put a poster in its window stating: 'Only two Asians allowed in the shop at any one time', yet we have become desensitised to prejudice against young people. Such punitive actions are reinforced by wide-scale use of the *Mosquito* (the electronic device which emits an unpleasant, high frequency sound that can typically only be heard by young people under the age of 25), set up in public places to deter young people from 'loitering', and the use of 'bot camps' if they fail to gain employment. The portrayal of young adults as 'scroungers' in TV reality programmes and in the tabloid press fuels intolerance towards young people, increasing their feelings of being marginal in British society.

References

BBC (2014) 'Young mothers face stigma and abuse, say charities', 25 February. www.bbc.co.uk/newsbeat/article/26326035/young-mothers-face-stigma-and-abuse-say-charities

BBC (2016) 'Winners and losers under the new state pension', Brian Milligan Personal Finance reporter, 4 April. www.bbc.co.uk/news/business-35928308

Blackman, S. (2014) 'Subculture theory: an historical and contemporary assessment of the concept for understanding deviance', *Deviant Behavior*, 35, 6: 496–512.

Buzzeo, J. (2016) 'Will the Youth Obligation work for disadvantaged young people?, *Employment Studies: The IES public employment policy research newsletter*, Summer, 24: 5–6.

Channel 5 (2015) *Benefits By The Sea*, Series 1, Episode 2.

Conservative Party (2015) 'Strong leadership, a clear economic plan, a brighter more secure future', Conservative Party Manifesto. https://www.conservatives.com/manifesto

Crisis (2015) *The withdrawal of support for housing costs under Universal Credit for young people: More pain for little gain?*, London: Crisis.

Daily Express (2016) 'Nearly 100,000 non-EU students STAYING in Britain after their studies', 29 January. www.express.co.uk/news/world/639092/students-britain-european-union-migration-uk-universities-theresa-may-home-secretary

Daily Mail (2016) 'How 93,000 non-EU students a year stay on in the UK: Abuse of system by those desperate to stay accounts for almost a third of net migration', 19 January. www.dailymail.co.uk/news/article-3422008/How-93-000-non-EU-students-year-stay-UK-Abuse-desperate-stay-accounts-net-migration.html

Department for Communities and Local Government (2016a) *English Housing Survey*, https://www.gov.uk/government/collections/english-housing-survey

Department for Communities and Local Government (2016b) Survey of English Housing, 2001-2 UK Government Web Archive, Table FC21010, http://webarchive.nationalarchives.gov. uk/20121108165934/http:/www.communities.gov.uk/documents/ housing/xls/

Department for Work and Pensions (2016) 'Jobseeker's Allowance and Employment and Support Allowance sanctions: Decisions made to March 2016', August. https://www.gov.uk/government/statistics/ jobseekers-allowance-and-employment-and-support-allowance-sanctions-decisions-made-to-march-2016.

Garthwaite, K. (2016) *Hunger pains: Life inside Foodbank Britain*. Bristol: Policy Press.

Guardian (2016b) 'EU referendum: youth turnout almost twice as high as first thought', 10 July 2016, https://www.theguardian.com/ politics/2016/jul/09/young-people-referendum-turnout-brexit-twice-as-high

Gillborn, D. (2013) 'Interest-divergence and the colour of cutbacks: Race, recession and the undeclared war on Black children', *Discourse: Studies in the Cultural Politics of Education*, 34, 4: 477-91.

Hatcher, R. (2011) 'The Conservative–Liberal Democrat Coalition government's "free schools" in England', *Educational Review*, 63, 4, 485-503.

Hebdige, D. (1979) *Subculture: The meaning of style*. London: Routledge.

Home Office (2016) 'Hate Crime, England and Wales 2015/16', *Statistical Bulletin 11/16*, 13 October.

Huffington Post (2016) 'EU referendum results: young "screwed by older generations" as polls suggest 75% backed remain', 24 June. www.huffingtonpost.co.uk/entry/eu-referendum-results-age-data-young_uk_576cd7d6e4b0232d331dac8f

Institute for Fiscal Studies (2015) 'Nearly two-thirds of children in poverty live in working families', https://www.ifs.org.uk/ publications/7880

Institute of Race Relations (2016) 'Post-Brexit Racism', 7 July. www. irr.org.uk/news/post-brexit-racism/

Joseph Rowntree Foundation (2014) 'Benefits sanctions are adding to bleak prospects for young people', https://www.jrf.org.uk/blog/ benefits-sanctions-are-adding-bleak-prospects-young-people

Mental Health Foundation (2013) *Young mums together: Promoting young mothers' wellbeing*, https://www.mentalhealth.org.uk/sites/default/ files/young-mums-together-report.pdf

Office for National Statistics (2016a) *UK Perspectives 2016: Housing and home ownership in the UK*, 25 May. ONS Digital.

Office for National Statistics (2016b) 'Conceptions in England and Wales: 2014, Annual statistics on conceptions covering conception counts and rates, by age group including women under 18', *Statistical Bulletin*, 9 March.

Poverty Site (2016) 'Low income by age group', www.poverty.org. uk/04/index.shtml

Rogers, R. (2011) '"I remember thinking, why isn't there someone to help me? Why isn't there someone who can help me make sense of what I'm going through": "Instant adulthood" and the transition of young people out of state care', *Journal of Sociology*, 47, 4: 411-26.

The Guardian (2016a) 'UK food prices set to rise after Brexit vote', 26 June. https://www.theguardian.com/environment/2016/jun/26/uk-food-prices-set-to-rise-after-brexit-vote-farmers-union

The Guardian (2016b) 'EU referendum: youth turnout almost twice as high as first thought', 10 July 2016, https://www.theguardian.com/politics/2016/jul/09/young-people-referendum-turnout-brexit-twice-as-high

The Guardian (2016c) 'Young remain voters came out in force, but were outgunned', 24 June. https://www.theguardian.com/politics/2016/jun/24/young-remain-voters-came-out-in-force-but-were-outgunned

The Guardian (2016d) 'Meet the 75%: the young people who voted to remain in the EU', 24 June. https://www.theguardian.com/politics/2016/jun/24/meet-the-75-young-people-who-voted-to-remain-in-eu

The Telegraph (2016a) 'Visa breaches by foreign students are "exaggerated" new figures suggest', 13 October. www.telegraph.co.uk/education/2016/10/12/visa-breaches-by-foreign-students-are-exaggerated-new-figures-su/

The Telegraph (2016b) 'Young people have a right to be angry at Brexit – but not at their parents who voted Leave', 28 June. www.telegraph.co.uk/education/2016/06/28/young-people-have-a-right-to-be-angry-at-brexit--but-not-at-thei/

The Times (2016) 'Lack of interest: Very loose monetary policy is creating problems for banks, savers and investors', 5 October. www.thetimes.co.uk/article/lack-of-interest-zdsskfms5

Index

Note: Page numbers in *italics* indicate figures, tables and boxes. Page numbers followed by an n refer to end-of-chapter notes.